1991

RELIGION IN THE POETRY AND DRAMA OF THE LATE MIDDLE AGES IN ENGLAND

Piero Boitani / Anna Torti (eds.)

RELIGION IN THE POETRY AND DRAMA OF THE LATE MIDDLE AGES IN ENGLAND

The J. A. W. Bennett Memorial Lectures
Perugia, 1988

D. S. Brewer

First published 1990 by D. S. Brewer, Cambridge

D. S. Brewer is an imprint of Boydell & Brewer Ltd
PO Box 9, Woodbridge, Suffolk IP12 3DF
and of Boydell & Brewer Inc.
PO Box 41026, Rochester, NY 14604, USA

ISBN 0 85991 303 1

British Library Cataloguing in Publication Data
Religion in the poetry and drama of the late middle ages in
England. — (The J. A. W. Bennett memorial lectures).
1. English literature. Special subjects : Religion — Critical
studies
I. Boitani, Piero II. Torti, Anna III. Series
820.9382
ISBN 0-85991-303-1

Library of Congress Cataloging-in-Publication Data
Religion in the poetry and drama of the late Middle Ages in
England : the J. A. W. Bennett memorial lectures,
Perugia, 1988 / Piero Boitani, Anna Torti (eds.).
p.   cm.
Includes bibliographical references and index.
ISBN 0-85991-303-1 (Brewer : alk. paper)
1. English literature—Middle English, 1100-1500—
History and criticism. 2. Christianity in literature.
I. Boitani, Piero. II. Torti, Anna.
PR275.R4R45   1990
820.9'382'09023—dc20   90-39926

This publication is printed on acid-free paper

Printed in Great Britain by
St Edmundsbury Press Ltd, Bury St Edmunds, Suffolk

Contents

Contributors

Douglas Gray   Oxford University
Domenico Pezzini   University of Sassari
Margaret Bridges   University of Berne
Przemysław Mroczkowski   University of Krakow
C. David Benson   University of Connecticut
†Paula Neuss   University of London
Saul N. Brody   City College, New York
Bruce Harbert   University of Sussex
Derek Pearsall   Harvard University
Richard Axton   University of Cambridge
Hans-Jürgen Diller   University of Bochum
Richard Beadle   University of Cambridge

Preface

A subject dear to the interests of J. A. W. Bennett was chosen for the sixth series of lectures organized in Perugia to commemorate him: religion, or rather the function of religious themes and problems in late Middle English literature. A twentieth-century Western audience may find it difficult to realize how fundamental religion was to what we would call medieval 'ideology' and the medieval 'imaginaire'. The papers which were read during the Symposium, and which are printed here with the changes the authors felt necessary to make, try to explore precisely the area where religious ideology and the religious 'imaginaire' meet in medieval England. For instance, Margaret Bridges is interested in the ways in which prayer may contribute to narrative flow or progress; Przemysław Mroczkowski deals with a central problem, that of the intellectual's, the artist's relationship to his faith; Richard Axton studies the ambivalence of Judas's function in narrative and drama, and discovers that this has important moral and theological consequences. Thus, the present volume begins with an essay where Douglas Gray examines the Book of Margery Kempe as an example of the vitality of fifteenth-century popular religion by focusing on the various meanings of the term, 'popular'. Domenico Pezzini completes this first section on the mystics in his article on the theme of the Passion (a topic, as is well known, which was very closely studied by Jack Bennett himself) in Richard Rolle and Julian of Norwich.

The second part of this book is devoted to Chaucer: after Przemysław Mroczkowski's piece, David Benson tries to define the aesthetics of the 'religious' tales, examining the stories of the Prioress, the Second Nun, the Man of Law, and the Clerk, while Paula Neuss reads the *Pardoner's Tale* as a moral play, thus anticipating themes which are dealt with in the third section of the volume. Saul Brody explores the complexities determined by the play of aesthetic and moral problems in the *Troilus* and in the *Nun's Priest's Tale*.

From Chaucer we move on to Langland, the religious writer *par excellence* of fourteenth-century England. Both Bruce Harbert and Derek Pearsall focus on the C-text of *Piers Plowman*. The former paves the way for the latter, by expounding the theology as such of the poem. The two essays also complement each other, Harbert's stressing the 'intellectual' side of the C-text, Pearsall's highlighting the role 'lunatyk lollares' play in the imaginative, spiritual texture of *Piers Plowman*.

The third part of our volume concentrates on drama, a most important, 'public' and 'popular' manifestation of religious ideology and imagination. Both Hans-Jürgen Diller and Richard Beadle study the theological features of mystery plays. The former, however, deals with 'popular' religion, showing how plays not only prefer the tangible or bodily aspects over the intangible, but even sacrifice the latter for the sake of the former. Richard Beadle, on the other hand, focuses on the York Creation and Fall of the Angels, underlining the remarkably close integration of their poetic, dramatic, and theological qualities.

We hope that readers will enjoy the present book and learn from it as much as the original audience of the papers and the editors themselves did in April, 1988. For both the Symposium and the volume we would like to thank the British Council, the City of Perugia (and particularly its Mayor, Mario Silla Baglioni, and Prof. Roberto Abbondanza), and above all the Regional Council of Umbria. Without the help of its President, Francesco Mandarini, and its Assessore alla Cultura, Pierluigi Mingarelli, such gathering of scholars from England, Poland, Germany, Switzerland, Italy, and the United States, and the publication of the present book would have been impossible.

6 November 1988   Anna Torti
                                                   Piero Boitani

POPULAR RELIGION AND LATE MEDIEVAL ENGLISH LITERATURE

DOUGLAS GRAY

My title deserves an apologetic and explanatory gloss. I do not intend to produce a list of the practices of 'popular religion' which are mentioned over the whole range of late medieval English literature.[1] I shall instead focus on one particular fifteenth-century book which I think owes much of its interest and its power to one kind of popular piety — that of Margery Kempe of Lynn. Its vivid narrative, intriguing character, and the glimpses of contemporary life it offers have given it a certain fame. It has been less happily received by intellectuals, by the historians of spirituality or of literature. Margery's behaviour provoked adverse comment in her own day, and has continued to excite strong reactions. There is a widespread tendency for commentators to take sides — to berate her as hysterical or to rush to her defence. As if to prove the truth of the remark attributed to Dr Thomas Szasz, 'if you can talk to God, you are praying; if God talks to you, you have schizophrenia', psychiatrists have been let loose on her (but although the evidence the *Book* gives is fascinating, it is surely not extensive enough for a convincing 'analysis').[2] Historians of mysticism, coming to her from Hilton with his intellect, his moderation, and his humility, are not surprisingly somewhat cast down. But it has never seemed fair to me to see her simply as the final degenerate example of the medieval English mystical tradition. Her *Book* is simply too full of energetic and unruly life to sit quietly in that pigeon-hole. Recent work on Margery[3] which seems to me to have produced a more sympathetic understanding of her has either

---

[1] For collections of popular beliefs and practices see, for instance, Owst 'Sortilegium in English Nomiletic Literature of the Fourteenth Century', *Studies Presented to Sir Hilary Jenkinson* ed. J. Conway Davies (London, 1957), or J. Burns, 'The Scotland of John Major', *Innes Review* 2 (1951) 65 – 77.

[2] But see the interesting attempt by Dr A. Ryle, in Stephen Medcalf, ed., *The Later Middle Ages* (London, 1981), pp. 114 – 5.

[3] Cf., for instance, Clarissa W. Atkinson, *Margery Kempe Mystic and Pilgrim* (Ithaca, 1983); S. Dickman, 'Margery Kempe and the English Devotional Tradition' in *The Medieval Mystical Tradition in England* ed. M. Glasscoe, I (1980), pp. 156 – 72; H. P. Weissman, 'Margery Kempe in Jerusalem: Hysterica Compassio in the Late Middle Ages' in *Acts of Interpretation . . . in Honor of E. Talbot Donaldson* eds. Mary J. Carruthers and Elizabeth D. Kirk (Norman, Okl., 1982), pp. 201 – 17.

concentrated on her as a woman writer (where, for instance the rather vague word 'hysterical' can be questioned — as it can be in the case of her more celebrated contemporary, Joan of Arc, though she preferred the sword to the pen), or has tried to see her in terms of medieval affective devotion. It is the second approach that I wish to pursue here. I do not believe that Margery can ever made into a 'typical' or an 'ordinary' figure, but I think she looks more comprehensible and slightly less bizarre against the background of 'popular religion' of an ecstatic and enthusiastic kind. Her *Book* seen in this way is a remarkable expression of the vitality and the stresses of fifteenth-century religion.

'Popular religion' is, I realize, an ambiguous and a slippery term, which raises all kinds of awkward questions,[4] As a literary medievalist, I am rather inclined simply to accept the ambiguity of 'popular' in the senses both of 'made by the people' and 'made for the people'. But who are the people? And what is 'un-popular' religion? It is clear that most of the practices of what is often called 'popular piety' — such as going on pilgrimage, venerating relics, etc. — were not confined to the lower orders or to the illiterate. Very few French peasants in the fifteenth century could have matched the enthusiasm for relics of their king, Louis XI. 'Un-popular' religion might be the official administration, the theological arguments of the 'clerks', the intellectual minority, who then as later were prone to comment crossly on 'popular superstition'. We must accept that it is very difficult to draw firm dividing lines between 'low' and 'high' culture. There is constant overlap and interaction. It is of course important that the intellectual minority were the governors of the Church, and that it is through their eyes that we see most medieval religion. And it is usually thanks to them that we can catch glimpses of the beliefs of the humblest and least learned strata of society. But it is important to remember that 'popular' and 'learned' or 'official' religion are aspects of the same thing, although they may sometimes represent notional extremes. Manselli has insisted on the unity of the 'fait religieux', claiming that any difference is not a qualitative one, but a matter of emphasis, which lies in the different ways the 'word' of the Christian revelation was accepted ('popular religion' being marked by 'une prééminance marquée des valeurs affectives et émotives sur les valeurs

---

[4] On 'popular religion', see, for instance, R. Manselli, *La religion populaire au moyen âge. Problèmes de méthode et d'histoire* (Conférence Albert-le-Grand, 1973), E. Delaruelle, *La piété populaire au moyen âge* (Turin, 1975), R. and C. Brooke, *Popular Religion in the Middle Ages. Western Europe 1000 – 1300* (London, 1984); on 'popular culture', see P. Burke, *Popular Culture in Early Modern Europe* (London, 1978), N. Z. Davis, *Society and Culture in Early Modern France* (Stanford, 1965) and 'Some Tasks and Themes in the Study of Popular Religion' in C. Trinkaus and H. A. Oberman, eds., *The Pursuit of Holiness in Late Medieval and Renaissance Religion* (Leiden, 1974), pp. 307 – 36, S. Kaplan, ed., *Understanding Popular Culture* (Berlin, New York, Amsterdam, 1984).

logiques'). Popular religion, he argues, cannot be systematized; it is like 'un encadrement, un canevas, dans lequel peuvent s'insérer les formes les plus diverses de l'expérience religieuse'.[5] It seems to me to be rather more positive and dynamic that that : 'popular religion' in the Middle Ages made a considerable contribution to 'official' religion. But Manselli is surely right in insisting that there is a constant interplay between 'learned' and 'popular' religion: 'un lien entre *deux* cultures qui demeurent perpétuellement dans un rapport dialectique mutuel d'influences réciproques, mais qui en même temps sont constamment à la recherche d'une possibilité de rencontre et de fusion'.[6] It is an essential point that there is a dynamic and symbiotic relationship between them.

It is tempting to say one knows 'popular religion' when one sees it — as, for instance in the Mexican Day of the Dead, or in a famous late medieval literary example, when the poet Villon makes his mother say:

> Femme je suis povrette et ancienne
> Qui riens ne sçay; oncques letteres ne leuz.
> Au moustier voy, dont suis paroissienne,
> Paradiz paint, ou sont harpes et leuz,
> Et ung enffer ou dampnez sont bouluz.
> L'un me fait paour, l'autre joye et liesse.[7]

It is significant, of course, that this latter example, so often quoted, comes to us through the imagination and the words of an intellectual 'clerk'. It is to this group in society that we owe the accounts of such famous unlettered English visionaries as Caedmon or Thurkill,[8] and most of our knowledge of the beliefs and practices of those strata where popular religion becomes indistinguishable from folklore and magic. England did not have energetic inquisitors like those who collected the materials for such modern studies as *Montaillou, The Cheese and the Worms,* or *The Night Battles,*[9] but moralists and preachers refer to a wide range of popular beliefs — in necromancy, in various forms of divination, in lucky and unlucky practices and meetings, and so on. They are later joined by Reformers lamenting and listing 'superstitious' and 'Popish' practices (like the ringing of church-bells in storms).[10] For a dramatic realization of such practices in their social

[5] Manselli, p. 19.
[6] Manselli, p. 20.
[7] *Testament*, ll. 893 – 8.
[8] See P. G. Schmidt, 'The Vision of Thurkill', *JWCI* 41 (1978) 50 – 64.
[9] E. Le Roy Ladurie, *Montaillou* (1975) tr. B. Bray (London, 1978); Carlo Ginzberg, *The Cheese and the Worms (Il formaggio e i vermi: Il cosmo di un mugnaio del '500,* 1976) tr. J. and A. Tedeschi (London, 1980) and *The Night Battles (I Benedanti: Stregoneria e culti agrari tra Cinquecento e Seicento,* 1966) tr. J. and A. Tedeschi (London, 1983).
[10] For example, 'Naogeorgus', *The Popish Kingdome* tr. B. Googe: see D. Gray, *Themes and Images in the Medieval English Religious Lyric* (London, 1972), p. 241.

context, however, we have to turn to the scenes or allusions of the writers, like Villon, or Chaucer, who not only satirizes the crooked Pardoner who preys on popular piety, but marvellously catches the spontaneity of 'popular religion' when he makes his credulous carpenter, who is so convinced of the blessedness of a 'lewed man / That noght but oonly his bileve kan', respond to a crisis, to what he interprets as 'some woodnesse or som agonye' in his lodger with a charm, a 'white paternoster',[11] just as he makes a miller's wife, rudely awakened by the falling body of her husband, instantly utter a pious ejaculation to a local wonder-working relic — 'Help! hooly croys of Bromeholm'.[12]

It is possible to distinguish certain patterns in 'popular religion': for instance, the folk practices that marked the movement of the seasons and the year, or the practices or rituals associated with the important events of the life of the individual (e.g. birth, marriage, child-bearing, death), or with the unpredictable events and anxieties of rural and domestic life, or with health and sickness. Here, for most ailments or problems, spiritual and physical help was available in the form of prayers, medical remedies, or charms (and our clear distinction between these categories was often not observed). A widespread prayer-charm against bleeding, for instance:

> Crist was born in Bethlem,
> And cristend in flom Jordane;
> And als the flome stode als a stane,
> Stand thi blode, N. (neven his name)
> *In nomine patris et filii et spiritus sancti* Amen[13]

seems to derive its physical power from the recalling of an event of great spiritual power at an especially sacred place: there was a legend that during the baptism of Christ the river Jordan miraculously stood still. The Biblical account itself has a powerful supernatural atmosphere, with its supernatural heavenly voice and dove, and the strange prophetic character of the Baptist. The fifteenth-century pilgrim Fabri informs us that the water of the Jordan was greatly sought after by pilgrims, who used to bring it back with them for a variety of medical and magical purposes (although, because of a rival popular belief, they had to smuggle it into their galleys past the watchful eye of the Venetian captains, who believed it brought bad luck).[14] The 'high' or 'official' practices and rituals and these coexist and interact. At childbirth, there were available for use prayers, charms, or amulets — like the 'birth-

---

[11] *Miller's Tale*, CT I, 3477 – 86.
[12] *Reeve's Tale*, CT I, 4286.
[13] D. Gray, 'Notes on Some Middle English Charms', *Chaucer and Middle English Studies in Honour of Rossell Hope Robbins* ed. B. Rowland (London, 1974), p. 62.
[14] *The Book of the Wanderings of Brother Felix Fabri* tr. A. Stewart (Palestine Pilgrims' Text Society, 1892 – 3), II, pp. 12 – 13.

girdles', parchment rolls with images of the Instruments of the Passion, the Five Wounds, the Crucifixion, that were wrapped around the woman's body.[15] At death, the church provided solemn rites and, in preparation for death, an elaborate literature of comfort and consolation. There is much evidence that there was a widespread fear of 'sudden death', an unprepared or untimely death. This could be averted by various pious practices — by looking at an image of St Christopher on the wall of a church (one such at Wood Eaton in Oxfordshire has the inscription 'Ki cest image verra le jur de male mort ne murra'), or by seeing the elevated Host — about which the Reformer, Becon, waxes satiric: '. . . if the priest be weake in the armes, and heave not up hye ynough, the rude people of the countrey in diverse partes of England wyll crye out to the Priest, holde up Sir Johne, holde up. Heave it a littel hyer.'[16] At a still more 'popular' level, the folk belief that the fairies 'took' children and others who seemed to have died an untimely death could perhaps afford a certain comfort analogous to that of the 'official' books of consolation. There seems to have been — as in most societies at most times — an intense curiosity about life after death. This surely is at least in part responsible for the great popularity of stories of visits to purgatory and hell or to the Otherworld, and for the numerous accounts of dreams or visions or 'sightings' of ghosts and revenants (who sometimes warn the living in a very orthodox, not to say didactic, manner about the need for confession, unction, alms, prayers or Masses for the departed, repentence, the folly of trusting in executors, etc., but sometimes demand vengeance, and occasionally behave in a decidedly odd way, like the spirit who at a crossroads would cry 'How! How! How!' before appearing as a pale horse).[17] The dead were very close to the living. The future — the unpredictability of what was to happen in this uncertain life here on earth — also seems to have produced a good deal of anxiety and curiosity, which is reflected in divinatory practices and in the intense interest in prophetic visions and dreams, and in prophecy generally (which, typically, ranges from the intellectual pole of Joachimism to the popular almanachs).

One thing that 'high' spirituality and 'popular' religion have in common is a belief that the world is filled by spiritual powers.[18] This is one reason for

---

[15] A number are preserved in the Wellcome Historical Medical Library: MSS 632, 804, 804a; see *Catalogue* ed. S. A. J. Moorat, I, pp. 491 – 3.

[16] Thomas Becon, *The Displaying of the Popish Masse*, in *Prayers and Other Pieces of Thomas Becon* ed. J. Ayre (Parker Soc. 1844), p. 270.

[17] See R. C. Finucane, *Appearances of the Dead. A Cultural History of Ghosts* (London, 1982), p. 80.

[18] This can be seen from almost any chronicle. For instance. *An English Chronicle of the Reigns of Richard II, Henry IV, and Henry V* ed. J. S. Davies (Camden Soc. 64, 1855)

the strong attraction that was exercised by sacred places — shrines, sanctuaries, places associated with miraculous power —[19] and by sacred persons, especially the saints (the Very Important Dead, as they have been called),[20] whose power was widespread (as Chaucer says, people come from every part of England to venerate the holy martyr that helped them when they were sick) and very long-lasting,[21] or by sacred relics. The journey to such a sacred place, the pilgrimage,[22] is of course one of the most distinctive and important forms of medieval devotion, and one that was shared by all levels of society. Its central importance is shown by the profoundly evocative nature of the word 'pilgrimage' and its image; it combined a desire for spiritual benefit and assistance, penitence, and curiosity. It was a solemn occasion — it was the image of man's earthly pilgrimage to 'Jerusalem celestial', and of his journey to death — and highly emotional,

records in the first 50 years of the fifteenth century besides the accusation of necromancy (1441) associated with the Duchess of Gloucester, a variety of portents: blood boiling out of wells (1409); the threefold ebbing and flowing of the Thames in one day (1410–11) accompanied by the appearance of strange fishes, 'that betokened fallyng of newe thyngis'; an eclipse of the sun (1433) 'wherof moche peple was sore aferd'; a blood-red sun (1449) 'wherof the peple hadde gret marvaille, and demed that it sholde betokened sum harme sone aftirward (which it did — Rouen fell later in the year, and in the following year 'alle Normandy was lost').

[19] For instance, holy wells; see R. C. Hope, *The Legendary Lore of the Holy Wells of England* (London, 1893); D. Gray, *Robert Henryson* (Leiden, 1979), p. 26.

[20] Peter Brown, *The Cult of the Saints* (London, 1981), ch. 4; cf. also his 'Relics and Social Status in the Age of Gregory of Tours' (Stenton Lecture, 1976, University of Reading).

[21] A sentence in the early sixteenth-century Vulgaria of Horman (ed. M. R. James, p. 150) records that 'they saye that alle the kynnered of theym that kyllyd saynte Thomas of Caunturburye have the wynde and the wether ageynste them where som every they go' (an earlier legend says that the knights were not able to set foot on the Holy Land, whither they had gone on a penitential pilgrimage, because of hostile gales (V. and E. Turner, *Image and Pilgrimage*, p. 7). In the seventeenth century J. Aubrey records some vestiges of belief in the power of saints (see Gray, *Themes and Images*, pp. 278–9). In the Middle Ages, a popular 'familiarity' with saints seems to have been widespread; cf., for example, the sets of mnemonic verses for the saints in each month of the calendar (see Bühler, *Studies in the Renaissance* 6 (1959) 229–35): eg.

David of Wales lo[v]eth wel lekes
That wil make Gregory lene chekes
If Edward do eate some with them
Mary sende hym to Bedlem

(here the 31 syllables represent the days of the month of March; the relevant feasts are on the 1st, 12th, 18th, and 25th days). Or cf. the way in which St Peter seems to become a comic porter or door-keeper in some merry tales; he dices for souls; gets rid of Welshmen, etc.; see D. S. Brewer, ed., *Medieval Comic Tales* (Cambridge, 1972), pp. 19 ff., 55, 80–1 (is this comic stereotype alluded to in the oath of the porter in *Sir Gawain and the Green Knight* 'ye, Peter!' [l.813]?).

[22] See, for instance, J. Sumption, *Pilgrimage. An Image of Mediaeval Religion* (London, 1975); D. J. Hall, *English Medieval Pilgrimage* (London, 1965); V. and E. Turner, *Image and Pilgrimage in Christian Culture* (New York, 1978).

and also a holiday, with an element of that 'game' and merriment which is, it should be noted, a common element in 'popular religion'.[23]

As with much of the 'high' spirituality of the period, popular piety was marked by intensity, by fervent enthusiasm (often further intensified, or exaggerated — the 'prééminence marquée des valeurs affectives et émotives') without its logical or theological framework. It shares the so-called 'affective devotion' appealing to the emotions and the will rather than the logical and speculative powers of the intellect, with its characteristic emphasis on the humanity of Christ, on the details of his suffering and Passion. Such an emphasis, intensified, produces sometimes ferocious descriptions of physical torment marked by a 'terrible precision', even to the detailing of the exact number of Christ's wounds, or the exact number of the drops of blood shed, or the exact dimension of the great wound in his side.[24] On the other hand, the equally strong emphasis on Love as the centre of the Redemption — as sermons and lyrics kept on stressing, it was Christ's love for man that led him to be wounded and tormented, and man should love Christ in return with equal intensity — can lead to a sort of familiar relationship with Christ, who is seen as a loving brother as well as a terrible Judge. This 'homeliness' is found in both Julian of Norwich and Margery Kempe.

Two important strands in this style of devotion need to be mentioned here, however briefly. Firstly, meditational and devotional books stress the need for readers or hearers to use the faculty of imagination: to imagine that they are actually present at the sacred scenes which are being recreated — thus Ailred of Rievaulx: 'with complete devotion follow the mother as she goes to Bethlehem. Go with her into the inn; stand by and assist her when she bears the child . . .'[25] and so on. A more popular audience could be no doubt similarly moved by words in a sermon or by visual images. Certainly, Villon's old mother seems to have used some imagination, and even Chaucer's John the carpenter has a vivid enough imagination to be moved by Nicholas's evocation of Noah's flood.[26] Secondly, there is an emphasis on the 'imitation of Christ' (significantly, the title of a famous devotional book), on following — in various ways — the pattern of Christ's life. The closeness of the imitation could be used as a test of true sanctity (it was so

---

[23] Manselli, p. 17.

[24] On the *mensura vulneris*, see L. Gougaud, 'La mesure de la plaie du côté', *Revue d'histoire ecclésiastique* 20 (1924), 223 ff.; Gray, *Themes and Images*, pp. 34, 236.

[25] Ailred, *De Institutione Inclusarum* ed. C. Dumont (Paris, 1961), p. 120; there are many well-known examples in the Ps-Bonaventura *Meditations on the Life of Christ*. There are some interesting remarks on the kind of 'devotional literacy' exploited by such works in V. Gillespie, 'Strange Images of Death: the Passion in Later Medieval English Devotional and Mystical Writing' in *Zeit, Tod und Ewigkeit in der Renaissance Literatur* ed. J. Hogg (Analecta Cartusiana 117, Salzburg, 1987), pp. 111 – 59.

[26] *Miller's Tale* CT I. 3611 – 17.

used as a sharp test of the prelates and the clerical establishment by medieval satirists and dissenters). St Francis was widely regarded as an *alter Christus*: one example is the vision of Pier Pettinaio after Francis' death — he sees a procession of apostles, saints and martyrs 'all walking carefully, and scrutinizing the ground with much earnestness, that they might tread as nearly as possible in the very footsteps of Christ'; at the end of the procession, however, came St Francis, barefoot and in his brown robe: he alone walked easily and steadily in the actual footsteps of Christ.[27] Not everything is as charming and lyrical as this, however. Some more enthusiastic and literal manifestations of this desire — like the behaviour of the fourteenth-century continental flagellant movements — will seem to most of us now (though they did not, apparently, seem so to many people then) disquieting, at the least.[28]

Mostly, personal practices seem to have been less spectacular, consisting rather — beside the liturgy and other services of the Church — in prayer, meditation, sometimes contemplation, and various penitential practices, including pilgrimage. The surviving written evidence suggests that late medieval private piety was intense, personal, and 'inward'. It would be rash to generalize about 'popular religion' from this evidence, but it is not hard to see that there could be a potential source of tension between the demands of private revelation and official orthodoxy or the approved rituals and services of the church. Certainly, some people kept demanding an apostolic purity in Christ's priests and Christ's church, and some people felt an intense need for emotional and spiritual 'fulfilment', for the exhilaration of an individual relationship with Christ.

I should briefly recall some of the ways in which the patterns of 'popular religion' were transmitted. These came by no means only through the official 'media', but also from parents, and from what now called 'peer groups' (the usual methods in a traditional society), through informal talk or discussion ('dalliance') with friends, spiritual advisers, and others. The official media, which clearly were of considerable importance, employed, firstly, the word: through books, which were not the exclusive property of the literate minority, since they could be (as the *Book* shows) read aloud to others, or paraphrased; through formal oral discourse (most obviously the sermon [we know that people flocked to hear charismatic preachers], but also other devotional or exemplary forms such as saints' lives, hagiographic or didactic romances, songs or carols). At least of equal importance was the

---

[27] Cf. F. Cristofani, 'Memorie del B. Pietro Pettignano da Siena', *Miscellanea Francescana* 5 (1890) 34 – 52; J. R. H. Moorman, *A History of the Franciscan Order* (Oxford, 1968), p. 223.
[28] They seem mostly to have been criticised for being 'illicit', *sine auctoritate Ecclesiae*; see Delaruelle, pp. 278 ff. The *Bianchi* were tolerated in Italy.

image, used sometimes in combination with the word, as in the cycle plays which presented the Christian 'myth' in dramatic form for a popular audience, or, combined with music as well, in liturgical processions and ceremonies, used sometimes alone, in statues or crucifixes,[29] in windows, in paintings, those 'laymen's books' that so affected Villon's mother. An interesting piece of evidence of the vivid impression that could be left in the minds of the totally uninstructed comes in one of the very last references to the Corpus Christi plays. At Kendal (Westmorland) in the early seventeenth century, a Puritan vicar, Shaw, was horrified at the ignorance of the parishioners, and cited the instance of an old man from Cartmel, who did not know about salvation by Christ:

> 'Oh, sir', said he, 'I think I heard of that man you speak of once in a play at Kendall, called Corpus Christ's play, *where there was a man on a tree, and blood ran down &c.* And afterwards he professed he could not remember that he ever heard of salvation by Jesus, but in that play.[30]

Let us consider Margery Kempe's *Book* in the light of all this. It is not an encyclopedia of the practices of popular devotion — far from it — although there are allusions to a number of the things I have mentioned (suggesting, perhaps, that a large area of popular piety is simply being taken for granted). On one occasion her devotion to the consecrated Host in one of those moments disapproved of by Becon brings a strange spiritual experience: the priest holds up the sacrament above his head, and 'the sacrament schok and flekeryd to and fro as a dowe flekeryth wyth hir wengys. And whan he held up the chalys wyth the precyows sacrament, the chalys mevyd to and fro as it shuld a fallyn owt of hys handys.'[31] Equally prominent are her devotion to saints, to relics (like Our Lady's kerchief at Assisi), or her interest in pardons. From time to time the *Book* gives us a glimpse of popular religious practices among the people around her. An obvious example is the excitement at Lynn (ch. 62) over the famous preaching friar whom people followed from town to town.[32] On another

---

[29] One of the uses of the crucifix was for comfort at the end of life; see the account of Julian of Norwich's grave illness at the beginning of her *Revelations*; cf. the Italian *tavolette*, shown to the condemned on their way to execution; see Samuel Y. Edgerton, *Pictures and Punishment* (Ithaca, N.Y., and London, 1985), especially pp. 172 – 92.

[30] I. Disraeli, *Curiosities of Literature* 2nd Series, iii, p. 343.

[31] *The Book of Margery Kempe* eds. S. B. Meech and H. E. Allen, EETS 212 (London, 1940), p. 47 (all quotations are from this edition, but I have modernised some spellings [þ, ʒ, x =sh, i/j, u/v] and made some changes in punctuation). This episode is not altogether unlike the appearance of the Grail in the account in Hardyng, where it flew about the hall 'flyghtrande full faste above thaym all on lofte' (quoted by Felicity Riddy, *Sir Thomas Malory* [Leiden, 1978], p. 128).

[32] 'He had an holy name and gret favowr of the pepyl, in so meche that summe men, yyf thei wiste that he schulde prechyn in the cuntre, thei wolde go wyth hym er ellys folyn hym fro town to town, so gret delite thei had to heryn hym'.

occasion, in Italy (ch. 30), she meets a woman who has an image of Christ, and who 'whan thei comyn in good citeys, sche toke owt the image owt of hir chist and sett it in worshepful wyfys lappys; and thei wold puttyn schirtys therupon, and kyssyn it as thei it had ben God hymselfe' (a practice which would have appalled a Lollard, but which Margery finds deeply moving). Soon afterwards (ch. 31), she gives to the good people in the house where she is lodged 'the mett [*measure*] of Cristys grave, the whech thei receyved ful goodly, havyng gret joy therof' (this would have been a cord or another object with the measurements of the sepulchre, rather in the style of the measure of Christ's wound).[33] Margery has the traditional pilgrim's scrip and staff, and we are told (ch. 49) that the staff was 'of a Moyses yerde whech sche had browt fro Jerusalem'.[34] There is nothing in the *Book* about Jordan water: the description of her visit to the Jordan concentrates rather on the unbearable heat and on the fact that her feet were killing her. Indeed, there is nothing about charms, the magical or folkloristic end of popular religion — nothing like the tree of the fairies that the young Joan of Arc used to visit with the other village children.[35] With Joan, of course, we are dealing with a genuinely peasant background, whereas Margery is thoroughly 'bourgeois', the daughter of a burgess, and the wife of one. But the nature of the *Book* may also have a good deal to do with the difference. It is a consciously exemplary and improving work, whereas Joan's memories of her childhood were extracted by inquisitors. Who knows what such inquisitors might have been able to discover about Margery?

But what is really important about the *Book* is that 'popular piety' is here given dramatic form in a narrative of singular vividness and intensity. Who exactly is responsible for this is a matter of some debate, and there is no time here for an elaborate discussion. Margery, I think, was not literate, or not fully literate. The priest who managed to cope with the first attempt of the Englishman living in 'Dewchlond' and eventually wrote the book clearly had some editorial role in the making of it.[36] It seems to be an example of a kind of 'collaborative authorship' (involving both the 'lettered' or clerkly and the 'unlettered') that was probably not uncommon in the Middle Ages. One suspects that the truth lies somewhere between the two extremes of a simple 'dictation' and a simple clerical organizing 'authorship'; though

---

[33] See Allen's note in EETS, pp. 297 – 8.

[34] See EETS, p. 312. Like the 'yerd of Moyses' and the 'virga Moysi et Aaron' referred to there, Margery's was probably a pilgrim's relic or memento (in the seventeenth century the phrase comes to mean a divining rod).

[35] *Procès de condamnation de Jeanne d'Arc. Texte, traduction et notes* ed. P. Champion (Paris, 1920 – 21) II, pp. 43 – 4, 124 (beside it was a well reputed to cure fever).

[36] See J. Hirsh, 'Author and Scribe in *The Book of Margery Kempe*', *Medium Ævum* 44 (1975) 145 – 50.

certain passages are obviously due to the priest (his expressions of doubt, for instance), many others seem to have the ring of a very individual voice and sensibility which it is impossible not to think of as 'Margery Kempe'.

However it was made, the *Book*'s qualities of energy and vividness are obvious — its liking for concrete detail, which often gives a distinctive sense of being close to contemporary life; for conversations which have the ring of the speaking voice; for dramatic scenes. Its immediacy is perhaps intensified by its curious and apparently unstructured form. Book II is a brief coda (begun by the priest in 1438, two years after he wrote the proem to Book I), an account of the grace wrought in her 'yerys that sche levyd aftyr; not alle, but summe of hem, aftyr hyr owyn tunge', which ends somewhat abruptly with her return to Lynn, and then gives an 'appendix' of her prayers. The much longer Book I is also based on reminiscences (some going back twenty years and more), but is not a direct transcription: it is selective;[37] sometimes her experiences were so high that she 'myth nevyr expressyn hem wyth hir bodily tunge liche as sche felt hem' ('sche undirstod hem bettyr in hyr sowle than sche cowde uttyr hem'); sometimes she had forgotten.[38] We are told at the beginning that the order is not chronological, 'but lych as the mater cam to the creatur in mend [*mind*] whan it schuld be wretyn'. There are perhaps traces of this — in the occasional impression of jerkiness;[39] in a certain repetitiveness; in the way that episodes vary in their intensity and vividness as if according to the working of memory; once even in the very immediateness of the narrative, when in the midst of a scene (ch. 15) with the Bishop of Lincoln, we appear to have a verbatim quotation; 'the Bysshop dede no mor to *us* at that day, save he mad *us* rygth good cher and seyd *we* wer rygth wolcome'.[40] But, on the other hand, scenes are sometimes grouped thematically (e.g. her experiences on pilgrimage; scenes of her 'ministry'; dialogues with Christ), and there is a sense that certain scenes are climactic (such as the various trial scenes, her experiences at Jerusalem or at Rome). And the *Book* has its own strange 'inner form', unified by themes and topics and above all by the personality of Margery herself.

---

[37] Apart from the exemplary story of her son in Part II we hear almost nothing of her numerous offspring, for instance; there are explicit indications sometimes that there is more to be said: cf. 'many mo swech revelacyons this creatur had in felyng; hem alle for to wryten it suld be lettyng peraventur of mor profyte' [ch. 23], 'and so sche was in many mo placys than sche wretyn. .' [ch. 30], etc.

[38] 'Yyf on of hir confessowrys come to hir whan sche ros up newely fro hir contemplacyon er ellys fro hir meditacyon, sche cowde a telde hym meche thyng of the dalyawnce that owr Lord dalyid to hir sowle, and in a schort tyme aftyr sche had foryetyn the most party therof and ny everydeel'[ch. 83].

[39] Cf. the abrupt introduction of the widow in ch. 18 (EETS, p. 45) which suggests that this episode may have got misplaced.

[40] Or, just possibly, a later scribe has been carried away by the spirit of the scene.

In 'genre' too, it seems something of a mixture. It is clearly, as it is often described, a 'spiritual autobiography' — albeit an incomplete one. But also, as well as being a record of visions and spiritual experiences, it sometimes sounds like a saint's legend or a pious romance with its adventures and its swings from tribulations to joy, almost as if it were a kind of contemporary version of a story from the *Golden Legend*. And at the same time it is clearly an exemplary book — it is described in the Proem as 'a schort tretys and a comfortabyl for synful wrecchys, wherin thei may have gret solas and comfort to hem and understondyn the hy and unspecabyl mercy of ower sovereyn savyowr Cryst Jesu'. In other words, it is a 'book of comfort', having something in common with other examples of the literature of consolation. Possibly — but not certainly — this emphasis is due to the priest. The book is implicitly, but rather heavily, 'authenticated' by Christ himself, when he tells Margery (ch. 88) not to worry that 'for speed of writing' with her writer she is spending less time praying than previously, since the book is going to turn many a man to Christ.[41] The priest is no doubt at least partly responsible for the feeling given to readers by constant reiteration that the book is to some degree a 'defence' of Margery and her feelings. She is 'justified' again and again — by Christ, who once even tells her (ch. 20) that 'my dowtyr, Bryde, say me nevyr in this wyse', by the way events turn out the way she has predicted, and above all in a series of 'trials'.

Her *Book* is almost obsessively concerned with the reactions of others, ranging from friendly to hostile, and this aspect certainly contributes largely to its characteristic sense of tension and restlessness. Varying explanations are given of her behaviour, some people clearly being of a mind with Dr Johnson later that 'enthusiasm' is 'a vain confidence of divine favour or communication', some believing that it was the work of an evil spirit, some that it was due to some bodily illness, like the falling sickness. These remarks are often quoted. It is clear that she could be extremely trying; it is hard not to sympathize with the exasperated Archbishop of York (in chapters 52 – 40): 'Wher schal I have a man that myth ledyn this woman fro me?' . . . 'What, woman, art thu come ayen? I wolde fayn be delyveryd of the' . . . 'I wote not what I shal don wyth the'. It may be that the strong tendency to divide the 'others' into 'enemies' and 'friends' owes much to her priest's defensive emphasis, but I suspect it also reflects Margery's own powerful conviction that her enemies were the enemies of Christ (Christ says as much to her in chapter 64 — any clerk that speaks against her life is

[41] And in the next chapter, Christ, the Virgin Mary and the saints are pleased by it. God helps with the writing of it by frustrating the devil who afflicts the priest's eyesight (EETS, p.5) so that in spite of his spectacles he cannot see to write the book.

not God's clerk but the devil's). Her numerous enemies[42] range from her vehement 'deadly enemy' the Mayor of Leicester,[43] who (in the account as given) seems to combine a bureaucratic fussiness worthy of local government with a deep-seated male animosity ('I wyl wetyn why thow gost in white clothys, for I trowe thow art comyn hedyr to han awey owr wyvys fro us and ledyn hem wyth the'), through those who preach against her or abuse her, to others who in varying degrees are persuaded — like the important prelates who conduct the various investigations into her beliefs. That the *Book* should demonstrate her essential orthodoxy so dramatically and at such length is hardly surprising, given its strongly defensive cast. And of course she was unfortunate in being so publicly active in a period of intense persecution of Lollards — the taunt 'Cobham's daughter' was hurled at her (ch. 54) at Beverley probably about the time Oldcastle was recaptured in 1417; she had just come from a similar experience in Leicester, a town which had had a history of Lollard connections.[44] There seems no reason to doubt the verdict of the *Book* that she was no Lollard, although it is quite likely that one or two of her convictions which came from her voices (for instance, that she was assured of salvation) might well have caused some comment from her interrogators had they been minded to pursue these matters[45] (although there is much discussion in the *Book* of her behaviour, the 'trials' are concerned with the investigation of her beliefs rather than with questions — of the kind put to Joan of Arc — about the nature of her spirits). These scenes have a good deal of interest for the historian of

[42] Backbiting and envy are commonly complained of (cf. e.g. ch. 44); the danger of such spiritual 'losengiers' to Christ's lovers is a theme found elsewhere (cf. the *Life* of Christina of Markyate ed. C. H. Talbot (Oxford, 1959; repr. 1987), pp. 131, 175. Visionaries (cf. e.g. St Bridget) often encounter hostility before their truth is acknowledged.

[43] If Margery was there in the summer of 1417, the mayor was John Arnesby. It would be intriguing if he himself had Lollard sympathies (though he calls her 'a fals loller'); he may well then have had a particular antipathy to a wandering enthusiastic ascetic apparently set on breaking up marriages.

[44] See K. B. McFarlane, *John Wycliffe and the Beginnings of English Nonconformity* (London, 1952), pp. 102 – 4, 121 – 5, 139 – 41, 172 ('the heretics' metropolis'), 177. It was a centre of Lollard book-production; see Anne Hudson, 'Some Aspects of Lollard Book Production', *Studies in Church History* 9 (1972), reprinted in her *Lollards and their Books* (London, 1985), pp. 183, 189 ('bills' copied by Thomas Ile of Braybrooke in 1414 were distributed round Leicester by William Smith).

[45] Although the line of questioning is clearly directed towards 'Lollardy', Anne Hudson has pointed out ('A Lollard Mass', repr. *Lollards and their Books* p. 114) that one of the questions at York seems designed to detect 'any leanings towards the beliefs of the Free Spirit'. A number of other tendencies might conceivably have aroused suspicion; for instance, her statement that Christ told her that he was above Holy Church [ch. 29], if put into a more hostile context, could have been made to cause trouble. She always answers correctly on the disputed question of the priesthood, but she clearly has her own idea of 'good priests' — in one case [ch. 33], for instance, she senses that a priest is a 'spiritual friend': 'hir thowt that the preste whech seyd Messe semyd a good man and a devowte'.

'popular religion'. They show that clerical suspicion — and indeed hatred — of her and her influence continued even when she has been doctrinally 'cleared': at York,[46] when the Archbishop declares 'sche knowith hir feyth wel anow. What shal I don wyth hir?', his clerks say 'We knowyn wel that sche can the articles of the deith, but we wil not suffyr hir to dwellyn among us, *for the pepil hath gret feyth in hir dalyawnce, and peraventur sche myth pervertyn summe of hem*'. Among other things, this distrust of 'popular religion' reflects a long-standing ecclesiastical concern about the formation of sects or conventicles. But such hatred and indignation is by no means confined to clerks — a series of potentially nasty mob scenes shows how violently ordinary layfolk could react to what they saw as a danger to traditional beliefs and ways of life: a little later, for instance, when she is arrested and brought to Hessle (ch. 53), 'ther men callyd hir loller, and women cam rennyng owt of her howsys wyth her rokkys [*distaffs*], crying to the pepil, "Brennyth this fals heretyk" '. These scenes should also form part of our 'picture' of popular religion.

Her friends[47] are as varied and as interesting a group. They range from her long-suffering husband through confessors and spiritual advisers to others she meets by the way who act 'kindly' towards her — they are, of

---

[46] Where many of the Archbishop's company had despised her, 'calling hir "loller" and "heretyke"', and swearing 'many an horrybyl othe that sche shulde be brent'. The antagonism runs high in this scene ('the clerkys seyden', etc.), with a hint of anticlerical satire — 'than seyd a gret clerke wyth a furryd hood' — which might remind us of the narrative of the interrogation of the Lollard Thorpe (MS. Rawlinson C. 208; ed. from an early 16th-century print in A. W. Pollard, *Fifteenth Century Prose and Verse* (Westminster, 1903); see A. Hudson, ' William Thorpe and the Question of Authority' in G. R. Evans, ed., *Christian Authority. Essays in Honour of Henry Chadwick* (Oxford, 1988). Perhaps there is a further feature of popular narrative in that the clerks are hostile figures of 'minor authority' — like the Sheriff of Nottingham in the Robin Hood ballads — whereas the great prelates — like the king in the ballads — come to see the truth.

[47] Cf. for instance, the good 'Duche' priest in Rome who gives up his office to support her [ch. 33 et seq.] or Dame Margaret Florentyne [ch. 38]. In ch. 52 she goes to confess to one Sleytham, the confessor of St John of Bridlington (d. 1379; canonised 1401); see Allen notes in EETS, pp. 315 – 6 (in one life of the saint, miracles are attributed to Sleytham, 'a fact which seems to show that Bridlington was in Margery's time a centre of ''saint-making'' enthusiasm'). One of the problems presented to the ecclesiastical authorities by 'saint-making' enthusiasm is illustrated by the case of Richard Wyche, an Essex vicar burnt for heresy in London (1440), 'for whoos deth was gret murmur and troubil among the peple, for some said he was a good man and an holy, and put to deth be malice; and some saiden the contrary; and so dyvers men hadde of him dyvers oppinions. And so fer forth the comune peple was brought in such errour, that meny menne and wommen wente be nyghte to the place where he was brend, and offrid there money and ymages of wax, and made thair praiers knelyng as thay wolde have don to a saynt, and kiste the ground and baar away with thaym the asshis of his body as for reliques . . .' [this was forcibly stopped, and many were imprisoned, including a London vicar — a bitter adversary of the friars — accused of manufacturing false relics by mixing ashes with sweet-smelling herbs] (*An English Chronicle* ed. J. S. Davies, p. 56).

course, friends of Christ. They are sometimes solitaries, like Julian of Norwich, anchorites or friars — like the Carmelite William Southfield of Norwich, ([ch. 18] the fame of whose simplicity and piety lived on; according to Bale, he had visions, and the Virgin Mary frequently visited and talked with him)[48], or the English Franciscan she met at Assisi, who said he had never heard of anyone living 'for to be so homly wyth God be lofe and homly dalyawnce as sche was' [ch. 31]. These 'friends of Christ' in no sense form a 'sect', but many of them seem to share an interest in an interior mystical or devotional closeness with Christ. One of the most interesting of her supporters is the holy man, Richard of Caister, the vicar of St Stephen's, Norwich, to whom is attributed a popular affective lyric 'Jesu, Lord, that madest me',[49] and whose sanctity was such that his tomb was venerated (after his death Margery weeps beside the grave of the 'good vicar' [ch. 60]). Later, Bale records a tradition that he was a Wycliffite. There seems to be no evidence to support this, but N. P. Tanner in his study of religion in the diocese of Norwich remarks that the unusual wording of his will (with no requests for masses or prayers, and instructions to give money to the poor) might suggest that he was a 'radical', who while not a Lollard probably had sympathy for some Lollard views.[50] One might suspect that others of Margery's 'friends' could be similar. Sometimes she falls in with odd, 'outsider' figures, like Richard the crookbacked man, who makes a memorable entry:

> Than anon, as sche lokyd on the on syde, sche sey a powyr man sittyng whiche had a gret cowche [? *hump*] on hys bakke. Hys clothis wer al forclowtyd [*heavily patched*], and he semyd a man of .l. wyntyr age. Than sche went to hym and seyde, 'Gode man, what eyleth yowr bak?' He seyd, 'Damsel, it was brokyn in a sekenes.' Sche askyd what was hys name and what cuntreman he was. He seyd hys name was Richard and he was of Erlong [*Ireland*].[51]

But it would be wrong to suggest that her friends were all like this — alongside Richard, or William Weaver, the old Devonshire man with the white beard, who is also sent by God to accompany her, there are figures like the English friar who is a master of divinity and the Pope's legate, who comforts and defends her at Constance. Similarly, there is the good priest at Rome, or the nuns at Venice among whom she had 'great cheer' [ch. 27]. A point that is insisted on in these sections is that she is often more honoured

---

[48] She calls him [ch. 18] 'a good man and an holy levar'. Bale's account is printed in EETS edn., pp. 374 – 5.
[49] No. 51 in D. Gray, ed., *A Selection of Religious Lyrics* (Oxford, 1975).
[50] N. P. Tanner, *The Church in Late Medieval Norwich, 1370 – 1532* (Toronto, 1984), p. 232. He appears in the *Book* as a very attractive figure, even once [ch. 17] making a gentle joke.
[51] Meech and Allen, p. 76.

and loved by foreigners than by her own countrymen 'for thei weryn evyr hir most enmys and cawsyd hir mych hevynes in every place ther they comyn' [ch. 33]. It is one of the grey friars at Bethlehem who fulfils Christ's promise to her — 'I shal makyn al the werld to wondryn of the, and many man and many woman shal spekyn of me for lofe of the and worshepyn me in the' — when he asks one of her companions 'yif that wer the woman of Inglond the which thei herd seyd spak wyth God'.

All this is presented as part of a providential plan. The early chapters of the *Book* are a vividly told 'conversion narrative'.[52] The account it gives of motives and forces working is not only of considerable psychological interest, but also recalls the 'media' through which popular religion and piety was transmitted. When Margery is 'vexed in spirit' and fearful of damnation, her imagination creates images like those which Villon's old mother observed:

> sche say, as hir thowt, develys opyn her mowthys al inflaumyd wyth brennyng lowys [*flames*] of fyr as thei schuld a swalwyd hyr in, sumtyme rampyng at hyr, sumtyme thretyng her, sumtym pullyng hyr and halyng hir . . .

whereas, in contrast, Christ appears to her

> in lyknesse of a man, most semly, most bewtyuows, and most amyable that evyr mygth be seen wyth mannys eye, clad in a mantyl of purpyl sylke, syttyng upon hir beddys syde, lokyng upon hir wyth so blyssyd a chere that sche was strengthyd in alle hir spyritys . . .[53]

The first stage of her conversion is triggered by sound:

> On a nygth, as this creatur lay in hir bedde wyth hir husbond, sche herd a sownd of melodye so swet and delectable, hir thowt, as sche had ben in Paradyse. And therwyth sche styrt owt of hir bedde and seyd, 'Alas, that evyr I dede synne! It is ful mery in hevyn.'

---

52 The word 'conversion' is used in ch. 18 (EETS, p. 44) and in ch. 85 (EETS, p. 208).
53 Margery prefers a distinctly male image of the Second Person (she does not use the idea of 'God as mother'). Her temptations to lechery (ch. 4 and ch. 59), though by no means unusual in the lives of ascetics (cf. Richard Rolle, for example), may possibly indicate a strong sexuality which may be linked with her energy and creativity. Cf. the case of Savonarola (see D. Weinstein, *Savonarola and Florence* (Princeton, 1970), pp. 79 ff.), where at the age of 22 after a rejection in love, his spiritual uncertainty and the conflict between flesh and spirit seems to have found expression in a symbolic dream in which the water of repentance extinguished the carnal heat of desire. Weinstein suggests that his conversion was his way of solving the dual problems of defeat in love and the guilt of physical desire, and had a larger significance: 'What made him no ordinary man, was not a particular prophetic insight into the state of things, but this ability to translate personal experience and inner struggle into creative and effective terms' . . . 'preaching would seem a natural outlet for this passionate puritan'. Possibly we may see a similar 'translation' in the case of Joan of Arc, and a more 'inward' example in the case of Margery.

When the change finally comes, it is a total one; as the Proem puts it: 'thus alle this thyngys turnyng up-so-down, this creatur whych many yerys had gon wyl [*waywardly*] and evyr ben unstable was parfythly drawen and steryd to entren the wey of hy perfeccyon.' Her new life is a reversal: she gives up her faith in worldly goods, and turns to a life of asceticism; and there is a reversal in the attitudes of 'others' to her — those who had been her friends now sharply reproved her. The 'way of high perfection' brings an absolute opposition between the will of God and the opinion of the world.

She is called — in an austere, rather Augustinian way — by a 'hidden God' (the phrase from Isaiah, *vere tu es Deus absconditus* is twice used) to be an outcast, an exile, a pilgrim in the world. Christ is a hard taskmaster: her lot is one of tribulation and suffering (as the Virgin Mary says to her at one point [ch. 29]: 'Yyf thu wylt be partabyl [*capable of partaking*] in owyr joye, thu must be partabyl in owyr sorwe'). Her sufferings range from the extreme (threats to her life, trials, sickness, poverty, abuse and ostracism) to the small, but no less aggravating — the Mayor of Leicester will not give her back her pilgrim's scrip; a 'rekles man, litil chargyng hys owyn schame, wyth wil and wyth purpose[54] kest a bolful of watyr on hir hevyd comyng in the strete'. To this, 'sche nothyng meved therwyth, seyd, "God make yow a good man," heyly thankyng God therof . . .' If her independence of mind and her constant wanderings make us think of Chaucer's Wife of Bath, her extraordinary patience and perseverance make us think of his Constance or Griselda. In the midst of her sufferings, Christ gives messages of comfort and consolation; suffering increases grace, and 'thys creatur thowt it was ful mery to be reprevyd for Goddys lofe' (often it seems that, for her, suffering is a necessary validating 'sign' — and, possibly, a psychological necessity). Certainly much of the stress of the narrative comes from the tension between these 'messages' (perhaps, as suggested above, one of the 'official' reasons for the book) and the events that she has to live through. There is also, however, a note of hope — she says to her confessor once, in a phrase that recalls Julian of Norwich, 'Ser, beth of a good comforte, for it shal ben ryth wel at the last'; and later in the book (ch. 85), she is rewarded with a vision of the book of life with her name in it.

She is so much an outcast, and behaves so strangely, that in the eyes of some she is mad. She has been likened to the traditional 'holy fool', and there is much to be said for this comparison.[55] Indeed at one point (ch. 26)

---

[54] The phraseology here sounds very like Margery's own.
[55] See R. Maisonneuve, 'Margery Kempe and the Eastern and Western Tradition of the "Perfect Fool" ' in M. Glasscoe, ed., *The Medieval Mystical Tradition in England* (1982), pp. 1 – 17. Cf. 1 Cor 3 : 18 'Let him become a fool that he may be wise'. The idea is found in penitential literature (cf. the fool Hobbe in the didactic romance *Sir Gowther*). Commentators took the white robe which Christ was forced to wear when mocked before Herod to be the dress of a fool (R. Woolf, *The English Mystery Plays* (London, 1972), p.

her fellow pilgrims literally make her into a fool: 'they cuttyd hir gown so schort that it come but lytil benethyn hir kne, and dedyn hir don on a whyte canwas in maner of a sekkyn gelle [*sacken* (?)*apron*], for sche shuld ben holdyn a fool', and make her sit at the table's end 'benethyn alle other'. She seems to lead a 'liminal' existence, to use the terminology of Victor Turner.[56] He notes that rites of passage in traditional societies are marked by three phases: separation, marginality, and aggregation. 'Liminality' is a betwixt and between state, where neophytes possess nothing, and must be humble, passive, and totally obedient to their instructors; among themselves they develop an intense comradeship and egalitarianism, which Turner calls *communitas*, a sense of unstructured 'community' which is outside the usual structure and ties of society. He says that liminal situations and roles are attributed with magico-religious properties, and that these are often regarded as dangerous or inauspicious ('manifestations of "communitas" appear dangerous and anarchical to those concerned with the maintenance of "structure" '). Among examples of the 'liminal' in non-traditional societies, he cites pilgrim groups and certain symbolic figures in folk-literature, like holy beggers, strangers, simpletons, and fools. Margery's mode of existence certainly seems to belong here, although, since she is an intensely 'interior' pilgrim, she strains the traditional *communitas* of the institutionalized pilgrimage to breaking point. Again, in a rather Augustinian way, she only finds her *communitas* with fellow spirits, the friends of Christ, who are true spiritual pilgrims; and her only 'aggregation' is with Christ and his saints in her visions.

Let me now quickly discuss some characteristic features of this 'liminal' pilgrim's way of life. (All are sent by, or required by, God; parallels to all of them can be found in other visionaries or *dévots*; but all, singly or in combination, cause criticism and suffering.) Firstly, like Joan of Arc and others in the late Middle Ages, she sees visions and hears voices.[57] God

---

249; cf. York Play xxxi, 337 ff.). Madness is an important strand in the *Book*. Margery takes her early breakdown as part of God's providential plan; in ch. 56 there is a fear that it will recur. (And, of course, her enemies often think that she has a devil in her). She heals a madwoman in ch. 75. Many of her actions are those of a 'fool for Christ' (for instance in the kissing of the lepers in ch. 74).

[56] See V. Turner, 'Pilgrimages as social Processes' in his *Dramas, Fields, and Metaphors* (Ithaca and London, 1974); V. and E. Turner, *Image and Pilgrimage*, ch. 1 (in his later work Turner refined this idea, seeing pilgrimage systems as 'liminoid' [open, optational, not conceptualized as religious routine] than 'liminal' [belonging to the mid-stage in a religious processual structure consisting of rites of separation, limen or margin and re-aggregation]).

[57] She sometimes specifies an apparition; sometimes the visions come 'in thought', or 'to her ghostly sight' (or once [ch. 85] 'hir ey-leyds went a lityl togedyr wyth a maner of slep, and sodeynly sche sey, hir thowt . . .'); sometimes God 'dalyd to hir sowle'. Her favourite term is 'feelings'. Cf. W. A. Christian, *Apparitions in Late Medieval and Renaissance Spain* (Princeton, 1981), p. 201: 'For modern Westerners, emotions are the signified, the net

speaks to her ('Our Lord [it is most often the second Person of the Trinity] said to her mind . . .'), and she speaks to God. Christ, the Virgin Mary, the saints, her good angel, and the devil all appear or speak to her (sometimes in sacred places of spiritual power — chapels (once, appropriately [ch. 41], St Jerome appears to her in the church of S. Maria Maggiore where his body is buried), before altars, the holy places at Jerusalem, etc. — but not always. Christ constantly speaks to her to comfort and console her (e.g. 'I have frendys in every cuntre and shal make my frendys to comfort the' [ch. 38]). He also gives her practical instructions — to stop bearing children [ch. 17], and therefore (!) to go to Norwich; he tells her to stop eating meat, and later to start again; to wear white clothes; to give away her money; to lay down her head so that she will not see the waves. He tells her what to say to people (so that the Bishop of Lincoln receives a firm rebuke [ch. 15]). He tells her what will happen, and what she should do (e.g. [ch. 28] not to travel in a particular ship). (Often we sense something of the simplicity that shines out so remarkably in the testimony of Joan of Arc.) He can speak in a very homely way ('Dowtyr . . . thu . . . clevyst as sore onto me as the skyn of stokfysche clevyth to a mannys handys whan it is sothyn [*boiled*]'[ch. 37]), or quote a proverb ('It schal be verifyed in the comown proverbe that men seyn, "He is wel blyssed that may sytten on hys wel-stool and tellyn of hys wo-stool" ' [ch. 32]). They have dialogues and conversations (in one interesting exchange on virginity when Christ reassures her by saying that he also loves wives — especially those that would live chaste — he invites the Virgin Mary to speak to Margery also). Margery is respectful but 'homely' in her speech to Christ and the saints, just as she is to her social superiors.

Secondly, her spiritual experiences are accompanied by various 'physical phenomena' which often excite comment or dismay in others; to her they are signs or 'tokens'.[58] These include [ch. 35] feeling the fire of love, seeing

result of experience and physiology, clear data that can be acted on. For these people five hundred years ago, certain emotions seem to have been moral indicators, or signifiers. Just what they meant was not always clear. Some emotions were unidentified . . . some emotions were not truths in themselves, but rather a form of obscure communication from God. Like dreams, they were messages to be deciphered.' (This study also casts light on the 'traditional' nature of Margery's visions and of the working of the 'media' transmitting popular religion: collections of exempla 'provided preachers and their audiences with patterns and motifs that seem to have been incorporated into the plots of local visions' [p. 71]). Margery's voices do not always urge her on to ascetic extremes, indeed, at the end of ch. 66 the Virgin tells her that she is weak enough from weeping and crying: 'I kan the mor thank to etyn thi mete for my lofe than to fastyn, that thu mayst enduryn thy perfeccyon of wepyng'.

58   For parallels, see EETS edn. notes, p. 302. Cf. H. Thurston, *The Physical Phenomena of Mysticism* (London, 1952). There is an interesting parallel to the white flying things in the English *Pilgrimage of the Soul* (ed. K. I. Cust (London, 1858), p. 4), where the soul as it is borne up sees the earth as if it were transparent, full of spirits, 'and also thyck they passyd

many white things flying about her (=angels); and [ch. 36] hearing a sound 'as it had ben a peyr of belwys blowyng in hir ere' which is transformed into the voice of a dove and then into that of a robin 'that song ful merily oftyntymes in hir ryght ere'. She would fall down in ecstasy and 'wrest' with her body [ch. 17]; on another occasion [ch. 57], she 'wex . . . al blew as it had ben leed and swet ful sor'. But it was her sobbing and crying that seems to have excited the greatest resentment. It is interesting to see what local or individual levels of acceptance were (obviously — as is still the case — social groups will vary in their tolerance of what seems to us extreme enthusiastic or charismatic phenomena as tarantism, trances, snake-handling, etc.). 'Religious' weeping was by no means uncommon in the Middle Ages; apart from the visionaries,[59] it is found among quite ordinary pilgrims in Jerusalem. The fifteenth-century German pilgrim, Fabri, says that his and his companions' eyes were 'full of tears and our cheeks wet with joy', and describes the behaviour of some at the church of the Holy Sepulchre:

> I saw there some pilgrims lying powerless on the ground, forsaken by their strength, and as it were forgetful of their own being by reason of their excessive feeling of devotion. Others I saw who wandered hither and thither, from one corner to another, beating their breasts, as though they were driven by an evil spirit. Some knelt on the earth with their bare knees, and prayed with tears, holding their arms out in the form of a cross. Others were shaken with such violent sobs that they could not hold themselves up, and were forced to sit down and hold their heads with their hands, that they might endure their thick-coming sobs. Some lay prostrate so long without motion, that they seemed as though they were dead. Above all our companions and sisters the women pilgrims shrieked as though in labour, cried aloud and wept. Some pilgrims, out of excess of devotion, lost all command of themselves, forgot how they should behave, and out of excessive zeal to please God, made strange and childish gestures

(in spite of this final remark, he reproves those in the company who criticised the behaviour of the pilgrims).[60] Margery's weeping, of course, first appears in Jerusalem on Calvary, and often recurs in 'sacred places',

---

on every syde to and fro, as motys fletyn in the sonne beme, as wel in the eyer above, as in the erth bynethe, wendyng alwey to and fro withoute ony cessyng.'

[59] There were various patterns and parallels for 'religious weeping': the Virgin Mary (implied in the critical remark 'sum gret clerkys seyden owyr Lady cryed nevyr so') or Mary Magdalen; and many examples in more recent times, such as Christina of Markyate (cf. *Life*, pp. 113, 159), St Bridget (who seems to have been taken as a model by Margery), Bl. Angela of Foligno, or Mary of Oignies (who is mentioned by the priest in his discussion of the phenomenon in ch. 62). See EETS edn, notes *passim*; A. Wilmart, 'Prières de compassion' in *Auteurs spirituels et textes dévots du moyen âge latin* (Paris, 1932).

[60] Fabri, I, p. 283. Emotional scenes were common at pilgrimage sites; see EETS edn. notes, pp. 256, 290 – 1, and the references given there.

but, again, not always there — there is a nice episode in Rome [ch. 39], when she weeps in the house of a poor woman who had a 'lytel manchylde sowkyng on hir brest', and Christ says to her 'thys place is holy'. It irritates people sometimes because it interrupts a service or a sermon, or because it seems to them inordinate and excessive. We are told that sometimes she wept softly and stilly, but often it seems to be a loud scream [e.g. in ch. 57], so that 'many men wondered and marvelled what ailed her' (and one friar thinks it may be a 'cardiakyl' or some other sickness). (The effect is curiously like that that would still be produced in many parish churches if a worshipper suddenly burst out in charismatic or Pentecostal 'tongues'.)[61] Whether the phenomenon is a gift of God or not (as some said [ch. 62] she had a devil in her) is much discussed in the book. Her priest collaborator, although he defends it (see, e.g. chapters 28 and 62) reveals that he once had doubts about it. Margery is convinced that it is God's gift; for her it seems necessary both psychologically and devotionally — during a period when it is withdrawn [ch. 82], 'sche cowde fynde no joye ne no comforte in mete ne drynke ne dalyawns but evyr was hevy in cher and in cuntenawnce', and 'hir thowt it was no savowr ne swetnesse but whan sche myth wepyn, for than sche thowt that sche cowde preyin'.[62]

Thirdly, she is an inveterate pilgrim and wanderer. After her near escape from death from a falling beam in church, she was 'mevyd in hir sowle to go vysyten certeyn places for gostly helth'. She does this with such zeal that she sometimes seems like a Wife of Bath who has 'got religion'. The account of her journeys vividly expresses the splendours and the miseries of pilgrim life, but she is a highly spiritual and 'interior' pilgrim. The common spiritual experience of pilgrims at the holy places is felt by her with a distinctive intensity — so that at Jerusalem she almost falls from her ass because of the sweetness and grace. She has none of the 'curiosity' of the pilgrim tourist: in one revealing moment [II, ch. 4] her scribe remarks of her final journey (which turns into a pilgrimage), à propos of 'a place whech is clepyd Strawissownd [*Stralsund*]', 'yf the namys of the placys be not ryth wretyn, late no man merveylyn, for sche stodyid mor abowte contemplacyon than the namys of the placys, and he that wrot hem had nevyr seyn hem, and therfor have hym excusyd'. As mentioned above, in the fellowship of the 'institutional' pilgrims she is separate and often persecuted — there is [ch. 27] a rather comic moment when she is 'readmitted' and must make a new covenant: '. . . ye schal not speke of the gospel; wher we come, but ye schal syttyn stylle and makyn mery, as we don, bothin at mete and at soper.' Poor Margery found it very difficult to

[61] See the interesting parallels adduced by John Hirsh, *The Revelations of Margery Kempe* (Leiden, 1989).
[62] In ch. 49, 'plente of devocyon' is cited as the cause of her weeping; for the idea in religious and mystical writing that excess of love is good cf. L. Spitzer, *Classical and Christian Ideas of World Harmony* (Baltimore, 1963) pp. 95 ff.

separate spiritual life from social life. She is also set apart by her ascetic practices and her white clothing.[63] She finds communitas only with rare 'friends', like the good priest in Rome; their parting is an emotional moment: 'and so departyd asundyr whom charite joyned bothyn in oon, thorw the whech thei trostyd to metyn ageyn, whan owr Lord wolde, in her kendly cuntre whan thei wer passyd this wretchyd wordelys exile.' Such moments of spiritual friendship heighten the austere and heroic Augustinian quality of her pilgrim's calling. Later in the *Book* [II, ch. 2] there is a sentence that makes us think of the Old English *Seafarer*: 'sche wolde a putt it [God's command] owt of hir mende, and evyr it cam ageyn so fast that sche myth not rest ne qwiet han in hir mende evyr was labowryd and comawndyd to gon ovyr the see'.

As the *Book* shows, it is not only 'over the sea' that she suffers; her wanderings in England bring constant criticism and persecution. The authorities both ecclesiastical and secular seem to have a widespread fear and dislike of vagabonds and of unlicensed religious wanderers[64] — though they certainly existed (in Norfolk, for example, there was the ex-Carmelite Thomas Scrope, who could be seen c. 1425 'clad in a hair shirt and a sack and girded with an iron chain, preaching the gospel of the kingdom of God and proclaiming that the New Jerusalem, the bride of the Lamb, was about to come down from heaven and that her spouse would soon be ready to meet her, adding that he himself had already, with much joy, seen her in the spirit')[65] — as potential troublemakers or sectarians. Again, her white clothing causes difficulties. Even more does the fact that she is a wife who is not conforming to the stereotype — at one point [ch. 53], many times 'men of the country' say to her with some kindness as she is escorted as a prisoner, 'Damsel, forsake this lyfe that thu hast, and go spynne and carde as other women don, and suffyr not so meche schame and so meche wo. We wolde not suffir so meche for no good in erthe' (they get a predictable reply).

---

[63] Christ simply tells her (ch. 15) 'I wyl that thu were clothys of whyte and non other colour, for thu shal ben arayd aftyr my wyl'; as Margery instantly sees, it will be the cause of slander and accusations of hypocrisy. See Allen note, EETS edn p. 273; 'more than one symbolism may be involved'. It was variously associated with virginity, purity, persecuted innocence or martyrdom, penitence (as with the Italian *Bianchi*) and the remission of sins. The Archbishop of York associates it with virginity ('Why gost thu in white? Art thu a mayden?' [ch. 52]). It could also suggest a separate calling or an unknown sect (Allen, EETS, p. 314, notes a 1399 proclamation against 'une novele secte des certeins gents vestuz de blanche vesture et soi pretendantz de grande seintetee', probably flagellants).

[64] On wanderers, see J. J. Jusserand, *English Wayfaring Life in the Middle Ages* tr. L. T. Smith (London, 1901); one cause of the hostility is that they are seen as a challenge to centres of stability — home, town, or parish.

[65] See Tanner, p. 61; cf. *DNB* s.v. Scrope, Thomas. According to Bale, he was frightened away into the life of an anchorite for twenty years, but later returned to the active life, and in the years before he died (1492) at the age of almost a hundred spent each Friday as a barefoot itinerant preacher.

However, the *Book* does not simply present an exemplary life of passive suffering. Margery is not only a positive person, she exercises a kind of ministry. This consists in prayer — 'good men' give her money to pray for them; she prays for souls in purgatory, for Jews, Saracens, and heretics; for her son, who is healed; and Christ says that she is to be a 'mirror' and that 'many thousand souls' shall be saved through her prayers — in counsel[66] — she converts Thomas Marchale of Newcastle [ch. 45], she consoles the dying (ch. 72); she kisses and consoles sick women (ch. 75); through her prayers a madwoman is healed (ch. 75) [that this 'right great miracle' is recorded at length might possibly suggest that Margery's priest may have been thinking of possible beatification?] — in instruction (here we sometimes get close to the tricky question of 'preaching'[67]: when she is charged with this in a nicely satiric scene in ch. 52, she is careful in her phrasing — 'I preche not, ser, I come in no pulpytt. I use but comownycacyon and good wordys . . .') — she tells tales (rather good ones: the Archbishop approves of the one she tells in ch. 52, and one of the clerks says 'this take smytyth me to the hert'; later, her good tales make women weep [ch. 53]), and speaks directly and sometimes sharply, like an Old Testament prophet.

She does indeed have the gift of prophecy, and is much sought after because of it. (This element of Margery Kempe, which again brings us close to 'popular religion' has usually been ignored.)[68] Her voices tell her of her own future (cf. ch. 40), and assure her of her spiritual power (ch. 78); events in her life are foretold by others (e.g. the holy anchorite prophesies that a broken-backed man shall lead her forth). She receives revelations ('secrets'), she can see into people's hearts, and has knowledge of the future [ch. 33]; that is to be an important feature of her life is indicated in the Proem: 'sche knew and undyrstod many secret and prevy thyngys whech schuld beffallen aftyward be inspiracyon of the Holy Gost'. Various examples are given in the course of the *Book*.[69] (She does not, it seems,

---

[66] Recluses seem to have been expected to act as counsellors (see Tanner, p. 63); Julian of Norwich and others do this in Margery's *Book*.

[67] Cf. the clerks' remark 'wot we wel that sche hath a devyl wythinne hir, for sche spekyth of the Gospel'. See Allen, EETS, p. 315.

[68] Prophecy seems to have been expected of a holy person (cf. St Bridget, Bl. Dorothea of Prussia); see EETS edn., p. 274. Christina of Markyate was also known for her prophetic power.

[69] Cf. For example, ch. 17 (Richard of Caister will die in seven years); ch. 23 (the vicar and his benefice, and other examples); ch. 28 (she warns her fellow pilgrims not to sail in a certain galley; this episode shows how seriously her powers were taken); ch. 42 (Christ tells her to hurry back to her hostel to avoid a storm), etc. Many are concerned with local and everyday matters (e.g., [ch. 25] the question of the font in the chapel — where her 'feeling' supports the family's side — or the question [ch. 71] of whether the Prior of Lynn will be replaced). She is once troubled [ch. 23] by these prophetic powers or 'feelings' ('thes felyngys . . . bothe of levyng and of deyng, of summe to be savyd, of summe to be

24   *Religion in the Poetry and Drama of the Late Middle Ages*

enter the more perilous world of millenarian — like Scrope — or political prophecy — like the later Maid of Kent.) She seems sometimes to be held in a kind of awe, as if she had second sight, and at one point is consulted almost as a medium [ch. 19] by a widow who wants to find out if her dead husband needs help.[70] She changes peoples' lives. She is a magnetic person as well as an exasperating and embarassing one: the best testimony to her 'charisma' comes from one of the men who arrested her [ch. 53] — 'Damsel, yf evyr thu be seynt in hevyn, prey for me'.

The characteristic emphases of popular piety mentioned above are found throughout the *Book*. Central to Margery's spiritual life and 'feelings' is the 'memory' of Christ's life; she sees it as if she were present, and she imitates it. The traditional devotional stress on 'being there' is taken literally. The pattern is introduced early in the *Book* and very dramatically. In chapter 6, she asks Christ 'of what shall I think?' He answers 'to her mind', 'Daughter, think on my mother'. Immediately she sees St Anne great with child, and asks to be her maiden and servant. The imaginative participation is complete: 'and anon ower lady was born, and than sche besyde hir to take the child to hir and kepe it tyl it wer twelve yer of age wyth good mete and drynke, wyth fayr whyte clothys and whyte kerchys' — and a little later 'went sche forth wyth owyr lady and wyth Josep, beryng wyth hir a potel of pyment [spiced wine] and spycys therto.' And so throughout, with an intense power of memory and imagination, the advice of the treatises and sermons and lyrics is put into practice; the statement of the lyric, 'The minde of thi passiun, suete Jesu, / The teres it tollid / . . . In herte sueteth',[71] is literally enacted in her weeping. There is no need to list the many examples. Later [ch. 79], she participates in the crucifixion scene, falling down as the Virgin Mary does, and speaking to Christ who consoles her. A very nice example occurs in a vision of the Virgin Mary dying [ch. 73], with all the Apostles kneeling before her asking for grace. Margery weeps loudly, and the Apostles command her to 'cesyn and be stille'. Rather typically, she answers back in the way she does with her contemporaries: 'Wolde ye I shulde see the modyr of God deyin and I shulde not wepyn? It may not be, for I am so ful of sorwe that I may not wythstonde it . . .'[72]

dammyd'; cf. ch. 59); and it is said there (and repeated, eg. ch. 71) that there were many more than those recorded.

[70] At the beginning of this chapter she tells another widow that her husband is in Purgatory. She is offended, saying that her husband was a good man and 'sche levyd not that he was in Purgatory'; however, her 'gostly fadyr', an anchorite, supports Margery 'and confermyd hir wordys wyth many holy talys'. For a good example of such holy tales, see the account of the shipman's vision in a chronicle (Gray, *The Oxford Book of Late Medieval Verse and Prose* (Oxford, 1985), pp. 19 – 20). Cf. also Finucane, *Apparitions*.

[71] Carleton Brown, *English Lyrics of the Thirteenth Century* (Oxford, 1932), no. 56.

[72] Again, this is a kind of homeliness or familiarity that is common in medieval 'popular' devotion. Cf. the more extreme example in the *Liber Exemplorum*: the son of a poor woman

The relationship of the spiritual and the temporal world is so close for Margery Kempe, that the two continually overlap. In Rome [ch. 32], she cannot find a priest who can understand English to hear her confession, and Christ sends St John the Evangelist to hear it ('and sche seyd "benedicite" and he seyd "Dominus" verily in hir sowle that sche saw hym and herd hym in hire gostly undirstondyng as sche schulde a do another preste be hir bodily wittys'). Throughout the *Book* there occur these extraordinary 'time-slips', in which she moves from the temporal present to an 'eternal present', in which she participates in the events of Christ's life. Thus, in chapter 49, when she sees the Abbot of Leicester and his brethren coming to welcome her 'anon in hir sowle sche beheld owr Lord comyng wyth hys apostelys'. And there is (chapters 79 et seq.) a 're-living' of the Passion narrative, in which she takes part, crying out against the Jews and [ch. 81] finding herself alone with Mary after Christ's death — 'and thowt a thowsand yer tyl the thryd day came . . .'[73] In these chapters, there is a strange effect of weaving in and out of the historical Biblical story. It is clearly a vivid 'dramatization' of affective piety, but also perhaps, in a curious way, a popular and enthusiastic reflection of a characteristic mode of 'high' spirituality, the sophisticated symbolic system of typology, in which as Auerbach says 'the here and now is no longer a mere link in an earthly chain of events, it is simultaneously something which has always been, and which will be fulfilled in the future; and strictly, in the eyes of God it is something eternal, something omnitemporal, something already consummated in the realm of fragmentary earthly event.'[74]

Almost as prominent is the devotional idea of the imitation of Christ, which is often made explicit, and is continually implicit in Margery's narrative. Christ, consoling her against one of her clerical enemies [ch. 34], remarks 'I have oftyntymes seyd to the that I schuld be newe crucified in the be schrewyd wordys . . .' The intensity with which this is felt is well illustrated by an incident on Corpus Christi day in Bristol [ch. 45], where she is following the sacrament as it is carried around the town 'wyth

---

who constantly venerated an image of the Virgin was hanged. When her prayer that he should be restored to life did not seem to have been granted, she upbraided the image, 'Is this the price of service to thee . . . If thou restore not my son, I will take away thy Son'. And as she reached out to take the image of the Christ child, her son stood by her, saying 'What dost thou, mother? Behold, the mother of God has restored me to thee . . .' (quoted by T. A. Heslop in J. Alexander and P. Binski, *Age of Chivalry* (London, 1987), p. 27.

[73] Cf. the 'touch me not' episode at the end of ch. 81; Margery's 'hevynes' at the command is genuine. Again, she carries an element of popular devotion to odd and literal extremes; in one of her visions [ch. 85] 'in a maner of slep' she saw Christ standing above her so near 'that hir thowt sche toke hys toos in hir hand and felt hem, and to hir felyng it weryn as it had ben very flesch and bon' (on the intense visualizing tendency in the Late Middle Ages, and the obsession with the touching of sacred images, cf. Edgerton, pp. 21–2).

[74] E. Auerbach, *Mimesis* (1946; tr. W. R. Trask, Princeton, 1953), p. 74.

solempne processyon, wyth meche lyth and gret solempnyte' weeping and
sobbing: 'than cam a good woman be this creatur and seyd, "Damsel, God
yef us grace to folwyn the steppys of owr Lord Jesu Crist" — than that
worde wrowt so sor in hir herte and in hir mende that sche myth not beryn it
that sche was fawyn [*fain*] to takyn an hows; and ther sche cryed, "I dey, I
dey". . .'

These various devotional strands are bound together by a number of
deeper unifying themes, usually expressed as sets of powerful opposites.
Thus, an omnipresent sense of sin is counterbalanced by the great stress
which Christ's words lay on love, as for instance in chapter 64: 'Dowtyr,
yyf thu knew now swet thy love is unto me, thu schuldist nevyr do other
thyng but lovyn me wyth al thyn hert . . .' Intertwined with this is the
opposition of suffering and sorrow (the token of the instability of this world)
with joy (the token of the stabilility of the world to come): Christ says to her
[ch. 78] when she suffers both from the effort of her crying and from the
abuse of the people 'Dowytr, this plesith me rith wel, for the mor schame
and mor despite that thu hast for my lofe, the mor joy schalt thu have wyth
me in hevyn, and it is rithful that it be so.' Sorrow is always with her and is
almost unbearable, but the moments of joy are intensely felt. There is
sometimes a 'merriment' that she shares with other visionaries (in Rome
[ch. 39] St Bridget's maiden tells her that the saint 'had a lawhyng chere'),
and which is a distinctively intense and interior form of the 'game' that has
been seen as part of popular religion. A nice example is a scene [ch. 54] in
which she puts down the Archbishop of York's steward. Offended because
she 'lowgh and made good cher', he says 'Holy folke shulde not lawghe', to
which Margery replies 'Ser, I have gret cawse for to lawghe, for the mor
schame I suffyr and despite, the meryar may I ben in owr Lord Jesu Crist.'

Finally, I should like to return briefly to the question of the 'media' by
which popular piety was transmitted, and see what light Margery's *Book*
throws on them. In her case, devotional stimuli come through both the ear
and the eye, through the books that are read to her ('as the Bybyl wyth
doctowrys therupon, Seynt Brydys boke, Hyltons boke, Boneventur,
Stimulus Amoris, Incendium Amoris, and swech other' [ch. 58]),[75] through
'dalliance', and through the power of the word in sermons (one example of
many is in ch. 68, where 'God of hys goodnes enspired the frer to prechyn
mech of hys passyon so compassyfly and so devowtly that sche myth not
beryn it . . .').[76] It is plain from the events of her narrative that she had a
highly sensitive imagination, and that the effects on it from aural stimuli
were very powerful and intense. But even more so are the effects of *visual*

---

[75] Cf. Tanner, pp. 111 – 2: books owned by laywomen in East Anglia include 'the book of St
Katherine', 'my English book of S. Margarets life', an 'English book of St Bridget', and 'a
book called Hylton'.
[76] She yearns for the word and for preaching; cf. ch. 58, ch. 61.

media, which have a quite remarkable importance throughout the *Book*. The sight of holy places, or, especially, of images (crucifixes, a pietà), or even of people (children — especially boys — or a seemly man), or scenes of pain (a man with a wound, a beast being whipped) act as visual 'triggers' for her imagination, and transport her to an 'eternal present' in which she sees Christ in his childhood or in his passion.[77] (The allegorical story she tells to the Archbishop of York in ch. 52 gives further evidence of a developed visual imagination.) Interestingly, religious ceremonies (which use both visual and aural stimuli)[78] are sometimes mentioned as having this effect — like the Corpus Christi procession just mentioned, or the deposition scene at the Easter sepulchre in Lynn [ch. 57], with 'preystys knelyng on her kneys and other worschepful men wyth torchys brennyng in her handys befor the sepulcre, devowtly representyng the lamentabyl deth and doolful berying of owr Lord Jesu Crist aftyr the good custom of Holy Cherch', which draws 'hir mende al holy into the Passyon of owr Lord Crist Jesu', or the ceremony [ch. 78] on Palm Sunday, when the priest beats with a staff on the church door, and enters with the sacrament, followed by the people — 'than thowt sche that owr Lord spak to the Devyl and openyd helle-yatys, confowndyng hym and alle hys oste . . .' Passages like these raise the question of whether mystery plays were among the media which formed her sensibility. There are references to plays at Lynn,[79] and, of course, we know that there was a flourishing dramatic tradition in East Anglia. Margery never mentions a play, but it seems most unlikely that she did not see one. The way she imagines and re-lives the Passion scenes (with such details as the stretching of Christ's hands and feet, the cruel dropping of the cross into the mortise) sounds rather like the 'ideal' audience reaction that some of the dramatists were striving for. But of course it is impossible to establish the relative importance that visual dramatic scenes, static visual representations, and verbal meditations — whether singly or in combination — had in the formation of her remarkable sensibility.

Margery Kempe presents an extraordinary example of 'homeliness' combined with intense visionary qualities, of mysticism rooted in everyday experience. If she sometimes makes us think of a Wife of Bath who has 'got religion', sometimes she reminds us of the young Blake announcing to his parents that he had just seen the prophet Ezechiel. In spite of her moments of spiritual peace and illumination, she remains a restless wanderer in this world; in book II, there is an aura of heroic fortitude about her as, old and much put upon, she walks back to Lynn across central Europe from

---

[77] See esp. ch. 35 (ch. 82 mentions that weddings recall the marriage of Joseph and Mary).
[78] Cf. also chapters 45, 72, 82.
[79] There was a Corpus Christi Guild at Lynn by 1400, and there are references to 'an interlude on Corpus Christi Day' (1385), 'a certain play at the Feast of Corpus Christi' (1462); E. K. Chambers, *The Medieval English Stage* (Oxford, 1903), II, p. 374.

Wilsnack, almost like a spiritual version of Mother Courage. To us, as to many of her contemporaries, she seems an extreme, impossible, but sometimes curiously sympathetic figure. 'Typical' she is not, but her *Book* shows one kind of popular piety 'in action'. And if 'popular religion' gives a more comprehensible context for this strange figure, then Margery Kempe offers a dramatic enactment of its fervours and enthusiasms. The *Book* is a fascinating example of the symbiotic interaction of 'high' spirituality with unlettered piety, and a most valuable 'window' into the personal religion of one laywoman. It has considerable importance for our 'picture' of religion in late medieval England: it is an example of the lay piety, which, it is often claimed, became increasingly important all over Western Europe, but which here finds expression not through the characteristic groups — con- fraternities, guilds, etc. — or in the common desire to be associated in one way or another with the established religious orders, but in an individualism which, although it seeks the companionship of a few sympathetic souls, is an individualism of an extreme form. More generally, it suggests that late medieval religious life is not decayed, benighted, or oppressive, but is rather surging with life, sometimes of a rather wild kind. N. P. Tanner concludes his survey of religion in late medieval Norwich with the observation that the growth of new movements alongside the still vital older institutions suggests both development and continuity:

> Religion in late medieval Norwich appears neither as a complete break with the religion of the early and high Middle Ages nor as a fossilized ritualism. It seems have been in contact with the aspirations of the citizens while remaining a stimulating, at best an elevating force — as Christianity should be. This conclusion is easier to accept if the Reformation in Norwich is seen as a development from within the late medieval church as much as a reaction against it . . .

The *Book* of Margery Kempe offers a good deal of support for this view, but it also shows some of the tensions between 'official' religion and popular religion; besides the vitality, the strains that were produced by charismatic energies like those that drove her on her strange and intense inner pilgrimage.

THE THEME OF THE PASSION IN RICHARD ROLLE AND JULIAN OF NORWICH

DOMENICO PEZZINI

At the very beginning of a work known under the title of *Fervor Amoris*, or *Contemplations of the Dread and Love of God*, one of the most important devotional compilations of the fifteenth century, we find a concise presentation of Christian doctrine which runs as follows:

> Amonge all creatures that euer god of his endeles myght made, was there none þat he so loued as he dyd mankynde, whom he made [to reioyce] euerlastynge blysse in stede of aungels, whiche dyd fal from blysse downe in to helle. But that good god loued so man, that for as moche as man had forfeyted that blysse thorugh synne of Adam, he of his plenteuous charyte became man, to bye body and soule that was lost. In what maner he bought vs, euery crysten man knoweth or sholde knowe: that no lasse pryce but suffred his owne precyous body to be all to-rente with bytter paynes of scorgynge. He suffred also a garlonde of sharpe thornes pressyd to his heed, whiche percyd so the veynes that the blood ran doune in to his eyen, nose, mouth & eeres. Afterwarde vpon the crosse his bones were drawe out of Ioynte, the veynes & the senewes were borsten for strayte drawynge, to þe crosse he was nayled honde & foot, and so fayled the blood of kynd with bytter paynes of deth. He betoke his spyryte to the fader of heuen, and than suffred at the last his gloryous herte to be thorugh-percyd with a sharpe spere for to gyue his herteblood to bye man body and soule into Ioye without ende.[1]

This passage is relevant at least for two reasons: first because it lays the foundations of the kind of spirituality described in the treatise; secondly, and more generally, as a witness to the typical devotional literature of late medieval England. The starting point is a theological summary, where it is said that God created the world out of pure love for mankind, and, after

---

[1] The treatise was printed by Wynkyn de Worde in 1506 as 'opus Ricardi heremyte de Hampull'. This edition was reprinted by C. Horstman, *Yorkshire Writers*, ii (London, 1896), pp. 72 – 105; the quotation is on p. 73. The ascription to R. Rolle cannot be proved: see H. E. Allen, *Writings Ascribed to Richard Rolle* (New York, 1927), p. 356. J. P. Jolliffe, *A Check-List of Middle English Prose Writings of Spiritual Guidance* (Toronto, 1974) lists 17 mss. of the *Fervor Amoris* under the items H.15, K.2, M.15. On the treatise and some of its sources see M.G. Sargent, 'Minor Devotional Writings' in A. S. G. Edwards, ed., *Middle English Prose: A Critical Guide to Major Authors and Genres* (New Brunswick, 1984), pp. 147 – 75, p. 160.

Adam's fall, he wanted to rescue man and restore him to eternal bliss, and did this by taking flesh and dying on the cross. A conclusion is drawn, and presented as man's natural response to the action of God: 'Yf god of his grete goodnes loued thus man . . . kyndely a man sholde nyght and daye with all his wyttes loue him'. Half the passage is devoted to recalling 'in what maner he bought vs', and this is a lengthy description of the sufferings Christ endured on the cross, in terms which ring familiar to any reader of the innumerable Middle English lyrics consecrated to the Passion. No one will fail to notice the extraordinary, unbalanced emphasis which is bestowed on the crucifixion scene. The reason is not difficult to find when we consider that the spiritual way proposed by this treatise consists in a progress through four degrees of love (ordained, clean, steadfast and perfect) based on the principle that to restore ruined man it is necessary to reorder his feelings and emotions which sin corrupts and deviates towards false and deceptive goods. Against such a background the meditation on Christ's sufferings appears as a powerful means to purify man's affectivity and redirect him to his true 'kynde', which is to love the real and true good.

The *Fervor Amoris* is not strictly speaking a mystical work: the treatise does not recount any supernatural experience and it is not even addressed to would-be contemplatives. But as a work of spirituality it is a good example of what circulated in England at the end of the Middle Ages, being in itself the original result of a compilation of some of the most popular classics of medieval spirituality: Bonaventure, Rolle, Bridget of Sweden, Suso, Mechthild of Hackeborn, etc. It is beyond question that the heart of this spirituality is love, and that the meditation on the Passion occupies a central place in the process of self-purification necessary to start any attempt to love God and one's neighbour.

The massive presence of the theme of the Passion in the spirituality of Western Europe at the end of the Middle Ages need not be demonstrated here.[2] The motif is so widespread that we find Chaucer's pagan heroine Criseyde swear 'by that God that boughte us bothe two',[3] a very popular expression which appears as the first line of one of the most famous Passion lyrics: 'Ihesu that hast me dere i-boght'. This fervour led to excesses and abuses: Hilton feels obliged to warn the reader of his *Epistle on Mixed Life* not to waste much time in imagining the Passion, but to practise it, since it is

---

[2] See R. Kieckhefer, 'Major Currents in Late Medieval Devotion' in J. Raitt, ed., *Christian Spirituality II* (London, 1987), pp. 75 – 108. The Passion of Christ as a main devotional theme is described on pp. 83 – 89.

[3] G. Chaucer, *Troilus and Criseyde*, III, 1165. Other manuscripts have the variant reading 'wrowte': see B. A. Windeatt, *Troilus and Criseyde* (London, 1984), where the expression with 'boughte' is rightly termed an 'anachronistic oath', being nevertheless chosen by the editor as the best attested reading. Anyway, the very fact of using 'boughte', be it Chaucer's choice or a scribal error, is in itself revealing of a habit of mind, and of speaking.

better to wash the feet of Christ's body when they are 'righte foule and stynkyng' in his members, the fellow-Christians, than to fancy an imaginary washing of Christ's own feet.[4] But this very warning shows how deeply embedded this devotion was in Christianity.

The purpose of this paper is to consider and evaluate to what extent and in what way two of the Middle English mystics are affected by this dominant element of the spiritual atmosphere of their age. I chose to focus on Richard Rolle and Julian of Norwich because, unlike the *Cloud*-author and Walter Hilton, they are deeply marked by the Passion in their life and spirituality.

To illustrate their doctrine I shall first describe in what sense I use the word 'theme' as applied to the Passion. I take it at three different levels of meaning, and these are: theology, spirituality, and literature. All three levels are essentially an interpretation of what is and remains historically an event: the death of a man, Jesus of Nazareth, condemned for religious and political reasons and crucified some day before Easter in a far province of the Roman Empire during the reign of Tiberius. By 'theology' I mean the exploration and description of the inner significance of that event; by 'spirituality' I mean the place the Passion has as memory and imitation in the growth of Christian life; by 'literature' I mean all the verbal ways by which the meaning and the exemplary force of the event is conveyed to the mind and heart of the faithful in order to elicit his response as a person deeply involved in the fact itself.

The Theme of the Passion

It is perhaps unnecessary to recall that the Passion is the governing event of the life of Christ: the fact is forecast with reiterated announcements, and then described with an amount of detail unlike anything else in the story of Jesus. The gospel of Mark has been rightly called 'a gospel of the Passion', or 'the story of the Passion with a detailed introduction',[5] and the haunting presence of this final tragedy is repeatedly suggested in the gospel of John by frequent allusions to an 'hour' which designates both the death of Christ and his glorification. This expression establishing a strong connection between Jesus hanging on the cross and the Son of God elevated above the earth and enthroned at the right hand of the Father, is one of the main characteristics of the fourth gospel, and it is also a useful reminder that the Passion narratives encapsulate the meaning of the facts they relate. Actually

---

[4] Horstman, *Yorkshire Writers*, i, p. 273.
[5] R. Schnackenburg in J. Feiner and M. Löhrer, eds., *Mysterium Salutis: Grundriss heilsgeschichtlicher Dogmatik* (Einsiedeln, 1970; Italian edition Brescia, 1971, from which I take my quotations), vol. 5, p. 350 and note 6ª. See also the entry 'Passion' in J. L. McKenzie, *Dictionary of the Bible* (New York, 1965).

all the New Testament literature is a theological interpretation of the life of Jesus, especially his death and resurrection, and at the same time it provides the spiritual path derived from this theology. When we hear Peter preaching to his Christians: 'Christ suffered on your behalf, and thereby left you an example that you should follow his steps' (1 Pt 2:21) we already have the double meaning of the Passion, afterwards so wonderfully summarized by Pope Leo the Great in the formula 'sacramentum et exemplum', in which he gathered the whole life of Jesus as both a 'sign' through which we can read what God has done for us, and as a 'model' of what we should do as a response to God's action.[6] This double pattern of interpretation, which I have called theology and spirituality, is clearly visible, as can be expected, in the passage from *Fervor Amoris* quoted above.

a. The Passion as Theology   I cannot enter here into much detail, but I think some points must be made to outline a sort of theological map against which we may better evaluate the different responses to this theme in Rolle and Julian.[7]

The Passion of Jesus can be properly understood only within a chain of events which form what is usually known as the Story of Salvation. The starting point is the creation of the world by a loving God, the fall of man through sin from an original condition of happiness, and the necessity for him to be rescued in order to regain his former state of innocence and immortality. Immediately after the Fall God declares his intention to save mankind, and according to the Holy Scriptures, this intention is carried out by means of many liberating actions, the most powerful being the release of the Hebrews from the Egyptian slavery, and the return of the exiled people from Babylon. These great events, yearly remembered and celebrated at Easter, were but a shadow and a foretaste of the greatest of all: the final victory over sin, death, and the devil obtained by Christ through his death

---

[6] 'Crux enim Christi, quae salvandis est impensa mortalibus, et sacramentum est et exemplum: sacramentum, quo virtus impletur divina; exemplum, quo devotio incitatur humana: quoniam captivitatis jugo erutis, etiam hoc praestat redemptio, ut eam sequi possit imitatio' (*sermo* lxii, 1: P.L. 54, 390). See G. Hudon, *La perfection chrétienne d'après les sermons de Saint Léon* (Paris, 1959), pp. 157 – 64, and D. Pezzini, 'Sacramentum et exemplum: il mistero della croce in un poemetto del sec. IX', *Rivista di Pastorale Liturgica* 10 (1972) 130 – 37, where the *Dream of the Rood* is analysed according to this double interpretative pattern.

[7] To draw this theological map I have used: M. Mellet, 'La Redenzione' in *Iniziazione Teologica*, vol. 4 (Brescia, 1956), pp. 134 – 78; M. Schmaus, *Dogmatica Cattolica*, vol. 2 (Torino, 1961), pp. 216 – 69; W. Dettloff, 'Erlösung II. Dogmengeschichtlich' in H. Fries, ed., *Handbuch Theologischer Grundbegriffe* (München, 1962), vol. 1, pp. 308 – 11; E. L. Peterman, 'Redemption (Theology of)' in *New Catholic Encyclopedia*, vol. XII (1967), pp. 144 – 60; J. Alfaro, 'Le funzioni salvifiche di Cristo quale sacerdote' in *Mysterium Salutis*, vol. 5 (Brescia, 1971), pp. 853 – 60.

and resurrection. As I have said, the New Testament literature testifies to the conviction that Jesus of Nazareth is the Son of God made man to save mankind, and that his death has something to do with us, that it is a death 'for' us. Around this very simple and basic theological statement a varied and complex theology of salvation came to be formed and was registered in the New Testament writings. Jesus' death is presented as 'a ransom for many' (Mk 10:45), where Christ acts as a substitute for us, since to redeem us from the curse of the law he was 'made a curse for us' (Gal 3:13), and even 'sin for us' (2 Cor 5:21) 'that we might be made the righteousness of God in him' (2 Cor 5:21); the cross is seen as an instrument of peace and reconciliation between God and mankind (Eph 2:16ff), by which we are liberated from darkness (Col 1:13), sin (Rom 6:18), and the law (Gal 3:13).

Two words enjoyed particular favour in the Christian vocabulary for expressing the theology of the Passion in the shortest possible way: *salus* and *redemptio*.[8] They do not simply coincide, nor are they, strictly speaking, synonyms. The idea of rescue is common to both, but whereas *salus* evokes the healing of wounds, or the restoring of health after an illness, an act which could hypothetically be totally gratuitous on the part of the healer, *redemptio* conveys the idea of a purchase, where some price has been paid, stressing thus not only the final result, but also the cost of the operation (see 1 Cor 6:20 'you were bought at a price'). The difference in meaning can be relevant, as can be seen by comparing the Anglo-Saxon gospels, where even *redemptio* is rendered by *lesnisse* or other derived words meaning 'liberation', with the Middle English lyrics, where the verb 'buy' is usually employed, as we have seen, very often qualified with the adverb 'dere'. The shift in stress corresponds to the difference between the theology of the *Dream of the Rood*, and that underlying the Passion literature of the late Middle Ages.

According to J. Rivière, the major expert in the history of the dogma of Redemption, it was around the 12th century that the theology of salvation was fixed and systematized.[9] By the end of the 14th century three main interpretations of Redemption were currently available, and are given here in a rather simplified form. Needless to say, all these theories are founded on the Scriptures, and they are by no means mutually exclusive, the difference being a matter of emphasis on single points, or the pattern of their organization in different hierarchies. Anyone can easily expect that the dogma concerning the Redemption of mankind, both for its scope in time and space, and for the intervention of God in human history in the person of

---

[8] The terms 'salus' and 'redemptio' are analysed by M. Mellet, 'La Redenzione', pp. 175 – 77.

[9] J. Rivière, 'Rédemption' in *Dictionnaire de Théologie Catholique*, Vol. 13/2 (Paris, 1937), col. 1950. See also J. Rivière, *Le dogme de la Rédemption au début du Moyen-Age* (Paris, 1934).

a divine-human being, creates a series of polarities and tensions that on the one hand make a comprehensive and balanced interpretation rather difficult, and on the other provide different temperaments and psychologies, both of theologians and spiritual writers, with abundant matter to diversify their responses to the truth they interpret and experience.

1. The theory of *recapitulation* is based on the idea that Christ is the new Adam from whom a new mankind originates: the old wounds are healed, and as soon as our flesh is united to God through Jesus' flesh we are saved, in principle at least, because we become rooted in God. The Fall is mainly seen as an ontological cosmic disorder, creating a fragmentation of being, hostility and division in the inner self and between one man and another. The union of divinity and humanity in Christ is already in itself the beginning and the founding principle of a great work of reconciliation which repairs the damage caused by sin. Redemption is included in the Incarnation of the Son of God.[10]

2. The theory of *redemption* is built on the idea that since the Fall man has become the devil's property, and Christ has to rescue him and pay for it. The very name of 'redemption' evokes something dramatic, conveying the images of slavery and prison, the theme of a dispute between God, or Christ, and Satan in this sort of commercial transaction, and within it the shrewdness Christ has to use to defeat the wiles of the devil. All this has been exploited many times in literary works: Langland and the York 'Harrowing of Hell' come immediately to mind, and we shall find echoes of this theme in Rolle and Julian. The problem with this theory is that the death of Christ, in which he acts as a substitute for us, remains rather extrinsic, a price paid, with no visible connection with the rest of Christ's life and, more important, with all of us and the world in general.

3. The theory of *satisfaction*, elaborated by Anselm[11] and revised by Thomas Aquinas among others, was the most common during the 14th century. The Fall is here seen mainly as a moral disorder: in that it is directed against God it is an infinite offence which demands an infinite expiation to restore the balance. This was realized when Christ died on the cross: his death was seen as the perfect expiatory sacrifice, because Jesus, being man, could die, and being also God, could give an infinite value to his death.

---

[10] See H. De Lubac, *Catholicisme* (Paris, 1938), pp. 1–22.
[11] The best concise presentation of this theory, together with a strong criticism of the theory of 'redemption', is the *Meditatio Redemptionis Humanae* by St Anselm: see F. S. Schmitt, ed., *S. Anselmi Opera Omnia*, vol. 3 (Edinburgh, 1946), pp. 84–91. According to J. Rivière (*Rédemption*, col. 1943), this meditation 'n'est qu'un résumé du *Cur Deus Homo* sur le mode affectif'.

This last theory was strongly opposed by the English Franciscan John Duns Scotus, who maintained that neither sin is infinite, being an act of a finite creature, nor is Christ's death, in that Christ was a man and died as a man. According to him the Passion acquires a redemptive value for all mankind only because God recognizes it as such out of a gracious act of his will. God did not need to be satisfied by the death of a man, he did not properly need a satisfaction: he could save mankind by simply deciding to. This doctrine helps to move the theology of salvation from a juridical, or even commercial perspective, to an affective one, where love becomes not only, as it had always been, the governing principle, but the explanation and justification of everything.[12] In fact why did God choose to die, and to die in that way, if that was not strictly necessary? The reason was that God wanted to show his love in the most convincing manner, or, to put it in Saint Bernard's terms, to touch man in his carnal affections, which was the only practicable way to convert him from his sins and to help him gradually grow towards spiritual delights.[13]

This concentration on God's gracious love had a counterpart in a spirituality heavily relying on emotions, and this is what happened. Everybody knows how central was the crucified Jesus in medieval piety, and how important was the preaching of the Passion to stir the heart of the faithful and lead them to repent and confess their sins.

b. The Passion as Spirituality   Although it is now widely used, the word 'spirituality' is not easy to define.[14] We can say that spirituality arises when truth is translated into life, when theological beliefs are applied to one's personal existence and become guidelines and rules of conduct. Subjectivity and historicity are important elements in it, whereas theology tends to be more objective and universal. This distinction is useful, but can also be very dangerous if we take the difference in terms of opposition between heart and mind, emotions and ideas. The danger has been, and is a real one, and

---

[12] See how Scotus explains the Incarnation of the Son of God, which, according to him, would have taken place in any case, even if man had not sinned: 'Dico igitur sic: Primo Deus diligit se; secundo diligit se aliis, et iste est amor castus; tertio vult se diligi ab alio, qui potest eum summe diligere, loquendo de amore alicujus extrinseci; et quarto praevidit unionem illius naturae, quae debet eum summe diligere, etsi nullus cecidisset': Rep. Par., Lib. III, dist. VII, q. IV, in *Joannis Duns Scoti Opera Omnia*, vol. 23, Reportata Parisiensia (Paris, 1894), p. 303.

[13] *Super Cantica*, sermo 20, 6, in J. Leclercq, C. H. Talbot, H. M. Rochais, eds., *Sancti Bernardi Opera*, vol. 1 (Rome, 1957), p. 118.

[14] See C. Jones, G. Wainwright, E. Yarnold, eds., *The Study of Spirituality* (London, 1986), pp. xxi – xxvi, especially the Note on 'Spirituality', pp. xxiv – xxvi. See also B. McGinn and J. Meyendorff, eds., *Christian Spirituality I* (London, 1986), where a descriptive definition is given: 'it deals with prayer, spiritual direction, the various maps of the spiritual journey, and the methods of advancement in the spiritual ascent', p. xiii.

although one cannot doubt that 'there can be no true theology without spirituality and viceversa',[15] it is also true that a positive and fruitful connection and interdependence of the two is not easy to reach and to maintain. A crucial point in the history of this difficult marriage is precisely the 14th century, and we can discover many signs of a sort of uneasiness in the writings of the Middle English Mystics. It is commonly acknowledged that the 'unity between the mind and heart reached its supreme expression in the West in the age of the monastic theology of Anselm and Bernard of Clairvaux', a balance still present in the works of Thomas Aquinas and Bonaventure. But in late scholasticism a fundamental split appears:

> Two theologies developed: one theoretical and 'scientific', the other devotional and affective and increasingly unrelated to solid doctrine . . . Spirituality, as a consequence, became increasingly subjective and individualistic. Its basic concern was with private consent to God. Personal faith was put beyond discussion and isolated from intellectual questioning. Experience easily became an end in itself.[16]

This situation must be kept in mind when we discuss and compare such writers as Richard Rolle and Julian of Norwich, who in different ways are witnesses to the problems raised by this crisis and at the same time examples of contrasting responses.

Once the idea of spirituality is clarified and explained in terms of a personal appropriation of the Christian beliefs influencing our life-style, we can describe the spirituality of the Passion as a particular form of spiritual life characterized by a fervent contemplation of the crucified Christ with an ardent desire to share his suffering to reach the same saving effects. Historically this form of spirituality was immensely popular in the late Middle Ages, being an essential part of the devotion to the humanity of Christ, which was the dominant element of medieval Christian piety. I need not repeat here what has already been said about a story going back to Anselm, Bernard, Ailred of Rievaulx, Francis of Assisi, Bonaventure and many others.[17] What is surprising is the presence in the list of the mystics of the Passion of a striking number of women, among whom I cannot help

---

[15] Ph. Sheldrake, *Images of Holiness: Explorations in Contemporary Spirituality* (London, 1987), p. 8.

[16] Sheldrake, p. 9. See also W. Pantin, *The English Church in the Fourteenth Century* (Cambridge, 1955), pp. 251 – 52, and W. J. Courtenay, 'Spirituality and Late Scholasticism' in *Christian Spirituality II*, pp. 109 – 120.

[17] See F. Di Bernardo, 'Passion (Mystique de la)' in *Dictionnaire de Spiritualité*, vol. 12 (Paris, 1983), cols. 312 – 28. See also 'Humanité du Christ', *ibidem*, vol. 7, cols. 1058 – 96 (12th – 15th cent.); Pantin, pp. 190, 251; J. Leclercq, 'La dévotion médiévale envers le Crucifié', *La Maison-Dieu*, 1963, n. 75, 119 – 32; F. Vandenbroucke, 'La dévotion au Crucifié à la fin du Moyen Age', *ibidem*, 133 – 43; E. Cousins, 'The Humanity and the Passion of Christ' in *Christian Spirituality II*, pp. 375 – 91.

mentioning the Cistercian Nuns at Helfta, the Italian Clare of Montefalco (†1308), Angela of Foligno (†1309), and Catherine of Siena (†1380), Bridget of Sweden (†1373), and, of course, Julian of Norwich.

The literature produced by many of these women is in the genre of 'revelation', the term referring to some 'mystical experience'. This gives me the opportunity to make a further distinction within the field of spirituality. It has become customary to call 'mystics' all the great spiritual writers of 14th century England, and I do not intend to question the use of this label. But for the sake of clarity I think it necessary to recall that 'spirituality' and 'mysticism' do not simply coincide.

Mysticism is a word which is applied to an extraordinary spiritual experience in which someone has a particularly vivid apprehension of the Deity. It is a gracious gift of God, which can be prepared and requested by prayer and meditation, but is never the result of one's own efforts, neither can it be simply merited or planned. The experience is highly personal and totally gratuitous, and so it can hardly be communicated and generalized, although this is done quite often on the principle that in the Christian community the gifts bestowed to a single person are in fact intended for everybody.[18]

Spirituality, on the other hand, is something meant for a large public, practically for anyone who feels that a certain spiritual doctrine appeals to his psychology. It has a target and organizes the faculties of man in methods and rules in order to reach it, it has steps and degrees because it can be taught, whereas mysticism cannot. This does not go against what I have said about the highly personal and subjective element which characterizes spirituality, because any significant interpretation of faith within a single temperament can be shared with any other people having a similar disposition. We have 'schools of spirituality' marked both by a particular historical background and the strong religious personalities who are their origin.

The distinction between spirituality and mysticism does not mean either separation or opposition. A particular spirituality can prepare a particular mystical experience, and from a mystical experience a particular spirituality may derive. In this case the message received during a 'vision', often enriched by a subsequent reflection, becomes the core of a spiritual doctrine: Julian of Norwich is a case in point. It is not mere chance that so many mystical experiences have the Cross at their centre in a period when both literature and the visual arts are imbued with the image of the crucifix, and so many devotional books and songs are devoted to stirring the memory

---

[18] To my knowledge the most articulate and updated description of mysticism is E. Ancilli, 'La mistica: Alla ricerca di una definizione' in *La Mistica: fenomenologia e riflessione teologica*, a cura di E. Ancilli — M. Paparozzi, I (Roma, 1984), pp. 17 – 40.

of the Passion in the mind of the faithful. It is impossible to say which influenced which, but it is highly probable that the influence went both ways.[19] Anyway, I think it useful, while affirming the connection, to maintain the distinction.

In the light of what I have just said, the Middle English mystics should be classified in a more articulate manner. Only Richard Rolle and Julian of Norwich had mystical experiences, and for Rolle the agreement is not general. That is why, for the purpose of my paper, I chose to analyse only these two writers. Walter Hilton and the *Cloud*-author should properly be called 'spiritual masters': they are teachers, whereas Rolle and Julian are better described as 'witnesses'.[20] These differences should be kept in mind in that they help to see the aim and the scope of their work, the richness and the balance of the different elements of their doctrine, and within this the role and the meaning of the Passion, in a better light.

c. The Passion as Literature   When theology and spirituality combine to create a text where the form and the images become very important we have literature. Such texts were produced first of all to be used in liturgical celebrations: the two hymns *Vexilla Regis* and *Pange Lingua* by V. Fortunatus are certainly the best known examples of the genre. But the writing of literary texts on the Passion was by no means confined to liturgy, and as far as English literature is concerned we cannot forget that extraordinary blend of theological truths, spiritual feelings, and literary beauties which is the *Dream of the Rood*, a poem which seems to have an almost mesmerizing effect on any consideration of subsequent works.

The Passion, then, can be studied as a literary theme, paying attention to its dramatic possibilities and to the numerous images used to express a very complex network of meanings. I will say very little about this, since the subject has been widely explored and described, although a lot of work is still to be done. In late medieval England the Passion theme appears everywhere: prayers, sermons, lyrics, devotional treatises, mystery plays form a huge corpus of texts which should not be studied independently, but considered in their interconnection and finally presented in a comprehensive history. Needless to say such history cannot ignore the theological and spiritual background of the Passion literature, as the best recent critics have

---

[19]   Julian of Norwich actually mentions in her Short Text 'the payntyngys of crucyfexes that er made be the grace of god aftere the techynge of haly kyrke to the lyknes of Crystes passyonn . . .', *A Book of Showings to the Anchoress Julian of Norwich*, edited by E. Colledge and J. Walsh (Toronto, 1978), p. 202.

[20]   The discriminating element is in fact the actual mystical experience. Hilton and the *Cloud*-author describe the highest degrees of contemplative prayers which customarily are termed 'mysticism', but unlike Rolle and Julian, they never mention a personal supernatural mystical experience. On Rolle's uncertain status as a mystic see B. McGinn, 'The English Mystics' in *Christian Spirituality II*, p. 197.

admirably shown.[21] As for the purpose of this paper I merely specify that the literary analysis of mystical texts such as Rolle's and Julian's will consist mostly in evidencing the images employed and the use made of them, their grouping into motifs, and their meaning within the tradition of the literature of the Passion.

Richard Rolle

To talk about the presence and relevance of the Passion theme in the writings of Richard Rolle is not an easy task, his works being so numerous and varied in genre and destination, and the theme appearing almost everywhere.[22] In order to reach a better description of his doctrine and a proper assessment of his ideas I shall divide my analysis in two parts: in the first I shall consider his most famous and most popular works, such as the *Incendium Amoris*, the *Emendatio Vitae*, and the *English Epistles*, whereas in the second I shall examine the rather neglected and undervalued *Melos Amoris*. Although in a writer like Rolle it is always difficult and risky to separate autobiography from teaching, I would say that this is the dividing line between the two groups, in that the attitude of the spiritual guide is much more prominent in the first group than in the *Melos*, a work which Rolle seems to have written for himself, casting his meditations in a fascinating and maddening alliterative style at times almost incomprehensible.[23]

Anyone familiar with the hermit of Hampole and his writings will not be surprised if I say that experience much more than ideas constitutes the foundation stone of his doctrine, and within his experience emotions and feelings are always in the foreground.[24] He is known for having a strong

---

[21] I refer to R. Woolf, *The English Religious Lyric in the Middle Ages* (Oxford, 1968); D. Gray, *Themes and Images in the Medieval English Religious Lyric* (London, 1972); J. A. W. Bennett, *Poetry of the Passion* (Oxford, 1982).

[22] For an updated survey of Rolle's biography, canon, criticism and bibliography see J. A. Alford, 'Richard Rolle and Related Works' in *Middle English Prose*, pp. 36 – 60, where the author correctly remarks that 'there is no comprehensive approach to his thought as a whole' (p. 49), a fact that severely hinders any investigation in Rolle's themes and ideas.

[23] H. E. Allen states that 'The *Melum Contemplativorum* is the most individual of Richard Rolle's writings, both in subject-matter and in style' (*Writings*, p. 116), and she finds it 'the most important of Richard's composition, but extraordinarily monotonous' (p. 118). More sympathetic opinions are expressed by Arnold in his edition of the work, and Vandenbroucke in the French translation, but to confirm a widespread neglect of the *Melos* it suffices to observe that in a specific work such as M. F. Madigan's *The Passio Domini Theme in the Works of Richard Rolle* (Salzburg, 1978) only two poor pages are dedicated to the analysis of the *Melos* (pp. 179 – 81).

[24] See N. Marzac, *Richard Rolle de Hampole* (Paris, 1968): 'Il entre de plein-pied dans son expérience sans jamais beaucoup se soucier de la doctrine formelle' (p. 108).

anti-intellectual bias, which can be questioned and limited by more sympathetic critics,[25] but cannot be denied, and this makes him a good example of the incipient divorce between theology and spirituality which we have seen as taking place towards the end of the Middle Ages. Rolle's highly emotional temperament is immediately visible in the way he tells about his conversion, where he says:

> As adolescence dawned in my unhappy youth, present too was the grace of my Maker. It was he who curbed my youthful lust and transformed it into a longing for spiritual embrace. He lifted and transferred my soul from the depths up to the heights, so that I ardently longed for the pleasure of heaven more than I had ever delighted in physical embrace or worldly corruption.
>
> (IA 15, 21)[26]

The vocabulary used here is very typical of Rolle and reveals the two main characteristics of his spirituality: an intense and pervasive affective tone on one hand, and the habit of conceiving the ascetic life according to a pattern of oppositions. Any significant Christian life has some form of conversion as its starting point, and the quality of this experience is likely to colour the subsequent spirituality. Rolle's crisis 'has plausibly been interpreted as an acute sexual temptation', and no wonder that this fact, together with his radical and totalitarian temperament, led him to think of spirituality as a violent turning away from the world to the point of choosing a solitary life, and to see conversion 'chiefly in terms of the re-orientation of our emotions'.[27] Actually this 're-orientation' means quite often stark opposition, since Rolle is convinced that 'love for God and love for the world cannot coexist in the same soul' (IA 1, 49), and for him 'love is truly pure . . . when there is not the least inclination to seek pleasure in the enjoyment of physical beauty'. (IA 37, 165).

The positive rejection of any theological discussion or investigation is boldly stated right at the beginning of the *Incendium*, since his book is not 'for the philosophers and sages of this world, nor the great theologians bogged down in their interminable questionings, but for the simple and unlearned, who are seeking rather to love God than to amass knowledge'. (IA Prol., 46).

---

[25] See M. F. Madigan, *The Passio Domini Theme*, p. 77.
[26] The quotations from the *Incendium Amoris* are, by chapter and page, from Richard Rolle, *The Fire of Love*, translated by C. Wolters (Harmondsworth, 1972).
[27] S. Tugwell, *Ways of Imperfection* (London, 1984), p. 163. See also the interesting remarks made by R. Woolf in comparing Augustine's and Bernard's idea of love with Rolle's: 'To the mystical school to which Rolle belongs . . . there can never be this tranquil relationship between love of God and man's natural desires, for love is violent, compelling, and unreasonable, and it does not make use of man's natural faculties, but possesses him by thwarting and overcoming them', *English Religious Lyric*, p. 161.

Given these premises, it is not surprising that Rolle's mystical experience appears unconnected with any point of Christian doctrine, but is expressed in terms of emotions, whose strongly physical quality is stressed by Rolle himself.[28] Unlike Julian, he has no vision or revelation of Christ on the cross or at any other moment of his life, but he feels warmth and sweetness, and hears melodious songs from heaven. These are 'pure' feelings, which anyone will experience once he has rectified the wrong ones. Rolle is never tired of repeating that man is fascinated by carnal pleasures, lust, riches, pride and vainglory: all these are false and deceitful goods, and running after them man is frustrated and damned. I shall quote an interesting passage from the *Incendium*, where, by the way, Rolle shows himself much more intellectual than he claims to be:

> Nothing is loved except for the good it contains or is thought to contain, whether real or apparent. This is the reason why those who love physical beauty or temporal wealth are deceived or, one could say, tricked. For in visible and tangible objects there does not really exist either the delight that superficially appears, or the glory that is supposed, or the fame that is pursued.   (IA 23, 116)

There is a very simple anthropology here, where man is defined by his need of love, and, consequently, by his search for some basic goods like beauty, wealth, pleasure, glory, fame. The only problem is that these goods are not real, but apparent, and by the fact that they are visible, tangible, and immediate, they may beguile man to his destruction. The correct judgement and the right choice are of the utmost importance, since 'it is not possible for a rational soul to be without love while it is alive', and consequently 'love is the foot, so to speak, by which after its pilgrimage on earth it will be carried either up to God or down to the devil, to be subject there to whom it served here' (IA 23, 116).[29]

Rolle sees no possible composition between the love of God and the love of earthly creatures, and he reaffirms again and again that 'God wants to be loved in such a way that no one else has a share in that love' (IA 23, 115). Statements like this reveal a passionate temperament, and should not be taken too literally[30], since at other times Rolle is ready to acknowledge the

---

28 'I felt my heart begin to warm. It was real warmth too, not imaginary, and it felt as if it were actually on fire' (IA prol., 45). W. Riehle invites to be cautious about a too realistic interpretation of this passage and other similar expressions in Rolle's works (*The Middle English Mystics*, London 1981, pp. 6 – 7).

29 A fascinating exploration into this image of love as a foot can be found in V. Gillespie, 'Mystic's Foot: Rolle and Affectivity', in M. Glasscoe, ed., *The Medieval Mystical Tradition in England* (Exeter, 1982), pp. 199 – 230.

30 F. Vandenbroucke gives us an interesting profile of Rolle's psychology in his introduction to the French translation of the *Melos Amoris* (R. Rolle, *Le Chant d'Amour*, Paris, 1971).

goodness of such natural comforts as eating, sleeping, being sheltered from heat or cold, and the spiritual delight derived from the 'presence and conversation and company and fellowship' of a friend, distinguishing these things from 'the foul, unclean, illicit comforts of the world' (IA 39, 177 – 8). Anyway it is true that the prevailing mood is one of suspicion and pessimism, and that man is repeatedly invited to reject the false and empty goods of this world, and to aspire to the lasting joys of heaven.

The basic principle of spiritual life is then to accept, or even seek, earthly sufferings to gain eternal bliss, and to reject earthly pleasures to avoid eternal damnation. In this attempt to overcome the various temptations of carnal delight, pride and vainglory, the meditation on the Passion is paramount in that it offers Christ's sufferings, and humiliation, and utter poverty as an example to be followed, and as a means to stir up our right feelings. This doctrine is wonderfully summarized in *The Commandment*:

> I wate na thyng, þat swa inwardly sal take þi hert to covayte Goddes lufe and to desyre þe joy of heven, and to despyse þe vanitees of þis worlde, as stedfast thynkyng of þe myscheves and grevous woundes of þe dede of Jhesu Criste. It will rayse þi thoght aboven erthly lykyng, and make þi hert brennand in Cristes lufe, and purches in þi sawle delitabelte and savoure of heven.[31]

Paradoxically this meditation will produce sweetness and delight in the heart of the faithful: this is not the effect of the mere contemplation of the pains Christ endured on the cross, but the result of the spiritual consideration which connects those pains with the theology of Redemption: they are a powerful and touching sign of his great love, and the soul feels sweetness as a consequence of feeling loved by her redeemer.[32]

To concentrate on the Passion, to hold it 'mykel in mynde', pertains to the second degree of love, in which the classical three enemies of man, the flesh, the world and the devil, are to be overcome. To his reader Rolle says that this meditation:

> wyll kyndel þi hert to sett at noght al þe gudes of þis worlde and þe joye þarof and to desyre byrnandly þe lyght of heven with aungels and halowes.[33]

He too remarks that 'Il importe de corriger Rolle par lui-même. Il faut tempérer ses affirmations les unes par les autres . . .' (p. 64).
[31] In *English Writings of Richard Rolle*, ed. H. E. Allen (Oxford, 1931), p. 80.
[32] See Gal 2:20: 'Christ loved me and gave himself for me'. The problem of how to be happy while meditating the suffering of Jesus is dramatically posed by St Anselm in his *Meditatio Redemptionis Humanae*: 'Quomodo gaudebo de vita mea, quae non est nisi de morte tua? . . .'. To which he gives this perfectly balanced answer: 'Illorum itaque debeo crudelitatem execrari, mortem et laborem tuos compatiendo imitari, piam voluntatem tuam gratias agendo amare, ac sic secure de bonis mihi collatis exultare' (Schmitt ed., p. 89).
[33] The quotation is from *Ego Dormio* in Allen, ed., *English Writings*, p. 65.

It is only obvious to remark that here we have the usual expectation of a reversed situation: the solitary man is in fact waiting for other joys, and above all for another company, the fellowship of angels and saints in that celestial barn, to speak in Hopkins' words, which houses 'Christ and his mother and all his hallows'.

By meditating on the Passion the believer not only purifies his soul, but he also learns how to imitate his master. Interestingly this imitation is given a theological reason: we are one with Christ.

> He will never attain the kingdom of heaven by way of wealth or fleshly delight and pleasure, especially when it is written of Christ, it was necessary for Christ to suffer, and so enter into glory. If we are members of Jesus Christ, our head, then we are going to follow him. (IA 18, 103)

The perspective is still essentially in terms of spirituality, and again we cannot help remarking that what is offered for imitation in the whole life of Christ is his suffering. This is even more apparent if we consider what is perhaps the best summary of Rolle's teaching on the Passion as matter for contemplation, a passage found in ch. 8 of the *Emendatio Vitae* which is consecrated to the practice of meditation. The people to whom Rolle addresses his advice are those 'þat nwly ar turnyd to Criste', and to them he suggests to concentrate on 'þe manhede of Ihesu criste', which is explained and summarized in this way:

> It is gude meditacion of cristis passion and his deed, and oft to recorde qwhat payns and wrechidnes frely he toke for our hele in goynge and prechynge, hongyr, þirst, cold, heet, repreuys and cursyngs, suffyryngys, so þat it be not greuus to an vnprofetabyll seruand to felo his lorde and emprour.[34]

The principle is the same as that of the *Incendium* passage, but it is more evident here that the life of Christ, as a subject both of meditation and imitation, is just a long Passion, since nothing else of what he did is recorded except hardships, pains and sorrows.[35] The fruit of this meditation is that the devil is overcome and his tricks are destroyed, fleshly temptations are slackened, the soul is enkindled to love Christ, the mind is raised, cleansed and purged. The balance is heavily in favour of the *pars destruens*, as it is in the presentation of the two opposite feelings which should accompany the meditation:

[34] I quote from Richard Mysin's translation published in R. Harvey, ed., *The Fire of Love and the Mending of Life*, EETS OS 106 (London, 1896), p. 119.

[35] See H. U. von Balthasar, 'Esistenza come anticipazione della passione?' in *Mysterium Salutis*, vol. 6, pp. 240–41. He quotes a work by Tommaso Leonardi, *Christus crucifixus sive de perpetua cruce Christi a primo instanti suae conceptionis usque ad extremum vitae* (Bruxelles, 1648), which resumes this theme in the title and traces its tradition back to Richard of St Victor and many others.

Ioy for sikyrnes of owr gaynbiyng, heuynes for filth of owr synyng, for þe
qwhilk it is to heuy þat so worþi a offirynge is offyrd.[36]

The death of Christ had to be so painful because the sin it had to repair had
been so heavy: this is the theology of satisfaction mentioned above, with a
notable stress on the cost of the redemption.

As a spiritual director Rolle did not limit himself to advise meditation on
the Passion, but he also provided a model for this practice with the poem
'My keyng þat water grette' inserted in his *Ego Dormio*.[37] Moreover two
versions of *Meditations on the Passion* are ascribed to him.[38] I do not intend
to analyse these texts here, either because this has already been done, and
above all because they do not reveal much about Rolle's own method of
prayer, but rather are witnesses to his ability to adapt a widespread and well-
established meditative tradition to the necessities of his readers.[39] A cursory
look at the *Ego Dormio* poem will immediately reveal the main
characteristics of this Passion literature: a strong emphasis on the sufferings
of Christ interspersed with exclamations of painful wonder for the contrast
between the beauty of Christ's flesh and the hard and bitter pains inflicted
on him, all this leading to tears of repentance and prayers of love-longing.

All in all, the most personal and most articulate text on the Passion theme
in Rolle's writings can be found in what is the most difficult and intriguing,
and accordingly the least read and quoted of his works, the *Melos Amoris*.
The section centred on the Cross is from ch. 30b to 32, and is introduced as
a typical meditation on the Passion:

> Plena prorsus pietas est cum compunccione Regem regum
> pro peccatis nostris perspicere perforatum   (90)[40]

> (Perfect piety is to contemplate with compunction the King of kings
> transfixed for our sins)

[36] Mysin's *Mending of Life*, p. 119.
[37] Analyses of this poem can be found in R. Woolf, *English Religious Lyric*, pp. 162 – 4, and
Bennett, *Poetry of the Passion*, pp. 37 – 41. For the disputed problem of the canon of
Rolle's poem see Allen, *Writings*, pp. 287 – 311, and Woolf, *English Religious Lyrics*, pp.
380 – 2. See also the chapter 'Richard Rolle and the Mystical School' in Woolf's work for a
good analysis of the Rollian lyrics.
[38] See Allen, *Writings*, pp. 278 – 87; M. M. Morgan, 'Versions of the Meditations on the
Passion Ascribed to Richard Rolle', *Medium Aevum* 22 (1953) 93 – 103; M. F. Madigan,
The Passio Domini Theme in the Works of Richard Rolle, pp. 92 – 117.
[39] Madigan, *The Passio Domini Theme*, p. 230. M. Sargent does not say a word about these
Meditations (except in the Bibliography) in his entry on R. Rolle in the *Dictionnaire de
Spiritualité*, vol. 13, cols. 572 – 90.
[40] All the quotations are from E. J. F. Arnould, ed., *The Melos Amoris of Richard Rolle of
Hampole* (Oxford, 1957). The only modern translation of this work is in French: R. Rolle,
Le Chant d'Amour, Coll. 'Sources Chrétiennes' nn. 168 – 169 (Paris, 1971). F.
Vandenbroucke, who wrote the introduction and the notes to this translation, provides a
good interpretation of the plan of the work, from which the 'section' on the Cross is taken.

Nothing new, apparently: a theological truth, the Son of God killed for our salvation, is proposed for meditation as a most high form of piety, and this is meant to stir in us repentance and conversion. The impression of hearing something familiar becomes stronger when we read that 'tam preciosum pectus in plagis puniri permisit' (God allowed this very precious heart to be punished with wounds), or that 'tenerrima caro cicatrices sustinuit' (his most tender flesh was rent with scars). But as we proceed, we are struck by the richness of the images and symbols employed, the deep theological density, the marvellous and, for Rolle, unusual balance between the various aspects of the theme. The result is an impressive mingling of theology and spirituality cast in a high literary style charged with a lot of biblical, liturgical and patristic echoes, together with Rolle's well-known peculiarities just described.[41]

The very movement of the section is worth considering. The text can be analysed according to the following pattern: (1) An invitation to contemplate the great paradoxes of the Incarnation and Redemption; (2) The Passion as meditation in the usual medieval style; (3) The Passion as theology, with all its saving effects; (4) The Passion as an experience in Rolle's own life; (5) An appeal to sinners to turn away from earthly delights and love God and heavenly goods.

The development of the first point is mainly theological, but one must not forget that the man who is invited to contemplate the wounded King of kings is someone who 'lives among honours and delights', whereas his Maker has come to this earthly exile to suffer humiliation and hunger. It is theological meditation marked by the urge to conversion, and the traditional paradoxes of God become man are not first of all subject for admiration and praise, but rather used to make man feel guilty for his sins. The language is a strong mixture of heroic and biblical vocabulary which soon gives place to and is quickly superseded by such affective oppositions as:

> flevit Felicitas infinita et Panis perpetuus fame affligebatur . . . mendicavit Maiestas mirifica et pauper appellari non erubuit ditissimus Dominator (91)

> (The infinite Happiness wept, and the everlasting Bread was starving . . . the magnificent Majesty became a beggar, and the most wealthy Sovereign was not ashamed to be considered poor)

Other fascinating images occur, such as

> Estus alget eternitatis et Sol celicus occasum habuit obscuratus, Organum angelorum obriguit inter impios et Psalterium Sanctorum subticuit cessando, sanguine suffusum. (91)

[41] 'In the *Melum* Rolle does not rely on assertion and autobiography alone to carry home his meaning: over and over again he brings texts from Scripture into the discourse . . .', Allen, *Writings*, p. 119.

(The Fire of eternity was freezing and the heavenly Sun died in a dark sunset, the Organ of the angels was silent before the wicked, and the Psaltery of the saints stopped playing, suffocated by his blood)

If the 'magnificent Majesty', or the 'Sun dying in a dark sunset' may be reminiscent of the heroic language of the *Dream of the Rood*, the images evoking happiness, poverty, fire, song and blood are unmistakably Rollian.

When we enter the second part, a meditation on the Passion, the landscape looks quite familiar. It is the typical contemplation of the crucified body, where each limb is named, encapsulated between the pain it has suffered and an affective adjective meant to indicate and involve the loving participation of the faithful. A few examples will suffice, since the triple pattern so defined is fairly regularly followed:

> capud confortabile spine pungent penaliter . . . dorsumque dignissimum in diris dolet verberibus, oculi obnubilantur amabiles, facies florida fuscatur . . . (91)

> (his comforting head is sorely pricked by thorns . . . his most noble back aches because of the cruel scourging, his lovely eyes are dimmed, his glowing face grows dark)

At times an adverb may emphasize the cruelty of the situation, or the affective adjective may be missing, but this is rare. At the end of this part we find two sophisticated paradoxes like those found in the first section: 'Languet eterna Lux et Leticia labitur in lamentum' (91) (The eternal Light grows faint, and Joy slides into a moan). They introduce the third part where everything is overturned, and we are given another list enumerating the positive effects of the death of Christ on the cross: this death reveals the great love of God, it is for us a source of infinite fecundity, and by its virtue our weeping will be transmuted into a jubilant song of joy. It is an admirable summary of the theology of Redemption which is worth quoting:

> Quamvis vita moritur, mors tamen occiditur, peccatum deletur, imago reformatur, ruina restauratur, regio redintegratur, captivus liberatur, homo salvatur, diabolus dampnatur, inferus remediatur, regnum aperitur, paradisum promittitur, Iratus placatur, resurgit Vita, mors in eternum interiit, ivit per iter irrevocabile . . . (91 – 92)

> (Although Life dies, yet death is killed, sin is destroyed, the image is reformed, the ruin is repaired, the native land is restored, the prisoner is set free, man is saved, the devil is damned, the people lying in hell are delivered, the kingdom is opened, the paradise is promised, God's wrath is appeased, Life rises again, death dies for ever, disappearing along a path without return . . .)

These triumphant but rather impersonal statements turn then into a highly emotional song of praise, much more involving in that the subject is now the crowd of the elected participating in the glory of the Resurrection. It is a new cosmic birth, by which the saved souls will receive the rest they have won, and will sing and laugh at last, having cried and wept during their earthly life. But Rolle the preacher lurks behind the curtain, eager to remind us that the invisible sweetness we experience in thinking of the world to come will make us insensitive to mundane dignities, and the fire of eternal love will destroy all worthless and deceitful delights.

In the fourth part Rolle comes to the foreground, to tell us how he escaped a dangerous temptation, and helped by the memory of the Passion, he was able to reject the attraction of a 'lustful delight' (leticia libidinosa) offered him 'in the world by a most loving woman' (93) (amicam in mundo amantissimam). We have already talked about this sexual temptation Rolle underwent in his youth, and have seen to what extent this experience determined his idea of spirituality. He says here that he chose then to suffer with the friends of God rather than rejoice with people who live an easy life on the earth but will cry for ever after Doomsday, killed by the very swords they have forged. The necessary strength to overcome the temptation came to him as a result of his continuous thinking on the blood Christ shed on the cross and on his bitter death. Again and again in this part we find many traditional images characteristic of the Passion literature: they reveal how familiar Rolle was with the liturgical texts and the theology of the Fathers. There is even the motif of the devil beguiled by the humanity of Christ, in whom he did not recognize the hidden divinity, which was the secret bait to which he fell victim.[42] This same theology of Redemption appears where Christ says: 'Emi te in hereditatem meam, ne sis possessio alterius' (97) (I bought you to be my heritage, do not become another's property), an idea referring to the theory of the 'devil's rights', stating that man had become the devil's property after the Fall. An echo of the Easter liturgy, where the Passion is described as a duel between life and death, Christ being the warrior, can be found where Rolle presents himself as a 'miles magnificus',[43] a stout and sturdy champion fighting against the devil. Apart from Rolle's protagonism, this heroic vocabulary together with the use of paradoxical language is again evocative of the *Dream of the Rood* and of the great Christian tradition, which no one will fail to notice reading such lines as these: 'Princeps populi patibulum perpessus arens apparuit deficiens

---

[42] This motif, which Bennett calls 'bizarre' (*Poetry of the Passion*, p. 47), goes back to St Augustine, who said in one of his sermons: 'The Redeemer came, and the deceiver was overcome. What did our Redeemer do to our captor? In payment for us he set the trap, his Cross, with his blood for bait. He (Satan) could indeed shed that blood, but he deserved not to drink it. By shedding the blood of One who was not his debtor, he was forced to release his debtors': *sermo* cxxx, 2: P.L. 38, col. 726.

[43] On the theme of the Christian as 'miles' see Riehle, *Middle English Mystics*, p. 52.

colore,[44] et videbatur vanescere virtus Viventis' (95) (The Prince of the people cruelly suffering on the gallows looked dried up, pale and wan, and the strength of the Living One seemed to vanish).

With the fifth and last part we are back to the medieval devotional world, and Rolle's invitation to conversion, following his own example, is cast in the typical genre called 'Complaint of Christ':[45] 'Clamat ad te Christus in cruce' (96), Rolle says, 'Peccare desine qui tam care redimeris' (97). Christ appeals to the sinner from the cross, reminding him how high was the price he paid to rescue him from damnation, and asking him to leave his sinful ways. The motif is the same as that found in the passage from *Fervor Amoris* quoted at the beginning, with an identical development: the Incarnation is the reason given to move man to repentance, but this is again nothing but a long Passion:

> Pro te incarnatus, pro te sum et natus, pro te circumcisus, pro te baptizatus, exprobratus iniuriis illatis, obprobriis saturatus, captus, ligatus, consputus, velatus, flagellatus, vulneratus, cruci affixus, aceto potatus et demum pro te immolatus. (97)

> (For you I took flesh, for you I was born, for you circumcised, for you baptized, rebuked and insulted, covered with abuse, captured, tied, spat upon, veiled, scourged, wounded, nailed to the cross, given vinegar for drink, and at last sacrificed for you)

It is perhaps important to remember that also the events listed here that seem to have nothing to do with the Passion were in fact interpreted as suffering and humiliation. In this same section Rolle talks about the Incarnation and birth of Christ in these terms: 'Imperator omnipotens in paupere puella formam . . . prendidit; in cunabulis clauditur Qui cuncta complere cognoscitur, Lumen indeficiens pannis involvitur' (91) (The almighty Emperor took shape in a poor maiden; he who is known for enclosing everything is enclosed in a cradle, the unfailing Light is wrapped in swaddling cloths). In the same way the circumcision was seen as the first occasion for Christ to shed his blood for us, and in the Baptism he had humbled himself under the authority of John the Baptist.

The balance is heavily in favour of sorrow and grief. Rolle wants to strike the imagination and the heart of his audience, and at times a threatening tone appears, as when he warns not to wait to turn to God when one is old,

---

[44] In Julian's *Revelations* the whole ch. 16 is devoted to describing 'the last petivous peynes of Christe deyeng, and discoloryng of his face, and dreyeng of his flesh'.

[45] See Woolf, *English Religious Lyric*, pp. 36 – 44, and Bennett, *Poetry of the Passion*, pp. 46 – 47. See also the poems collected under the heading 'Complaints of Christ' in D. Gray, *A Selection of Religious Lyrics* (Oxford, 1975), pp. 25 – 31.

because this means that, after wasting the flowers and fruits of life, one is left with bran and straw to offer to God:[46]

> Et quomodo tu paleas porrigis Potenti, putans quod placabis Principem iratum, offerens ei quando aliud non habes nisi quod est omnibus exosum? (99)

> (How dare you offer straw to the Mighty One? Do you think that you can appease the angry Prince by giving him what everyone finds detestable and useless?)

He says instead that he has offered his adolescence to God, and thanks him because, unlike other young people, he has remained chaste. The reason is again the memory of the death of Christ: his Passion has pierced Rolle's heart, and his blood has struck him like an arrow ('Pectus meum pietas tue passionis penetravit, et sagittavit me sanguis quem sudasti': 98). Everybody else should do the same, and anyone following Rolle's example will win the same reward: a radiant rest in a haven of peace, where he will reign with kings, be seated with the heavenly people on thrones of serenity, glorifying Christ whom he has loved beyond all measure.

I shall conclude this part with two remarks. If we consider Rolle's more popular writings we may be deeply disappointed: his treatment of the Passion is theologically very poor, and even in terms of spirituality it appears unbalanced and one-sided: suffering is overemphasized, and the glorious aspect of the Paschal mystery is hardly mentioned. This is because he views the meditation on the Passion practically only in connection with the purgative stage in the spiritual journey, 'a stage which the learner in contemplation made use of and then left behind':[47] this constitutes the severest limitation of his treatment.

On the other hand the long section of *Melos Amoris* which has been examined shows that he was well acquainted with the liturgical, patristic and theological tradition, and was capable of making a good use of it to describe his spiritual experience. The result is a treatment of the Passion which, while remaining characteristically Rollian, is rich, varied, and balanced. John A. Alford affirms that 'Rolle's most striking and difficult ideas lie in his Latin works, especially in his *Melos*, which despite the edition by

---

[46] Julian's outlook on this point is totally different. Of course she knows that those who 'wylfully and frely offer ther yowth to god' are rewarded and thanked supremely and wonderfully, but she adds that 'when or what tyme þat a man or woman be truly turned to god, for one day servys and for hys endelesse wylle he shall haue alle these thre degrees of blesse' (ch. 14, p. 353 of the Colledge-Walsh edition).

[47] Woolf, *English Religious Lyric*, pp. 160–61.

Arnold (1957) continues to be ignored. Scholars who are not able or not willing to read through this formidable body of material probably should leave evaluations of Rolle's mysticism to those who are'.[48] I think he is right.

Julian of Norwich

At the start in Julian's perspective the Passion is essentially viewed in terms of spirituality, and not merely as a part of it or an initial stage, but as the very keystone of the plan she sets up to organize her spiritual life. In fact she understands the showings as an answer to a prayer she had made expressing a desire to receive 'thre giftes by the grace of God. The first was mynd of the passion. The secund was bodilie sicknes. The thurde was to haue of godes grace thre woundys' (2, 285).[49] The language she uses is ostensibly that of the Passion for all three gifts: the bodily sickness is actually meant to give a fleshly consistency to the mental and visual meditation, and the wounds evoke quite naturally the crucified Christ. These three wounds, interpreted as 'verie contricion', 'kynd compassion', and 'willfull longing to god' (288), symbolize three substantial aspects of the spiritual journey: in this, as in the marked reference to the Passion as an all-embracing devotion, Julian is undoubtedly a daughter of her time.

A new insight, however, is suggested when we try to understand why she used the term 'wounds' to qualify these aspects of spiritual life.[50] In the Short Text of the *Revelations* she says that this idea came to her mind when hearing the story of Saint Cecilia, but this reference is suppressed in the Long Text. I should like to think that this was when and because she had a better understanding of the showings, and what could have been a colourful detail became instead a theological truth cast in an iconic structure.

It is a well-known tenet of traditional theology that God has redeemed mankind by using the same means that had caused man's ruin. This is what Fortunatus beautifully says in his *Pange Lingua*: after the sin of our progenitors God wanted to rescue them from death, and so 'ipse lignum tunc notavit / damna ligni ut solveret', and the scheme of our salvation required that 'medelam ferret inde / hostis unde laeserat'. So, if the term 'wound' evokes immediately the crucifix, at a deeper level it is also suggestive of the

---

[48] Alford, 'Richard Rolle and Related Works', p. 49.

[49] All quotations in this part are from the Long Text of Julian's *Revelations*. The edition used is E. Colledge and J. Walsh, eds., *A Book of Showings to the Anchoress Julian of Norwich* (Toronto, 1978). The two numbers refer to the chapter and the page respectively.

[50] For the development of the motif of the 'wounds' in medieval devotion see Colledge-Walsh, *Showings*, p. 205, and W. Riehle, *Middle English Mystics*, pp. 45–48. The image is interpreted in connection with the Song of Songs and is usually taken as a symbol of love. Julian's originality consists in making it the basic interpretative pattern of the whole spiritual life, comprising not only love, but also contrition and compassion.

'wounds' man suffered as a consequence of the Fall, and of the way God chose to heal him. Man had been affected in his mind and in his will, and had lost the grace of God: by the wounds Christ has suffered in his Passion man will be restored to his original condition, but this will be realized only if and when man becomes, so to speak, himself wounded. T. S. Eliot works in this tradition when he calls Christ 'the wounded surgeon', and the wounds Julian is talking about are in fact 'healing wounds', by which the mind will be purified by the memory of the Passion, the will strengthened by experiencing the pains of Christ's agony and death, and the grace of God recovered by a constant longing for him. This is actually what Julian says when the meaning of the image becomes more explicit, and the three wounds reappear as three 'medycins', by which man understands that 'his woundys begynn to heele and the soule to quycken' (39, 449):

> By contryscion we be made clene,
> by compassion we be made redy,
> and by tru longyng to god we be made wurthy.
> Theyse be thre menys wher by that alle soule com to hevyn. (451 – 52)

Right at the beginning of Julian's book we have a wonderful example of her way of treating the theme of the Passion: theology, spirituality and literature merge into one another, the three levels being present in a somewhat cryptic manner which needs careful reading to be discovered.

The same theological perspective linking the fall of man with his restoration using the same means but with the reverse effect, is more clearly described and more widely applied in the long parable of ch. 51 which Julian calls 'a wonderfull example of a lorde that hath a servannt'. Here a servant runs to do his lord's will, but in running 'anon he fallyth in a slade, and takyth ful grett sorow; and than he gronyth and monyth and wallowyth and wryeth, but he may nott ryse nor helpe hym selfe by no manner of weye' (51, 515).

Who is this man? A quick answer, prompted by the biblical hint about the servant of the Lord who has come to do his Father's will,[51] would be that Julian is talking of Jesus fallen on his road to Calvary. On the other hand the absolute impossibility of the servant's rescuing himself is evocative of fallen man, sorely wounded and weakened as a consequence of the original sin.[52] Julian tells us that she remained for a long time rather confused, trying

---

[51] See John 4:34: 'My meat is to do the will of him that sent me'; see also 5:30, 6:38 – 40.
[52] There is a striking similarity between this passage of the *Revelations* and the way St Anselm describes the condition of fallen man in his *Meditatio Redemptionis Humanae*. Julian's servant is 'blyndyd in his reson and stonyd in his minde', and Anselm says: 'In tenebris eram quia nihil, nec meipsum sciebam'; the servant falls in a 'slade' (valley, boggy place), and Anselm writes 'in lubrico eram . . . in descensu super chaos inferni'; the servant is 'full febyll and vnwyse' after the fall, like Anselm, who sees himself 'imbecillis et fragilis ad lapsum peccati'; Julian's servant cannot rise nor help himself because of 'þe hevynesse of

52   Religion in the Poetry and Drama of the Late Middle Ages

to understand the meaning of the parable, where the servant appeared at times like Adam, at other times like Christ, without ever corresponding perfectly to either of them. The solution to the mystery is reached after long investigations into the showing, and is clearly stated with these words:

> In the servant is comprehendyd the seconde person of þe trynyte, and in the seruannt is comprehendyd Adam, that is to sey all men. And therfore whan I sey the sonne, it menyth the godhed whych is evyn with the fader, and whan I sey the servannt, it menyth Crystes manhode whych is ryghtfull Adam . . . When Adam felle godes sonne fell; for the ryght onyng whych was made in hevyn, goddys sonne myght nott be seperath from Adam, for by Adam I vnderstond alle man. Adam fell fro lyfe to deth, in to the slade of this wrechyd worlde, and aftyr that in to hell. Goddys son fell with Adam in to the slade of the meydens wombe, whych was the feyerest doughter of Adam, and that for to excuse Adam from blame in hevyn and in erth; and myghtely he fechyd hym out of hell.   (51, 533 – 34)

As with 'wound', another key word is used here, 'fall', with a double contrasting meaning, since it indicates both 'sin' and 'incarnation' viewed as a fall from the glorious state of divinity to the wretched condition of humanity. To see in Adam-Christ all mankind gives Julian's treatment of the Passion a note of universal sympathy most peculiar to her and very different from Rolle's rather individualistic approach: this is all the more interesting if we consider that Julian was a recluse. Moreover, a very important theological point is made here: Julian sees Redemption not in terms of substitution but of solidarity, in accordance with the wide approach of the theory of recapitulation.[53] In fact, although the Passion is unquestionably the starting point and the radiating centre of her book and of her spirituality, she is positive in stating that among the many means God has ordained to help us 'the chiefe and principall meane is the blessed kynde that he toke of the maiden, with all the meanes that went before and come after, which be langyng to our redemption and to our endles saluation' (6, 305). In a sense Julian is like Rolle in considering the redemptive value of the whole life of Christ,[54] but unlike him this is not turned into a long list of endless sorrows,

his body', a condition which Anselm evokes saying: 'Pondus originalis peccati dehorsum me trahebat'.

[53] See Ephesians 1: 9 – 10. 'Dieu n'a pas voulu opérer le sauvetage de l'humanité, comme d'une épave: il a voulu susciter en elle une vie, sa propre Vie. La loi de la Rédemption réproduit ici la loi de la Création: il fallait que l'homme concourût à sa fin sublime, il faut maintenant qu'il concoure à son rachat. Le Christ n'est donc pas venu se substituer à nous — ou plutôt, cet aspect de substitution n'exprime que le premier temps de son oeuvre — mais nous mettre en mesure de nous hausser, par lui, jusqu'à Dieu. Non nous obtenir un pardon extérieur . . . mais nous transformer intérieurement': De Lubac, *Catholicisme*, p. 167.

[54] See J. Alfaro, 'Funzioni salvifiche di Cristo' in *Mysterium Salutis*, vol. 5, p. 855, who mentions St Bonaventure, *In III Sent.*, dist. 18, art. 1, q. 2: in *S. Bonaventurae Opera Omnia*, t. III (Quaracchi, 1887), pp. 382 – 5.

rather it becomes a cosmic joy flowing down from the Trinity over all the world. God the Father, Julian says, 'is wele plesyde with alle the dedes that Jhesu hath done about our saluacion; where for we be nott only hys by his byeng, but also by the curteyse gyfte of hys father' (22, 384). The idea of the Cross as the price Christ had to pay to buy us back from the devil is maintained, but the image of a strictly commercial transaction is happily counterbalanced by the added reason of the Father's courtesy who gives us to his Son as a present,[55] to be 'his blysse, his mede, hys wurshype, his crowne' (ibid.). Our being his crown is called by Julian 'a syngular marveyle and a full delectable beholdyng'. Why does she stress this detail? We are probably not far from the truth if we think that she has been fascinated again by the double possible meaning of the word 'crown', the garland of thorns becoming the crown of glory, the price and the reward connected in the same image.

This connective mentality helps Julian to set the Passion in a much larger context, to see it as a part of a much wider operation: the Passion is in fact a Trinitarian enterprise. To illustrate this I shall use one of those astonishing statements so typical of Julian where we find a high concentration of thought together with a sparkling stylistic clarity, and where again theology, spirituality and literary technique are fused in an admirable result:

> He is the enlesshead / and he made vs only to him selfe / and restored vs by his precious passion / and ever kepeth vs in his blessed loue / and all this is of his goodnes. (5, 303)

The sense of connection is strongly emphasized by the repetition of the particle 'and', perhaps the most common feature of Julian's syntax. The unity of God is rendered by using the single subject 'he', the Trinity appears in the three verbs describing God's operation towards the world, two in the past referring to the creation and the restoration of the world, and the third in the perennial present of his loving goodness, to which the first sentence gives an infinite extension. Thus the syntactic structure becomes, so to speak, a pictorial rendering of the theological truth, where the Passion is placed at the centre of God's activity, whose effects go far beyond that event and reach eternity.

[55] In specifying that we are saved and become one with Christ not only because of his redeeming death ('his byeng'), but also 'by the curteyse gyfte of hys father' Julian seems to be influenced by the Scotist theory, which J. Rivière sums up in these terms: 'L'oeuvre du Sauveur n'a, par rapport à nous, qu'une valeur *de congruo* et ne peut s'appliquer à notre profit que moyennant son acceptation par Dieu' (*Dict. Théol. Cath.*, vol. 13/2, col. 1951). As a matter of fact Julian does not totally agree with this idea, in that we are *already* restored to God's friendship through Jesus' sacrifice, and so God's acceptance of it does not seem absolutely necessary, as Scotus argued. Perhaps, by mentioning the courtesy of the Father as a second, equivalent reason for our redemption, she is trying to reconcile the two different theological theories current in her time.

To see the Passion within a creational and trinitarian perspective is only a logical consequence of a deep sense of harmony and unity between God and the world which Julian manifests over and again in her book:

> Thus I vnderstode that all his blessyd chyldren
> whych be come out of hym by kynd
> shulde be brought agayne in to hym by grace.   (64, 619)

She is imbued with the magnificent Pauline prologues to the Ephesians and the Colossians where the multiplicity and fragmentation of the created world gathers into unity to form a body of which Christ is the head in that he is both the source and the achievement of being.

Against this vast background Julian is able to view sin not only in terms of moral transgression, but as a disruption of the original harmony, a lack, a want of being, and, accordingly, she includes in it what Christ suffered for us, 'and hys dyeng and alle hys paynes, and passion of alle hys creatures gostly and bodely' (27, 405). We are far from the interpretation which considers sin and redemption as two separate things. Julian seems to fuse everything: 'synne — she says — had no maner substannce, ne no part of beyng, ne it myght not be knowen but by the payne that is caused therof. And thys payne is somthyng . . . for a tyme, for it purgyth and makyth vs to know oure selfe and aske mercy; for the passion of oure lorde is comfort to vs aȝenst alle thys' (27, 406 – 07). This metaphysical idea of sin is directly derived from the idea of God as the ground of our being, in whom only there is our full happiness and rest, since we are 'made only to him selfe'. More than a positive transgression, sin is perceived as a distressing failure: we do not reach our true being, and so we suffer, but this suffering is providential in that it makes us know ourselves, and discover that through sin we cannot achieve our welfare. In the scheme of redemption Christ bore our sins as much as he bore our death, the two fusing into one in Julian's perspective. Death is the utmost manifestation of sin in that it is the total destruction of being. By accepting death Christ destroyed it and restored mankind to the fullness of being. In this and for this the Passion is comfort to us.

Julian's treatment of sin shows how extraordinary is her capacity to blend high theology and intense affectivity. Another example of this can be found in the advice she gives on how to meditate on the Passion. Quite traditionally she invites us to consider *who* suffered, then *what*, and finally *for whom*. But two remarks she makes deserve our attention. The first reveals her humane and realistic attitude: in speaking of Christ during his Passion she mentions 'þe lothfullnesse that in our kynde is to suffer peyne' (20, 276), a reluctance she knew very well herself and which she frankly admits when she says that had she known what to suffer with Christ meant, she would not have asked for that 'gift' (17, 364). In the same vein she says that of the three joys that come from the Passion the first is that Christ is happy because it is over, 'and he shalle no more suffer' (23, 393).

The other remark goes back to what we have already said about the communional aspect of the Passion, which is a theological truth with strong affective overtones. In specifying for whom Christ died, Julian says that 'for every mannys synne that shal be savyd he sufferyd; and every mannes sorow, desolacion and angwysshe he sawe and sorowed, for kyndnes and loue' (20, 376), and this is not an event forever past, but a compassion which flows into every living man, since 'he sufferyth with vs' (377) now. The Incarnation has united Christ to all men, and he is one with us by 'kyndnes', that is by nature, and by love: as a consequence the Passion of Christ becomes the Passion of all mankind, and even more, the Passion of the world:

> Here saw I a grett onyng betwene Crist and vs, to my vnderstondyng; for when he was in payne we ware in payne, and alle creatures that myght suffer payne sufferyd with hym. That is to say, alle creatures that god hath made to oure servys, þe fyrmamente and erth, feylyd for sorow in ther kynd in the tyme of Cristes dyeng, for it longyth kyndly to ther properte to know hym for ther lorde, in whom alle ther vertuse stondyth. And whan he feylyd, then behovyd nedys to them for kyndnes to feyle with hym, in as moch as they myght, for sorow of hys paynes. (18, 367)

This cosmic participation in the Passion is clearly reminiscent of the *Dream of the Rood* and of the best tradition of the early Christian centuries.[56]

After saying what to meditate on, Julian goes on to describe 'iij maner of beholdyng of his blessyd passion' (20, 378). The first is the hard pain he suffered with contrition and compassion (20, 378); the second is the love that made him suffer it (22, 386); the third is the joy and the bliss that makes him like it (23, 389). The meditation appears as a process which is both an enrichment and a purification using in different measures the three faculties of the soul. In the first stage the imagination is at work, with a highly emotional contemplation of the Passion reviewed in a kind of slow-motion film of which Julian herself gives us such impressive and moving examples; but the heart too is there, with the spiritual accompaniment of contrition and compassion. In the second stage the heart is joined by the intellect to find out the reason which brought Christ to die for us, and it is typical of Julian to give such a simple answer as 'love'. In the third and highest stage of contemplation the intellect is dominant, since nothing visible is offered but

---

[56] 'Weop eal gesceaft' (l. 55). Pope Leo the Great, one of the best witnesses of the patristic tradition, writes with his usual, admirable clarity: 'Pendente enim in patibulo creatore, universa creatura congemuit, et crucis clavos omnia simul elementa senserunt' (While the Creator was hanging on the gallows, all creation was in tears, and all the elements together felt the nails of the cross piercing them), *sermo* lvii, 4: P.L. 54, 330. See also Bennett, *Poetry of the Passion*, p. 14.

the pure beholding of God's joy believed in faith. It is not mere chance that we find joy at the end of this meditation, and that, unlike the other two stages, here the verb is in the present tense. It is perhaps important to observe that these are not three stages to be run chronologically, but three different ways of meditation to be kept together so that they can interact on one another. Incidentally Julian does not bother to specify to what degree of love or to what stage in the spiritual journey the meditation on the Passion belongs.

Joy, then, is the fruit of this meditation, and this is but another way to commune with God through Christ. In fact the Trinity rejoices in the Passion (23, 392), and Christ rejoices, for three reasons: he will not suffer any more, he has rescued us from the pains of hell, and has brought us up into heaven (23, 393). It is only to be expected that Julian prays that the joy of the Trinity may become our joy too, and that 'the lykyng of our saluacion be lyke to the joy that Christ hath of oure saluation, as it may be whylle we be here' (23, 391).

The mention of hell and the reference to our salvation leads us to take up again an important aspect of any theology of Redemption, that is, the relationship between the Passion and sin, particularly between the death of Christ and that very personification of sin which is the devil.

This sub-theme of the devil can also be analysed according to the three levels of interpretation established at the beginning. Theologically it is the materialization of the war engaged between God and evil in order to redeem mankind; spiritually it means the personal temptations Julian underwent during the showings and more generally during her life; literally it is a presence embodied in powerful images which show the same love of vivid pictorial detail visible in the scenes of the Passion.

The devils appear around the cross, 'oglye and ferfull', right at the beginning of the showings, as the personification of the darkness which, according to Mt 27:45, is said to have covered all the world when Christ was dying. But the Passion marks the victory of Christ, and the devil is defeated and scorned:

> I see thre thynges, game, scorne and ernest. I see game, that the feend is ovyrcome, and I se scorne, that god scorneth hym, and he shalle be scornyd, and I se ernest, þat he is overcome by the blessydfulle passion and deth of oure lorde Jhesu Crist, that was done in fulle grette ernest and with sad traveyle. (13, 349 – 50)

The defeat of the devil becomes a source of strength for the believer, because the victory obtained through the Passion of Christ is shared with all who are united to him through faith:

> And ryght as in the furst worde þat oure good lorde shewde, menyng his blessyd passyon: Here with is the fende ovyr come, ryght so he seyde in

the last worde with full tru feytfulnes, menyng vs alle: Thou shalt not be ovyr come. (68, 646)

It is perhaps needless to note again the perfect parallelism of the clauses which emphasizes the force of God flooding triumphantly on all his lovers and enclosing them with him in the field of victory, and the repetition of the same verb 'ovyrcome' to mark the spectacular opposition between the devil and 'vs alle'. Together with the communional aspect of Julian's spirituality, which is so different from Rolle's individualism, another of her character-istics comes out here: the words God reveals to her are both 'lernyng' and 'tru comfort', 'sekernesse agaynst all trybulacyons that may come' (646, 647). This is the crucial point where theology turns into spirituality, and to understand the place and the meaning of the Passion in the idea Julian had of spiritual life we must consider, as we did with Rolle, the kind of temptation she underwent.

At first sight uncovering Julian's psychology looks like a very difficult operation. Unlike Rolle, who is so willingly autobiographical and even at times a bit too obtrusive, Julian tends to cancel herself, to disappear behind her visions, to want to mix with the crowd of her fellow-Christians. But careful reading of her book will give us unexpected clues to get a glimpse of her inner personality, and through that have a better understanding of her version of the spirituality of the Passion.

The first surprising discovery is that we find in her no word about carnal lust or the danger of riches, and even pride and vainglory are but very rarely mentioned. When she talks in the first chapter of her project of spiritual life, she seems to have an enthusiastic temperament, but more mature consideration leads her to see that beneath this fire of love there hides the opposite tendency: fear of physical suffering, and more than that, sloth, reluctance, inertia. These two apparently contrasting moods coexist in her, they fight against each other, and they give her a deep sense of insecurity. The two key-words, 'wele and wo', appear quite often in her book, and in the seventh Revelation we find an admirable illustration of these feelings which quickly and unpredictably come and go as the sun and the clouds in a windy spring sky:

> I was fulfyllede of the evyrlastyng suernesse . . . I was all in peese, in eese and in reste . . . This lastyd but a whyle, and I was turned and left to my selfe in hevynes and werynes of my life and irkenes of my selfe, that vnneth I could haue pacience to lyve. (15, 354)

There is a striking similarity with the agony of Christ,[57] in which he felt fear, tedium and a deep sadness, and it may mean that in her communion

---

[57] Mark 14:33 – 34 'he began to be sore amazed, and to be very heavy; and saith unto them, My soul is exceeding sorrowful unto death'.

with the dying Christ Julian re-enacts exactly what he suffered. To add to the sense of despair Julian says that she could not feel any comfort:

> Ther was no comfort ne none eese to my felyng, but feyth, hope and cheryte; and these I had in truth but fulle lytylle in felyng.   (15, 354 – 55)

It may seem that this alternation of contrasting emotional conditions is just an experience she had during a revelation. In fact this is not true. In ch. 64 she tells us about a distaste she felt for this world, because of the 'woo that is here and þe wele and the blessyd beyng that is there', and she goes on to say: 'this made me to morne and besely to longe, and also of my owne wretchydnesse, slowth and werynesse, þat my lykyd not to lyue and to traveyle as me felle to do' (64, 620). In the same chapter we have other glimpses of her interior portrait where she lists the pains from which she will be liberated:

> thou shalte nevyr more haue no manner of paynne, no manner of sycknes, no manner mysselykyng, no wantyng of wylle . . .   (64, 621)

Physical pain and mental disease go side by side, and against these evils the Passion is 'comfort and pacyens' (64, 620) at the same time, comfort for the certitude of a victory already obtained over every cause of sorrow and grief, patience as a capacity to suffer directly derived from the example of Christ.

Next to this indolence and despondency comes fear as another important aspect of Julian's psychology. She devotes an entire chapter (ch. 74) to analysing four different types of fear, carefully discriminating between those which are good and those which are not, and teaching how to use them for our profit. The first is fear of physical pain, and the second 'drede of payne, wher by man is sterid and wakyd fro slepe of synne' (671): these two are to be taken instrumentally, in that the physical pain is a training to learn patience, and the 'drede of payne of bodely deth and of gostly enemys' helps the man who is 'harde of slepe of synne' to repent and be converted. The third, a 'doughtfull drede' which draws us to despair, is to be rejected: 'god wyll haue it turnyd in vs into loue by tru knowyng of loue . . . for it may nevyr plese oure lorde that his servanntes douȝte in his goodnesse' (673). The fourth kind of fear is the only one which is totally good: Julian calls it a 'reverent drede', a feeling full of love and respect for a homely and courteous God. 'It is softe — Julian says — for þe more it is had, the lesse it is felte, for swetnesse of loue. Loue and drede are bredryn, and they are rotyd in vs by the goodnesse of oure maker' (673 – 74).

This fear, as we have seen, may become utter despair: this is the worst temptation, it is the characterizing condition of hell and the very personification of the devil. Again this seems to be at first only a temptation Julian felt during her agony. In ch. 67 she tells of an 'vgly shewyng' in which the devil, with a face 'reed lyke þe tylle stone whan it is new brent'

(636), grasps her throat and tries to kill her. This attack was expected, because Julian knew she would be tempted by the devil before dying. The devil returns 'with his heet and with his stynch' and appears in the form of two people talking incomprehensibly at one time, 'as they had holde a perlement with greate besynes', and, she says, 'alle this was to stere me to dyspeyre' (69, 648).

As with the sense of insecurity, which she described first as an experience had during a vision, but which must be intended, as we have seen, as a normal general condition, so it is here: the temptation to despair may come again and again, and for this, as for insecurity and fear, Julian has a general teaching:

> Oure curtesse lorde wylle nott that hys seruantys despeyer for ofte fallyng ne for grevous fallyng; for oure fallyng lettyth nott hym to loue vs.   (39, 453)

In this quotation despair does not come from fear of eternal damnation, but from seeing oneself wretched and unworthy because of our invincible tendency to sin. But here too Julian responds with her usual positive attitude. God does not want us to fall into despair: that is why he shows us our sin only 'by þe lyght of his mercy', so that 'by gracious knowing we may se oure synne profytable without dyspeyer' (78, 696 – 98). As a consequence a good use may be made of this feeling of our wretchedness: by contrition and 'by touchyng of the holy gost' we may turn this 'bytternesse in to hope of goddes mercy' (39, 449), and by considering our sin in the light of God's grace we can use it to break down our pride and presumption (79, 704). The point is to maintain a right balance, countering the feelings of guilt and unworthiness induced by the memory of our sins with the stronger feelings derived from the contemplation of the unfailing love of God, where by the word 'balance' one has to understand a much heavier stress on God's love than on our sins.

I may have indulged too much in trying to describe Julian's psychology as it can be derived from the temptations she underwent, but this is the clue which explains why she does not interpret the Passion as a means to frighten man from seeking delight in earthly goods, but views it mostly in terms of comfort, trust, joy and consolation on one hand, and as an example of how to learn patience, that capacity to suffer which helps us to live in peace and to offer compassion to our fellow-Christians.

In sketching Julian's spirituality of the Passion I would like to show how skilfully she combines theology and affectivity on one side, the individual and the community on the other.

To connect the Passion with joy and comfort is a well-known characteristic of Julian's: 'it is goddes wylle — she writes — that we haue true lykyng with hym in oure saluacion, and ther in he wylle that we be myghtly comfortyd and strengthyd' (23, 390). If we ask why we should rejoice in contemplating the Passion Julian gives the traditional answer: Christ's death has rescued us from sin and damnation and brought us to eternal bliss. But this is only one reason. 'That other is for comfort in oure payne, for he wylle that we wytt that it shalle be turned vs to wurshyp and to profyȝte by the vertu of hys passyon, and þat we wytte that we sufferyd ryght nought allone, but with hym, and see hym oure grownde' (28, 410 – 11). This is theology, and Julian affirms quite clearly that 'we be now in our lordes menyng in his crosse wyth hym in our paynes and in our passion dyeng' (21, 379 – 80), but no one will fail to notice the affective overtones: being with Christ we realize not only that our suffering becomes meaningful and profitable, but also and above all that we are not left to our solitude and desolation. In fact Julian adds that 'the well beholdyng of thys wylle doth saue vs from grugyng and despeyer in the felyng of our paynes' (28, 411). Moreover we find in the passage from which I am quoting another element of Julian's psychology, her sense of guilt: this too is softened and healed by the memory of the Passion, because God's love excuses our sin, 'and of hys gret curtesy he doth away alle oure blame, and beholdeth vs with ruth and pytte, as chyldren innocens and vnlothfulle' (28, 411).

The Passion is also a remedy against the two types of spiritual sickness which Julian calls 'specyall': the one is 'vnpacyens or slouth', the other is 'dispeyer or doughtfulle drede' (73, 666):

> And for helpe agaynst thys, full mekely oure lorde shewd the pacyens that he had in his harde passion, and also the joy and þe lykyng that he hayth of þat passion for loue. And this he shewde in example þat we shulde gladly and esely bere oure paynes. (73, 667)

Julian carefully specifies that Christ is happy 'now', but the endurance he showed in his Passion in view of the future reward and of the saving effects of his death is an example for us to do the same: 'for this lytylle payne that we suffer heer we shalle haue an hygh endlesse knowyng in god, whych we myght nevyr haue without that' (21, 381).

The crucified Christ who talks to Julian is not a reproachful and revengeful God, but a caring friend who offers support and healing, and who wants her to share with him a deep feeling of satisfaction and fulfilment: 'If thou arte apayde — Jesus says to her from the cross — I am apayde' (22, 382). And this leads to another important aspect of Julian's spirituality, the Passion as a school of compassion. In the thirteenth Revelation she writes:

> Thus I saw how Crist hath compassyon on vs for the cause of synne; and ryght as I was before in the passion of Crist fulfyllyd with payne and compassion, lyke in thys I was in party fulfylled with compassion of alle my evyn cristen,

. . . And than saw I that ech kynde compassion that man hath on hys evyn cristen with charyte, it is Crist in hym.   (28, 408, 410)

To contemplate the Passion means then to draw compassion from Christ and pour it on our fellow-Christians. This marvellous circularity, which also shows Julian's strong sense of the church, is grounded on the fundamental unity by which we are branches of Christ, who is the vine. As long as we remain united to him, and through him to the whole community of the faithful, we cannot break down:

> For one singular person may oftyn tymes be broken, as it semyth to þe selfe, but the hole body of holy chyrch was nevyr broken, nor nevyr shall be with out ende. And therfore a suer thyng it is, a good and a gracious to wylle mekly and myghtly be fastenyd and onyd to oure moder holy church, that is Crist Jhesu. For the flode of mercy that is his deerworthy blode and precious water is plentuous to make vs feyer and clene. The blessed woundes of oure sauiour be opyn and enjoye to hele vs. The swet gracious handes of oure moder be redy and diligent a bout vs; for he in alle this werkyng vsyth the very office of a kynde norysse, that hath not elles to done but to entende about the saluation of hyr chylde.   (61, 607 – 08)

This passage is noteworthy in that we see some of Julian's favourite themes fusing into one another. The church and Christ are united in the image of 'oure deerworthy mother in solas' and the crucifix changes gradually into a gentle nurse who washes us fair and clean, opens his wounds to heal us, and is busy about us with his sweet and gracious hands. One may even forget that Julian is talking about blood and wounds, and it is not easy to recognize the old solemn motif of the arms of Christ outstretched on the cross to embrace all the world behind the sweet hands of this careful and busy mother.

The way Julian employs traditional images to render her theology and spirituality brings us to consider her particular contribution to the treatment of the Passion as literature.

R. M. Wilson has rightly argued that her highest literary value is to be seen in terms of sentence-structure,[58] and the examples I have quoted cannot but confirm this view, especially if we consider the functional character of these patterns in evidencing and stressing the theological meaning of the sentence. In artistic terms she is more an architect than a painter, although this is only partly true: in depicting the Passion scenes she has no rival in English literature for the vividness of detail and the intense emotional participation. To this we should add a small group of images used as similes, and which are well-known: the drops of blood 'lyke to the droppes

---

[58] R. M. Wilson, 'Three Middle English Mystics', *Essays and Studies* n.s. 9 (1956) 96 – 104. See also what I have written in my introduction to Giuliana di Norwich, *Libro delle Rivelazioni* (Milano, 1984), pp. 44 – 46.

of water . . . after a grete shower of reyne', and round 'lyke to the scale of heryng' (7, 312); the body of Christ 'broken on pecys as a cloth and saggyng downwarde' (17, 362), and 'hangyng vppe in the eyer as men hang a cloth for to drye' (17, 363); the skin and the flesh 'rympylde with a tawny coloure, lyke a drye bord when it is agyd' (17, 363).

But the true peculiarity of Julian's imagery consists in selecting some details of the Passion scenery and treating them as symbols of theological truths or spiritual attitudes.[59] We have already seen this in the way she uses the wounds and the fall of Christ on the road to Calvary: both are double-sided in that they signify first the condition of ruined man, and secondly the way chosen by God to restore mankind to its glorious state. A triple meaning can be seen in the symbolic interpretation of the kirtle in the parable of the lord and the servant: at the beginning it is the poor clothing of a labourer, and it means 'þe manhode of Adam with alle the myschefe and febylnesse þat folowyth' (51, 534); then it is Christ's flesh, and the kirtle that was 'at the poynt to be ragged and rent' evokes 'the roddys and the scorgys, the thornes and the naylys, the drawyng and the draggyng, his tender flessch rentyng' (541); finally this 'Adams olde kyrtyll, streyte, bare and shorte' is made by our Saviour 'feyer, new, whyt and bryght, and of endlesse clennesse, wyde and seyde' (543).[60] Incidentally we may notice that Julian abounds in adjectives of positive meaning to show that the restoring goes far beyond the previous ruin.

Some of these symbolic images are quite traditional. So is, for example, the thirst of Christ on the cross intended both physically and spiritually as the desire he has to gather all of us in his bliss (ch. 17 and 31). The same could be said of the wounded side, which appears to Julian as a door letting in 'a feyer and delectable place, and large jnow for alle mankynde that shalle be savyd and rest in pees and in loue' (24, 394 – 5), a sort of new Eden.[61] Where Julian seems to be more original is in her treatment of the face, the crown of thorns and the blood. In the face of the dying Christ she sees 'a fygur and a lyknes of our fowle blacke dede, which that our feyre bryght blessed lord bare for our synne': this is the theology of the Trinity who has created man to his image and likeness, an image that was ruined by the Fall and that had to be restored by no one else 'but thorow hym þat made man' (10, 327 – 29). So in the Incarnation Christ assumes the likeness of our foul, black death, he bears our sins, to destroy sin and death. 'And he that made man for loue, by the same loue he woulde restore man to the same

---

[59] According to Riehle (*Middle English Mystics*, p. 47) this is a tendency 'which is present in all the qualitatively better texts'.
[60] On this traditional motif see the many patristic references collected by De Lubac in *Catholicisme*, pp. 13 – 15, 20 – 22.
[61] See D. Gray, *Themes and Images in the Medieval English Religious Lyric* (London, 1972), pp. 133 – 4.

blysse and ovyr passyng' (10, 329 – 30), with the word 'same' to mark the unfailing fidelity of God's love.[62]

In the same chapter a reference to the Vernicle of Rome and to its changing of colour, sometimes more comfortable and lively, sometimes more rueful and deadly, is used as a symbol of a spiritual condition, the fluctuating feelings of fulfilment and deprivation: 'And thus I saw him and sought him, and I had hym and wantyd hym; and this is and should be our comyn workyng in this life' (10, 326). With her usual consistency Julian sees in the experience she had during the showings a common condition, and reacts to it by a positive acceptance: our mutability may be very uncomfortable, but she learns that 'sekyng is as good and beholdyng' (332 – 33), because 'The sekyng with feyth, hope and charitie plesyth oure lord, and the fyndyng plesyth the sowle, and fulfyllyth it with joy' (332).[63]

I have already hinted that the crown of thorns hides the crown of glory, which Julian sees not as a vain trophy, but as the church gathered around his leader, since 'we be his crowne' (22, 384). R. M. Bradley suggests that this is the meaning of the second crown which appears on the crown of thorns in the eighth Revelation:[64] it is the suffering church, which 'shalle be shakyd in sorow and anguyssch and trybulacion in this worlde as men shakyth a cloth in the wynde' (28, 408). By taking part in Christ's Passion we shall share his victory and triumph. Again we have an image where theology and spirituality meet.

To end this list I shall quote a long passage from ch. 12 in which one does not know whether to praise the condensation of theological themes, or the splendour of biblical and liturgical imagery, or the fluency of rhythm which transforms prose into poetry. The key-image here is the blood, but Julian is superb in showing what can be made of it: instead of falling into morbid emotionalism like many devotional texts of her time, around this image she builds a powerful summary of the theology of Redemption written in a high, solemn style.

> The dere worthy bloude of our lorde Jhesu Crist,
> also verely as it is most precious,
> as verely it is most plentuous.
> Beholde and see the vertu of this precious plenty of hys dere worthy blode.
> It descendyd downe in to helle and brak her bondes,

---

[62] The rich theology of the image of God in the soul is analysed by Riehle, *Middle English Mystics*, pp. 142 – 50, especially pp. 146 – 48.

[63] For a more detailed commentary see Colledge-Walsh, *Showings*, pp. 81 – 83, where this ch. 10 is said to be 'a truly remarkable and wholly professional performance'.

[64] R. M. Bradley, 'Julian on Prayer', in R. Llewelyn, ed., *Julian Woman of our Day* (London, 1985), pp. 66 – 67.

and delyuerd them all that were there
which belongh to the courte of hevyn.
The precious plenty of his dere worthy blode ovyrflowyth all erth,
and is redy to wash all creatures of synne which be of good wyll,
haue ben and shall be.
The precious plenty of his dereworthy blode ascendyth vp into hevyn
in the blessed body of our lorde Jesu Crist,
and ther is in hym, bledyng, preyeng for vs to the father,
and is and shal be as long as vs nedyth.
And ovyr more it flowyth in all heauen,
enjoying the saluacion of all mankynd that be ther and shall be,
fulfylling the number that faylyth.   (12, 344 – 45)

It is impossible to analyse here the rich theology of this passage and the numerous biblical echoes which can be found in it. It sounds like a highly-wrought liturgical prose behind which it is not difficult to glimpse some powerful baptismal images. This blood hints at the destroying waters of the Red Sea when the Hebrews were saved from the Egyptians; it is also a sort of reversed flood, purifying the world not by destruction but by washing all creation;[65] it is finally the 'well of water springing up into everlasting life' (John 4:14) which Christ promised to the Samaritan woman, meaning by that water himself as a source of life. If my interpretation is correct, we could draw an interesting conclusion: although Julian, like many other medieval mystics, does not derive her spirituality from the sacraments, nevertheless she seems to be well aware of their complex liturgical imagery rooted in the Bible and the patristic literature. This would further testify to her highly-refined theological education. Needless to say, before concluding this part, neither the ideas nor the images are original, but the way she connects and amalgamates them is peculiar to her.

The great theologian Hans Urs von Balthasar, in a recent survey of the literature of the Passion repeatedly affirms that *the* problem with this literature is the difficulty in reaching a proper balance between affectivity and speculation, between personal devotion to the crucified Christ and the great patristic vision of the Cross as the peak of the work through which the Trinity redeemed mankind and God disclosed his inner being.[66] I would not venture to say that Julian has achieved this balance, but I am convinced that

[65] The motif of Christ's blood as a cleansing flood can be found in Fortunatus' *Pange Lingua*: 'terra, pontus, astra, mundus / quo lavantur flumine' (the earth, the sea, the stars, the world are washed by such a flood). Incidentally, I feel inclined to think that we need not go too far to search for the sources of Julian's theology, in that many basic ideas were cast in poetic form in the liturgical hymns, which she knew and used in the monastic office.

[66] H. U. von Balthasar, 'Mysterium Paschale' in *Mysterium Salutis*, vol. 6, pp. 197 – 203, especially p. 202.

she has gone very near it,[67] evoking thus that other masterpiece which is the very beginning of the history of the poetry of the Passion in England, the *Dream of the Rood*.

The main reason for her success is that she does not see the Passion in isolation neither in theology nor in spirituality. She starts from the Passion as a substantial part of her spiritual programme, she goes through it in a deeply felt mystical experience, and she meditates on it for a very long time. The result of this happy marriage between emotions and intellect is that she views the Passion first within the whole life of Christ (Incarnational aspect), then in the whole process of creation and restoration of a fallen world (Creational aspect), and finally in the whole work of the Trinity (Trinitarian aspect), thus going beyond any limit of space and time and flowing into eternity. The Passion comes gradually to be seen as the centre of a series of widening concentric circles, and cannot be properly evaluated without considering the whole setting and the movement leading to and originating from the death of Christ. These are the reasons why we find in Julian an unrivalled realism in the description of the Passion scenes, and at the same time the richest and most profound theology of the Passion among the English mystics.

The same can be said of her spirituality, in which the Passion is not a part of the purgative moment, a stage to be left behind, but a memory to be continually revived. If Julian's spiritual life seems at first to concentrate on the Passion, we soon discover that in fact it radiates from the Passion. Through this event she reaches out to God and to her fellow-Christians, she learns how to interpret and accept her emotions and feelings, she experiences hope and trust, joy and consolation and is gently brought to patience and compassion. Where Rolle's psychology seems to operate by contrasting blocks of values which cannot but fight against each other, Julian shows a much more conciliatory attitude by which, to use one of her favourite expressions, all things come to be enclosed[68] in one another. One has only to read that marvellous description of the development of spiritual life which she calls significantly 'forth bryngyng' (61, 601 – 602), where the 'blessed passyon' has its place, but within a series of actions which are all to be ascribed to God's tenderness in keeping us.

---

[67] J. Leclercq rightly praises Julian's sense of balance in his Preface to a modern edition of the *Showings* translated and annotated by E. Colledge and J. Walsh in 'The Classics of Western Spirituality' (London, 1978): 'Both in her method and in her teaching, she presents an integration of elements which have not always been so easily unified' (p. 13).

[68] In the Index of Subjects appended to my Italian edition of the *Revelations* I have collected under the item 'Racchiudere' (Enclose) many passages where Julian uses this verb: see Giuliana di Norwich, *Libro delle Rivelazioni* (Milano, 1984), p. 340.

In Christian theology the Cross was readily understood as a symbol of universal reconciliation.[69] This is perhaps the point where theology and Julian's personal temperament meet to create a spirituality of reconciliation. In fact this is her main characteristic: she gathers multiplicity into unity, she does not polarize the tensions she feels, but keeps them in an acceptable and practicable balance, she does not reject the negativity she experiences, but redeems it by discerning and accepting the positive side hidden in it. In this way the Cross is both the core and the colour of her spirituality.

Together with the cross as a meeting place where oppositions fuse into peace, the circle is perhaps the other basic image which helps us to understand and describe Julian's attitudes. I shall end this paper with a quotation which struck me the first time I read Julian, and has done ever since. It is where she depicts the relationship between God and us by using a series of inward-moving concentric circles:

> For as þe body is cladd in the cloth, and the flessch in the skynne, and the bonys in þe flessch, and the harte in the bowke, so ar we, soule and body, cladde and enclosydde in the goodnes of god. Yee, and more homely, for all they vanyssche and wast awey; the goodnesse of god is ever hole and more nere to vs, withouȝte any comparison.   (6, 307)

This is the starting point of Julian's theology and spirituality. The end will be an everlasting union with God who has created mankind as 'þe nobelest thyng that evyr he made' (53, 560), who has restored it after the Fall by knitting his Son to all men, and wants us to be in heaven with him forever, 'knytt in this knott,[70] and onyd in this oonyng, and made holy in this holynesse' (53, 560).

---

[69] See J. Daniélou, 'Le symbolisme cosmique de la Croix', *La Maison-Dieu*, n. 75 (1963), 23 – 36; see also D. Pezzini, 'Teologia e poesia: la sintesi del poema anglosassone Sogno della Croce', *Rendiconti dell'Istituto Lombardo* 106 (1972) 268 – 86, especially pp. 109 – 12, where, starting from Colossians 1:19 – 20, I show how the doctrinal principle of a world reconciled through the blood of Christ becomes one of the governing poetic principles of the *Dream of the Rood*. This truth has entered the English vocabulary: since the time of More and Tyndale the Redemption is usually called 'Atonement'.

[70] On this image of the 'knot' and the concept of 'nodus amicitiae', going back to Ailred of Rievaulx's *Speculum Caritatis*, see Riehle, *Middle English Mystics*, pp. 51 – 2.

NARRATIVE-ENGENDERING AND NARRATIVE-INHIBITING FUNCTIONS OF PRAYER IN LATE MIDDLE ENGLISH

MARGARET BRIDGES

A recent tagmemic analysis of prayers in the *Aeneid* attributes to Virgil's epic 116 prayers, not counting those speeches introduced by tagmemes with verbs of prayer (like *orare*) which were not pronounced 'in a religious spirit'.[1] Since the pioneering work of E. R. Labande in the nineteen fifties, French medievalists have inventoried and classified many a prayer appearing in the *chansons de geste*: the *Chanson de Roland*, for example, is said to contain about thirty prayers.[2] Even if the late Middle English inheritors of the epic tradition do not always so generously punctuate their narratives with prayers, which sometimes occur in so secularized a form as to make them all but unrecognizable *as* prayers, their continued presence, whether obtrusive or discreet, still raises questions about their narratological status. Can we content ourselves with observing, as do the above-mentioned studies, that these prayers, through their contextualization, serve to characterize those who formulate them (as, say, pious or vengeful) while at the same time constituting a moral or religious commentary on the narrative events in connexion with which they are formulated? To treat prayer as a form of discourse that characterizes the speaker and glosses his deeds hardly does justice to recent developments in discourse analysis and narratology.

At least one close-reading literary scholar has formulated an approach to prayer that is more pertinent to the not-so-narrative poetry of John Lydgate, much of which comes over as one extended hymn or prayer of praise. I am referring to Derek Pearsall's insight into what he calls Lydgate's temptation to escape 'the onward pressure of narrative' through the stasis of prayer or of complaint, which we might regard as a secularized version of prayer.[3] Pearsall's perception of how prayer may contribute to *inhibiting* narrative

---

[1] R. Jeanneret, *Recherches sur l'hymne et la prière chez Virgile* (Brussels, 1973).

[2] Jacques De Caluwe, 'La prière épique dans la tradition manuscrite de la *Chanson de Roland*', in *La Prière au Moyen-Age*, *Senefiance* 10 (1981) 147 – 86. Labande's seminal article on 'Le "Credo épique". A propos des prières dans les chansons de geste' appeared in *Recueil de travaux offerts à M. Clovis Brunel* (Paris, 1955) 11, pp. 62 – 80.

[3] See Pearsall's *John Lydgate* (London, 1970), pp. 92 – 3, 179 *et passim*.

flow does not, however, lie at the centre of my present preoccupation, which is rather with ways in which prayer may, on the contrary, *contribute* to narrative flow or progress.

One way in which literary prayers may be said to do this is when they are the expression of a wish of which the subsequent course of narrative events constitutes the fulfilment. A comprehensive typology of prayers might include, in addition to the petition (which is thought by historians of religion to be the oldest form of prayer), several prayer types that we don't directly associate with the expression of a wish, like prayers of thanksgiving, confession or benediction. The widely prevailing psychological definitions of prayer, however, subordinate prayer content, on which such a typology is based, to the common emotion in which all prayers are thought to originate. This results in such a comprehensive definition of prayer as an expression of 'the soul's sincere desire' (Friedrich Heiler),[4] which, when understood as the desire to influence or alter the course of events, leaves the door wide open for a conception of prayer as magic spell, incantation or charm. While plenty of work remains to be done if we wish to establish the status of late medieval narratives as magical narratives, in the way that Fredric Jameson has done for the Western novel,[5] the case for much late medieval narrative as a narrative of wish-fulfilment hardly needs to be argued, after the works of Northrop Frye, A. C. Spearing, Anne Wilson and Derek Brewer.[6] The love-visions of the fourteenth and fifteenth centuries in particular have come to be recognized as narratives springing from a dream-frame which acts 'as a signal that the dreamer was in a state of need, [and leads] the audience to expect that need to be fulfilled in [the course of] the vision'.[7] But when love-visions are centered *around* the frozen gestures of complaint, instead of springing *from* complaint, they are surely unsuitable for a study of the relationship between prayer and narrative flux, which they tend to replace by icons of complaint. So most of my examples will be taken from two other dominant narrative modes in late medieval England, the chivalric romances and the legends of the saints. I shall be arguing that these have plot-

---

[4] Quoted from Sam D. Gill's remarkable entry on 'Prayer' in *The Encyclopedia of Religion* (New York and London, 1987) 11, pp. 489 – 94.

[5] Jameson touches on the status of romantic narrative as wish-fulfilment in many of his writings, but I am thinking here in particular of his 'Magical Narratives: Romance as Genre', *New Literary History* 7 (1975) 135 – 63.

[6] See: Northrop Frye, *The Secular Scripture: A Study of the Structure of Romance* (Cambridge, Mass., 1976); A. C. Spearing, *Medieval Dream-Poetry* (Cambridge, 1976); Anne Wilson, *Traditional Romance and Tale: How Stories Mean* (Ipswich, 1976); Derek Brewer, *Symbolic Stories: Traditional Narratives of the Family Drama in English Literature* (Cambridge, 1980).

[7] Quotation adapted from Judith M. Davidoff's study 'The Audience Illuminated, or New Light Shed on the Dream Frame of Lydgate's *Temple of Glas*', *Studies in the Age of Chaucer* 5 (1983) 103 – 25, p. 107.

structures whose principal episodes are engendered by the expression of a wish, which as often as not takes the form of a prayer.

Although not all medieval romances thematize the ability of prayer to engender narrative to the extent that, say, Chaucer's *Knight's Tale*, following the *Teseida*, does, one could well argue that there are very few medieval romances that are not impelled by the wishes of their protagonists, expressed in pleas and prayers. It is tempting to attribute this function of prayer to the continuity of the epic tradition in Western culture. In view of the numerous metamorphoses undergone by the *Aeneid* in the course of its medieval retellings, we might, however, choose to examine Middle English readings of Virgilian prayer and petition with a certain degree of suspicion. Was Chaucer accurately reflecting Virgilian usage when, in his summary of the *Aeneid* in *The House of Fame*, he represented many of the narrative episodes as fulfilments of an earlier plea or supplication? The pictures on the walls of the temple of Venus tell Chaucer's dreamer the following tale: Aeneas is prompted to flee from burning Troy as a result of his divine mother's bidding. (The Middle English verb *bidden* used by Chaucer in this passage had added the connotation of *beden*, 'command', to its primary meaning of request or petition, resulting in an ambiguity to which I shall return). Aeneas subsequently sets out to Italy at the bidding of the dead Creusa's ghost (185 – 92). The storm at sea, unleashed by Juno's furious petition to Aeolus (202 – 8), only subsides as a result of Venus' supplication to Jupiter (212 – 20). Once landed in North Africa, the Trojan proceeds to Carthage in response to the prayers of a huntress, who turns out to be Venus in disguise. The sequence of plea-engendered episodes continues until Aeneas' adventure reaches its successful conclusion, in spite of Juno's antagonism, through Jupiter's providential *cure*, itself effected by Venus' prayer. Given the Chaucerian persona of the unfulfilled love-poet, one might suspect this to be a biased reading of Virgilian epic, intent on foregrounding a posture of supplication, which is also that of the medieval poet as lover and courtier. My own reading of the Latin epic, however, suggests that heroic action in the *Aeneid* is frequently subordinated to the pleas and prayers of mortals and immortals. The wishes expressed in these prayers often acquire the force of prophecy, as they proceed to spell out events before those events actually take narrative form. When in Book IV (607 – 29) the abandoned Dido enjoins the Sun, Juno, Hecate and the Furies to accomplish her desire for revenge, in spite of the protection which has ultimately been guaranteed Aeneas by virtue of previous supplications to Jove, she calls for a series of struggles and misfortunes which will effectively constitute the bulk of the plot of the second half of the epic. I suspect that the frequent use of prayer in Virgil may therefore have something to do with the trajectory of prophecy within which all the epic hero's deeds are inscribed. I also suspect that the hierarchical network of communication established by the supplications in the *Aeneid* serves to demonstrate power relations that are consonant with the political purpose of the epic and that have little in common with Chaucerian self-conscious reflection on authorial stance and status.

A single instance of Virgilian plea engendering narrative must serve to demonstrate what I mean. Leaving aside for the time being the poet's initial invocation of the Muses — itself a literary use of prayer that deserves further attention — the plea to which I refer is in fact the first to change the course of events for Virgil's hero as he is seen in the opening lines of narrative merrily ploughing the foaming brine with brazen prow, on his way from Sicily to Latium (34 – 5): lines 65 – 75 of the first book of the *Aeneid* are, in fact, concerned with Juno's plea to Aeolus that his winds may disperse and shipwreck hated Aeneas' fleet and with the weather king's reply. The structure of Juno's plea is typical of many literary prayers in that it establishes the power of the addressee to perform the desired deed (65-6) before requesting, indeed requiring (through the threefold use of the imperative) its performance:

> Him Juno now addressed thus in suppliant speech: 'Aeolus, for to thee hath the Father of gods and king of men given power to calm and uplift the waves with the wind, a people hateful to me sails the Tyrrhene sea, carrying into Italy Ilium's vanquished gods. Hurl fury into thy winds, sink and o'erwhelm the ships, or drive the men asunder and scatter their bodies o'er the deep'.[8]

To increase the chance of seeing her wish fulfilled, Juno, like many a literary supplicant, throws in a promise of reward: her beautiful nymph Deiopea will marry Aeolus and bear his children (71 – 5).

Less typical, but for our purposes more interesting, is Aeolus' reply, through which he transforms the plea of Juno supplex into a command. This involves the reverse distribution of power that we usually associate with supplication, where it is customary to assume the inferiority of the supplicant, whose wish cannot be fulfilled without the agency of the addressee. Although the fulfilment of Juno's wish may indeed depend on Aeolus' willingness to grant her request, the weather lord tells Juno that by virtue of her power over him her request has the force of command (76 – 80):

> Thus answered Aeolus: 'Thy task, O queen, is to search out thy desire; my duty is to do thy bidding. Of thy grace is all this my realm, of thy grace my sceptre and Jove's favour; thou grantest me a couch at the feasts of the gods, and makest me lord of clouds and storms'.

---

[8] Translations here and elsewhere are taken from the Loeb edition of *Virgil*, trans. H. R. Fairclough (London, 1932).

Command (*iussa*) and desire (*quid optes*) are then a function of power, and the distinctive vocabulary that we have here for these two semantic fields is perhaps more suitable for conveying reflections of this kind than is the essentially ambiguous vocabulary of supplication that we have in Old and Early Middle English. (It is only through the introduction of new words like *preien*, for 'to pray', towards the end of the thirteenth century, that *bidden* begins shedding some of its ambiguity on its long journey towards its relatively unequivocal Modern English reflex).[9]

In the Chaucerian summary of the *Aeneid*, Juno's plea to Aeolus is not the first but the third narrative-engendering prayer, owing to the medieval preference for narrating the fall of Troy, related by Aeneas to Dido in Virgil's second book, *before* the hero sets out on his journey, by virtue of the principle of *ordo naturalis*. The variety of Chaucer's vocabulary of supplication is well brought out by his choice of verb for the shrieking of the shrewish goddess who 'cries on' Aeolus to attack the Trojan heroes:

> Ther saugh I thee, cruel Juno,
> That art daun Jupiteres wif,
> That hast yhated, al thy lyf,
> Al the Troianysshe blood,
> Renne and crye, as thou were wood,
> On Eolus, the god of wyndes,
> To blowen oute, of alle kyndes,
> So lowde that he shulde drenche
> Lord and lady, grom and wenche,
> Of al the Troian nacion,
> Withoute any savacion.[10]

It is perhaps not surprising that Aeolus' judicious response is omitted by Chaucer, who, in this as in other passages of the *House of Fame*, associates his poetic narrative with supplication or complaint as the stance of the love poet at the mercy of the capricious dispensers of inspiration and fame, who are most impolitic in their arbitrary granting and refusing of their supplicants' requests.

Comparison with a later Middle English version of this Virgilian plea, in Caxton's *Eneydos* (dated 1490), yields some revealing resemblances and differences. Towards the end of his ninth chapter — Caxton replaces the twelve books of the *Aeneid* by 65 chapters — we read that

> (. . .) whan eneas, sone of venus, & nygh kynnesman of paris wold departe from troye / after the siege of ye same, for to goo into the conquest of the

---

[9] In Modern English usage the connotations of the verb *to bid* are only extended to the notion of request in specialized contexts such as those of auctioneering and card games.

[10] *The House of Fame*, 198 – 208, in F. N. Robinson, ed., *The Works of Geoffrey Chaucer* (2nd edn, London, 1957).

72   *Religion in the Poetry and Drama of the Late Middle Ages*

prouynce of ytaly, to hym promysed by the goddis at request of his moder; &
Iuno, ye ryght noble goddesse, wyllynge tempesshe and lette his gooynge /
dyd doo calle and assemble yolus and Neptunus, goddis of the wyndes and of
the see, prayenge & exhortynge theym moche swetely, that it myghte playse
eche of theym to putte theym in payne, & doo theyr deuoyr, to empesshe the
goynge of the sayd enterpryse, and makynge to breke and destroye alle the
nauye, in plongynge vnder the water and parellys ayenst the roches, for
hastely to drowne and destroye alle the hooste of Enee, the sone of venus,
whiche enforced hym to make werre in the goode Royalme of ytalye, whiche
was in his desire pryncypally aboue alle other. In whiche thynge soo doynge,
she wolde rewarde theym wyth suche guerdons as apperteyneth to grete and
hie goddys to be stypended / and shall doo honoure to theyr frendes / and
treate theyr lygnage and veray alyes / and socoure theym wyth alle hir myghte
/ whiche that the goddys hadde graunted to hir right gladly. And they made
theyr preperacyon, everyche in his regyon / for to warre upon Eneas.[11]

This amazing sequence of subordinate clauses contains a participial clause
modifying the object of Aeneas' desire, Italy, in terms which subordinate
the epic hero's career to his mother's request to the Gods. Their granting of
her request promises the fulfilment of mother and son's wish, as it contains
a promise of closure for the epic narrative. Juno's plea, or counter-request,
is, like all speeches in this passage, reported indirectly only. Since the
addressee of her plea is no longer simply Aeolus, but also Juno's brother
Neptune, who cannot be considered subservient to her in the way Aeolus is,
Caxton prevents his characters from playing the Virgilian power game of
the mutually dependent supplicant and addressee. Yet Caxton's Juno is not
wholly at the mercy of those to whom she addresses her plea, for although
the English author avoids using the ambiguous verb *bidden* throughout, he
has given us a word pair for the goddess's prayer which can hardly be said
to be tautological; not only is the notion of prayer as request rendered by
prayenge, while that of prayer as constraint is rendered by *exhortynge*, but
the reported plea also seems to hover deftly between these two
communicative modes, suggesting that the granting of Juno's request is
dependent on her addressees' pleasure (*that it myght playse eche of hem
. . .*) yet that they would somehow only be doing their duty (*deuoyre*) by
exerting themselves on her behalf. Finally, the large gap between the
relative pronoun introducing the Gods' glad acquiescence, and its
antecedent, the request itself, is filled by Juno's promise of reward on which
the Gods' acquiescence is syntactically dependent: the effect is, I think, to
suggest the efficacy of Juno's plea as bribe. Although the history of bribery
must be coextensive with that of postlapsarian man, it is perhaps appropriate
to recall the frequency with which fifteenth-century writers, like Caxton

[11] W. T. Culley and F. J. Furnivall, eds., *Caxton's Eneydos*, EETS ES 57 (London, 1890), p. 38.

himself, characterize their works as commissioned by patrons who have promised to follow up their requests for authorial activity by pecuniary reward. In similar metaliterary statements the authors of commissioned works characterize their narratives as the fulfilment of another's wishes, which, through the pressures of social and economic realities, necessarily become identified with the wishes of the author.

One such characterization of his work as plea-engendered and economically secured occurs in Caxton's preface to his translation of the *Legenda Aurea*, a collection of popular saints' legends to which I now turn, for the use of prayer to further narrative — whether in the form of narremes, narrative episodes or extended narrative sequences — is of course not confined to epic. In terms of genre, the late medieval saints' legends are curious hybrids, descended not only from such illustrious ancestors as the gospel narratives and classical biography, but also from the less prestigious hellenistic romance and the folktale, whose 'bastardizing' influence increases as the Middle Ages progress and whose wish-fulfilling function was acknowledged long before recent psychoanalytical criticism.[12] Analysis of their plot-structures suggests that the folktales circulating in medieval England, like those circulating in twentieth-century Russia, typically used prayer or supplication at key moments of the story without which the plot could not unfold further. It might be useful to recall how Vladimir Propp's syntagmatic analysis of Russian fairy tales outlined the traditional stages of the folktale in terms of recurrent functions performed by the *dramatis personae*. I am here primarily concerned with two of these stages, or functions, insofar as they frequently involve supplication.

The first of these initiates the hero's quest proper, although it may not occur at the outset of a tale, much of which relates an initial situation in narrative form (Propp's function A). That initial situation is characterized by a lack, which, when made known through a function that Propp calls mediation, leads to the hero's quest for the lacking object. Propp's caption to function IX ('Misfortune or lack is made known; the hero is approached with a request or command; he is allowed to go or he is dispatched') resolves the ambiguity of supplication as request or command into alternative story-types.[13] This key function of the folktale presides over the making of such *dramatis personae* as dispatcher and hero, who are related to one another as supplicant and addressee. In one variant listed by Propp (B3) the initiative for departure comes from the hero himself, and there is no dispatcher, no supplicant; in that case, however, mediation between the occasion for lack and the occasion for its elimination still involves the hero's

[12] I am thinking in particular of a work like Bruno Bettelheim's *The Uses of Enchantment* (London, 1976).

[13] All references to Propp are from Laurence Scott's translation of the *Morphology of the Folktale* (Austin, 1968).

desire to eliminate that lack and as such affords ample opportunity for prayer in the psychological sense defined above.

There is one other stage of the folktale in which supplication may play a central role. In Propp's twelfth section, on the function of the donor who furthers the hero's counteraction (or action countering the initial lack), we see the hero being tested, interrogated or attacked, as a preparation for his receiving either a magical agent or a helper. Propp's list of variants for this stage of the folktale shows the hero being tested by various forms of request: a prisoner begging for his freedom, a captured or virtually-captured animal requesting mercy, animals asking to be fed, burdened creatures begging for assistance, and so forth. As in the earlier stage of the narrative, the hero is therefore the addressee of a supplication, but where in the earlier stage the dispatcher's plea could initiate the hero's journey as quest, at this stage the donor's requests function as a judgment which may go either way, spelling — in narratological terms that we do not find in Propp — more adventures, more narrative for the hero and his agent or helper, but finality and closure for the false hero, whose failure to respond to the donor's plea precludes his heroic functioning in further narrative. We might also note how equivocal these tales are as to whose wishes are actually being fulfilled: morphological analysis suggests that it is the wishes of the supplicant, whether dispatcher or donor, that are being fulfilled in the course of events, whereas the hero-centric narratives themselves in fact never fail to suggest that the object of the narrative coincides with the hero's desires.

I have allowed myself to dwell on the stages of the folktale in which prayer may be the condition of further narrative because so many of the late Middle English hagiographical writings reflect this morphology of the folktale, and this use of prayer, as any random selection of such writings would demonstrate. From the many works which could serve to illustrate my point, I have chosen the legend of St Margaret of Antioch, partly because this virgin martyr's passion exemplifies the commonplaces of romantic and popular narrative so forcefully, and partly for the peculiar charm of some of its fifteenth-century English redactions.

Among the features that the heroine of this hagiographical legend shares with the heroes and heroines of folktale, is the fact that she is an outcast, banned from family and society alike (in this case on account of her Christian faith). It is precisely in the course of the mediatory stage of the narrative, outlined above, that both the seeker heroes and the victimized heroes of folktale leave the community of the initial setting of their own volition or through their forceful removal. In fact, it is the particular form taken by removal at this stage of the tale which determines the heroic category — seeker or victim — to which the protagonist belongs. But the virgin martyr's classification as one or the other of these two types of hero is problematical, as was pointed out by Cinzia Marino in connexion with the

Old English version of the legend of another virgin martyr, Juliana.[14] The
fact is that Propp's categories tend to resolve ambiguities on which the
hagiographical legends themselves — and indeed many of their romance and
folktale analogues — thrive. The heroine of the virgin martyr's legend is
both seeker *and* victimized. She both generates narrative through her own
desire to eliminate a lack, and she generates narrative by the fact that she
constitutes an object of desire, whose lack is experienced and countered by
other *dramatis personae*. The victimized virgin martyr is forcefully
removed from family and society, and is sexually persecuted by a lecherous
pagan representative of social order, whose sequestration of the saint is
obviously analogous to the abduction of the romance heroine. The seeker
virgin martyr's struggles against adversity in a hostile environment are
triggered by her desire for martyrdom, frequently figured in Middle English
hagiography as union with the bridegroom Christ.[15] Christ then properly
represents the lacking object, or rather missing person, whom the heroine
ends up marrying. But where hagiography of course differs from the other
kinds of narrative under consideration is in its displacement of the objective
of the quest, which is not to restore, through marriage, the 'victimized
seeker' to the society from which she was originally abducted, but to replace
that society into which the couple is integrated by another, superior society
or family, constituted by the heavenly communion of saints; the remains of
the dead saint, however, do return to the community of the living, which
benefits from its status as privileged possessor of the restored object of its
desire, in the form of the saint's miracle-performing relics.

The question pertinent to the function of prayer in the opening stages of
these legends relates to the way in which the saint formulates, or mediates,
her desire for the lacking object (martyrdom) or person (Christ). If the
expression of the saint's desire for martyrdom is not always clearly marked,
by formal prayer or other means, at the outset of hagiographical narratives,
it is presumably because of the potential theological problem posed by the
saint who invites martyrdom with the eagerness of the pagan suicide
triumphing in his own death. Treading this narrow path between sanctity
and presumption, the Margaret of the *South English Legendary* spends the
nights and days of her fifteenth year, before she has been singled out as the
object of the prefect's sexual desire, praying God for steadfastness and
desiring to be put to death for love of her Lord (31 − 8).[16] In the version of

---

[14] 'La *Giuliana* e l'*Elena*, Una Proposta di Analisi', *Filologia Germanica* 23 (1980) 101 − 20.
[15] Therein lies another ambiguity, that of *desiderio passionis*, as was so eloquently pointed out
by Eric Auerbach in his *Literatursprache und Publikum in der lateinischen Spätantike und
im Mittelalter* (Bern, 1958), pp. 54 − 63.
[16]   Þis ȝonge mayde þat was þer · in þe on ende of Acie
Priueliche niȝt and day · in oure Louerd gan crie
Þat he sende hure studefast herte · and in oure Leuedi Marie

her legend by Osbern Bokenham, written a century and a half later,
Margaret voluntarily leaves the company of her pagan father, receiving his
reprobation and hatred in exchange for her worship and love of Christ
(390 – 5).[17] Her desire to join the communion of saints is voiced in a formal
prayer addressed to God at a key stage of her legend, when she has just been
approached by messengers from the pagan prefect Olibrius, informing her
that he wishes either to marry her or to take her as his concubine, depending
on her social condition, which his messengers have come to ascertain. Her
prayer as a request for divine protection from sexual defilement and for
acceptance in the heavenly community is conventional enough, but
Bokenham's *Life of St Margaret* is the only version known to me which
makes the expression of protagonistic desire coincide with the expression of
the antagonist's desire, thereby telescoping the functions of the heroine as
seeker and as victim. This prayer is also interesting not just for the response
it triggers in the petitioners, who flee from her as though she were a witch
(496), but, coming as it does immediately after Olibrius's petition for sexual
possession of the saint, it does not so much answer that petition as force
Olibrius to restate his plea and redefine the object of his desire. In the
opening stages of the verbal exchange between the virgin and her suitor, the
prefect promises to reward her consent; in modern romantic jargon his plea
could be summarized as 'if you will love me, I will make you happy and
rich'. In her continued affirmation of her fidelity to the rival lover Christ,
Margaret converts the romance into theomachia, causing Olibrius to
reformulate his plea as threat: 'if you won't worship my Gods, I'll make you
miserable' (554 – 60).[18] The sequence of Olibrius's pleas thus underlines
the transition of the saint's status from one of desired object to one of hated
object of frustrated desire, or, in other words, the prefect, from having
desired her maidenhead, comes to wish for the maiden's head. (She will,
like most saints, end up decapitated, and use of the sword, to which Olibrius
explicitly refers, of course lends itself to interpretation as a sexual symbol.)

Wiþoute fentise in hure name · þe tormenes of deþe drie . . .
He[o] wilnede euere to be[o] ido · for oure Louerdes loue to deþe
(From Charlotte D'Evelyn and Anna J. Mill, eds., *The South English Legendary*, EETS OS
235 (London, 1956)).

[17] All references to Bokenham's text are taken from Osbern Bokenham, *Legendys of Hooly
Wummen*, M. S. Serjeantson, ed., EETS OS 206 (London, 1938).

[18] The ambiguity of Christ as God and Christ as lover is well brought out in Lydgate's version
of the legend, where the crucified God seems to Olibrius to be unworthy of the
noblewoman's love:

To thi beaute it were a ful grete loos,	For-sake his feithe, and do as I the rede;
To thi youthe and to thi maydenhede,	First lat that God of the be denyed
To leve on him that deied on a croos,	Which on a tre was hange and crucified.
I holde it foly; wherfore take goode hede,	

This quotation of lines 177 – 82 of *The Legend of Seynt Margarete* is from Henry Noble
MacCracken's edition of *The Minor Poems of John Lydgate*, EETS ES 107 (London, 1911).

The subsequent narrative of the saint's tortures can be said to be generated by this reformulated wish to persecute the martyr, a wish that is reiterated alongside the contrary wish — formulated in the petitions of the horrified bystanders — that she may preserve herself from bodily harm and pain by relinquishing the original object of her desire:

'Margrete, for the we sorwe this tyde!
Olibrius in his ire the hastyth to spylle.
Beleue hym, we counsele, & lyue yet stylle'. (586 – 8)[19]

At this stage of the narrative, in the course of, or in between, tortures, the devil himself usually appears, either adding a cosmic dimension to the persecutors' threats or, in the attractive guise of an evil counsellor, adding his diabolic plea of dissuasion to those that have already been voiced by his pagan followers. Although it is possible to read this temptation in terms of psychomachia — the devil's invitation to desist at a moment of great physical and psychological stress would then be a projection of the saint's repressed wishes — one is also reminded of the testing of the folktale hero through request or attack. It is in their handling of this phase of her passion that all versions of the Margaret legend are of special interest to us. For the devil (at first in the overtly aggressive shape of a dragon, then in the more insidious form of an Aethiops, or black man) appears as a result of Margaret's plea to God that she may come face to face with her true adversary, and not just with the wicked counsellors and cruel dogs who are his puny representatives on earth (638-40). On no less than three occasions Bokenham's version reminds us of the instrumentality of the saint's prayer in conjuring forth a *dramatis persona* who has hitherto remained behind the scenes. The first and longest of these three prayers, pronounced as Margaret's tender flesh is being torn to shreds, conveniently includes Bokenham's commentary on the didactic benefits of the saint's wished-for encounter with the devil:

And also, lord, if it plese the,
I wold beseche wyth al myn herte
That I myht onys myn aduersarye se
Wych wyth me fyhtyth & me wold peruerte,
And I hym shuld make ful sore to smerte,
And yeuyn exaunple be my victory
Alle virgynys to truste in thy mercy. (645 – 51)

Bokenham seems to be rationalizing a plea whose consequences proved to be problematical for many readers, shocked by the extravagant appearance of a fiery dragon, who obligingly bursts apart when the saint (whom he

---

[19] See also lines 579 – 81.

swallows whole) makes the sign of the cross in his belly. Although many authors go to great lengths to minimize this episode, Bokenham, far from being bothered by the extravagances engendered by the saint's prayer, has her repeat that prayer when she is removed from her place of torture and transferred to prison. This second prayer, which reaffirms her desire that she may be confronted with her true enemy, also includes a prayer-within-a-prayer insofar as it incorporates the wronged saint's complaint to the devil:

> And graunt that I may myn enmy se,
> Wych wyth me fyhtyth, face to face,
> Geyn whom I not what I trespace.
> Of alle thyngys, lord, thou art iuge.
> Twyn hym and me deme ryhtfully.
> And for thou art only my refuge,
> On hym I pleyne that hurt am y
> And woundyd also ful greuously.   (677 – 84)

No sooner has her prayer given birth to a huge, garish, hairy monster than the frightened saint lapses into humanity by forgetting that the dragon comes in fulfilment of her wishes. But that is something Bokenham will not allow his reader to forget:

> Whan Margrete hym sey, ful pale of cher
> She was, and for very fer trewly
> She had foryete that god hyr preyer
> Had herd, in wych she thus dede cry:
> 'Shew me, lord, onys myn enmy
> Er than I deye.'   (701 – 6)

If the dragon's appearance is engendered by the saint's pleas, so in Bokenham's version is his defeat. Fearful, and forgetful of her earlier resolution, Margaret cries to God for the protection which he never fails to grant His saints; her cry 'lete not this dragoun, lord, noyen me' (707) initiates the miraculous episode in which the dragon effectively proves his incapacity of harming her by exploding.

Although Bokenham perhaps shows more awareness than most hagiographers of the narrative-engendering function of prayer and of the literary possibilities this affords, almost any other hagiographical text of the late Middle Ages could be used to demonstrate that the saint's life, like the epic, like romance and like the folktale, is a narrative of wish-fulfilment. This is not only signalled by the fact that medieval narratives use prayers or petitions to further the development of the plot, but also by the fact that these narratives frequently prefigure their closure by a specific use of prayer or petition. Given the capacity of prayers of thanksgiving for signalling the completion of narrative units generated by desire, it is perhaps surprising that we find so few of them in the texts under consideration. More frequently narrative closure is signalled either by a kind of prayer that I shall be calling intercessory prayer, or simply by the failure of petition to elicit the desired response. In the examples we have seen only successful pleas of course guarantee the continuation of narrative as wish-fulfilment. If Emily's prayer to Diana in *The Knight's Tale* does not meet with the goddess's approval, and therefore fails to determine the course of the narrative, that is not just because the wish she expresses is incompatible with the wishes expressed by Palamon and Arcite in their prayers, but also, I suggest, because her desire to remain unmarried thwarts the dynamics of a romantic narrative whose goal is constituted by marriage understood as the recuperation and consummation of the object of sexual desire.

Similarly, one might argue that Gawain, in Malory's version of the *Morte Darthur* and in his stanzaic Middle English source, precludes further chivalric deeds and their narration when during the siege of Benwick he prevents Arthur from granting Lancelot's petition for peace. The rejection of this petition consecrates the split among Arthur's knights which will lead to the destruction of the flower of chivalry in the battle against Modred, just as Arthur's own elimination from the battlefield, and from heroic narrative, can be attributed to his failure to comply with the terms of another famous request, put to him in the course of a vision by Gawain's ghost. In substance this posthumous petition of Gawain's is grounded on the straightforward strategic observation that Arthur's army does not stand a chance without the support of Lancelot and his knights. But that has all the force of an injunction, originating as it does not in Gawain but in God:

> Thus much hath gyvyn me leve God for to warne you of youre dethe: for and ye fyght as to-morne with sir Mordred, as ye bothe have assygned, doute ye nat ye shall be slayne, and the moste party of youre people on bothe partyes. And for the grete grace and goodnes that Allmyghty Jesu hath unto you, and for pyté of you and many mo other good men there shall be slayne, God hath sente me to you of Hys speciall grace to gyff you warnyng that in no wyse ye do batayle as to-morne, but that ye take a tretyse for a moneth-day. And proffir you largely, so that to-morne ye put in a delay. For within a moneth shall com sir Launcelot with all hys noble knyghtes, and rescow you worshypfully, and sle sir Mordred and all that ever wyll holde wyth hym.[20]

The fact that the speaker characterizes his speech as a *warnyng* and uses a vocabulary of constraint rather than of request (*in no wyse . . . but . . .*) might lead us to question the status of this passage as petition. Its status as prophecy, however, is equally open to doubt, inasmuch as it entertains the

[20] E. Vinaver, *The Works of Sir Thomas Malory*, 3 vols. (2nd edn, Oxford, 1967), p. 1234. All quotations from Malory refer to this edition. The supplication to Arthur was preceded by an intercessory prayer insofar as the attendant ladies had pleaded to God to be allowed to accompany Gawain's ghost.

illusion that an alternative course of events is possible, and not just desirable.[21] As with the plea, everything is made to depend on how the addressee responds to the speech, which is repeated in its essentials by Lucan, when he, Arthur and Modred are among the last survivors of the last battle reported in Arthurian romance. Although the battle is over, Lucan suggests the possibility of further events — he speaks of revenge — if only Arthur will *leue of* and *let [Modred] be* until the *wycked day of Desteny ys paste*. (The verb *let* must be the petitioner's verb *par excellence*, and there can be no doubt about the formal status of Lucan's speech as plea).[22]

Whatever Arthur's inadequate response may mean in terms of the King's responsibility for the final turn of events, it is clear that this ungranted plea puts an end to the narrative of the knights' exploits. But although this petition of Gawain's, repeated and varied by Lucan, signals closure by virtue of the fact that it remains ineffective, an earlier petition pronounced by Malory's Gawain as he lay *in a greate boote* (. . .) *more than halff dede* is remarkable for its demonstration of yet another literary function of prayer, most often evidenced in connexion with the protagonists of hagiographical narrative on the point of death. Expressed succinctly, this function consists in linking the *dramatis personae* of a narrative to its author and audience in a chain of intercession. Bokenham's St Margaret, before being decapitated, addresses a long intercessory prayer to God in which she prays not just for personal salvation but also 'for them specially that my passioun / other rede, or wryte, other do teche...' (835 – 6). How is the prayer of the dying Arthurian knight comparable to the virgin martyr's linking of self, audience, author and exponent of her legend in a common hope of redemption?

Gawain initially confesses his guilt to Arthur before requesting paper, pen and ink with which to address his written prayer to Lancelot. After repeating in writing his responsibility for present circumstances, Gawain begs Lancelot to return to England, not just to redress a hopeless military situation, as we saw in connexion with his posthumous plea, but in order to pray for Gawain's soul:

> . . . I beseche the, sir Launcelot, to returne agayne unto thys realme and se my toumbe and pray som prayer more other les for my soule. (p. 1231)

In short, Gawain on the point of death has prayed Arthur to help him pray Lancelot to pray for him. But the intercessory chain is extended even further when Lancelot is finally in a position to grant Gawain's plea, which he does

---

[21] Mark Lambert in *Malory. Style and Vision in 'Le Morte Darthur'* (New Haven, 1975), p. 169, makes the same observation in connexion with his notion of tragic multicentricity, which sees Malory as multiplying the causes for the final catastrophe.
[22] *The Works of Sir Thomas Malory*, pp. 1236 – 7.

not only by praying on Gawain's tomb, weeping heartily, but also by
pray[ing] the people to pray for the soule of Sir Gawayne.[23]
We cannot fail to be reminded of that famous colophon to the *Morte
Darthur*, in which Malory addresses his audience as follows:

> I praye you all jentylmen and jentylwymmen that redeth this book of Arthur
> and his knyghtes from the begynnyng to the endynge, praye for me whyle I
> am on lyve that God sende me good delyveraunce. And whan I am deed, I
> praye you all praye for my soule. (p. 1260)

In spite of the peculiar circumstances in which it is thought to have been
written, and which lend political overtones to the concept of deliverance,
such a colophon is of course related to the hagiographer's hope, most often
appended to the concluding episode of his work,[24] that both the audience and
the hagiographical protagonist, whose prayers author and audience
celebrate and imitate, will intercede with God on his behalf.

This is not the place to explore the theological concept of intercession,
which lends efficacy to prayer by ensuring that its divine addressee, God, is
addressed indirectly, through the mediation of the saints and the not-so-
saintly, all of whom are simultaneously petitioners and addressees, with the
exception of the supplicant who initiates the chain of intercession. It must
here suffice to point out that the intercessory prayer performs a function that
strikes me as being related to the question of narrative closure in more ways
than one. Through the use of intercessory prayer, both in the mouth of his
protagonist and in his own colophon, the author points to the effects of his
work beyond the continuity of the narrative proper. At the same time,
through its self-referentiality, the prayer to others that they may pray —
besides the fact that it suppresses the direct object of prayer who might grant
wishes, and therefore wish-fulfilment narrative — suggests the inability of
prayer or plea to produce anything other than further acts of prayer or
pleading. The invitation to imitation of course makes good theological
sense. Yet the protagonists and authors of hagiographical narratives are not
just allowing prayer to function as a vehicle for a didactic message about the
need for intercession in a hierarchical religion where salvation can only be
acquired by degrees. Beyond this didactic function of intercessory prayer,
which, like ritual prayer, is essential to the continuity of orthodox tradition,
lies its inability to contribute to the renewal of narrative. The self-referential

---

[23] *Ibid*, p. 1250. This particular prayer to the people is secured economically by Lancelot's
distribution of twelve pence to every 'volunteer'.

[24] This authorial hope is occasionally expressed at the beginning rather than at the ending of a
work, but is always detached from the narrative proper, as when Bokenham prays his friend
to pray to St Margaret both for himself and his patroness towards the end of his preface to
the entire collection of *Legendys of Hooly Wummen*. This prayer is actually initiated by a
concluding formula: 'But for to drawe to a conclusyoun/ Of thys long tale now fynally,/ I
you beseche . . .' (ll. 226 – 8). The 'long tale' referred to here is his preface.

nature of intercessory prayer, which contrasts so strikingly with the narrative-engendering power of supplication, surely accounts for the popularity of this kind of prayer as a device of closure in the texts under consideration, as it accounts for stasis and repetition in a number of late medieval texts whose status as narratives of wish-fulfilment begs further study.

FAITH AND THE CRITICAL SPIRIT IN CHAUCER AND HIS TIME

PRZEMYSŁAW MROCZKOWSKI

I

The paper will deal with the description and relationship of two contrasted, sometimes opposed, and, in the perception of some, even contradictory attitudes and interests in the writings of Chaucer. To some extent the general situation in European culture will be borne in mind and treated as introductory to the subject. It will be assumed, in agreement with what now seems the prevalent view among critics, that the author of the *Canterbury Tales* remained an adherent of the orthodox religious doctrine still dominant in his country and on the continent. This will be dealt with in the section devoted to Faith. The term will accordingly denote acceptance by intellect and will, supernatural in character, with the assistance of divine grace, of what the Church proclaimed as God's revelation. Entailed also is the readiness to follow as authoritative the doctrine and the discipline of the Church.

It is equally obvious, particularly in view of the text of Retraction, taken as authentically Chaucerian,[1] that the poet's later work, notably *Troilus and Criseyde* and above all the *Canterbury Tales*, contain texts strikingly 'uninhibited', describing, as every reader knows, human portraits and actions markedly 'unaware', as it were, of Christian doctrine and ethics, though never expressly or intentionally so — at times in a way opposed to either, at times professedly 'emancipated' from both or at least illustrating pagan beliefs or conduct.

It is with this body of portraits, dialogues, and narratives that the second part of the formula in the title is concerned. The 'critical spirit' is meant as a comprehensive pointer to whatever lies outside the strict exposition of creed

---

[1] I am content to follow the balanced opinion of Robinson, p. 772 in Explanatory Notes of his *The Works of Geoffrey Chaucer*, 2nd edn. (London, 1957). A. David in his *The Strumpet Muse* (Bloomington, Ind. and London, 1976) deserves consideration as he tries to look honestly and seriously on the text, finding in it '. . . a deeply moving statement of the limitations of art . . .', p. 238, as set beside the ultimate realities see p. 239. See also *The Riverside Chaucer*, gen. ed. Larry D. Benson, 3rd edn. (Boston, 1987), pp. 956 and 965.

and conduct, without combating it. It grows partly out of the mental activity
that analyses and scrutinizes all that it encounters or whatever is submitted
or dictated to it, considering it against the comparative context and assessing
its reasonableness. Naturally, it also grows out of other psychological
factors and gifts but, as something contrasted with Faith, it may include a
certain amount of sceptical questioning of any assertions, especially
metaphysical ones; it may feed intellectually some impulses towards satire.
Conversely, in view of its universal 'position', it may react against
excessive or unjustified criticism of the said assertions, against too much
scepticism.

II

I shall begin with a note on the background, with a cursory view of the
maturation of medieval culture, its growth in power, variety, and depth,
from the days of St Bernard (1090 – 1153), the beginnings of Gothic under
Abbot Suger (c. 1081 – 1151) and the earliest universities, chiefly as a
process of the fairly conscious planning and building of *civitas terrena*,
meant to reflect and embody *civitas Dei*, a design not always envisaged in
the days of monastic ascendancy. The varying measure of disparity between
the vision and the reality will be taken for granted. This was growth and
development, the 'Age of Iuventus'. On the other hand, the attempts also
meant culturally restrictive activity in various fields. For example, we will
never know how many 'pagan' manuscripts were destroyed by zealous
clerks or monks. The turn of the new, crucial thirteenth century could
contain more opposed phenomena than before: both the vocation of the two
founders of the epoch-making mendicant orders, so strikingly expansive,
and the tragic smashing of the meridional culture in France. There was the
Church, and there was the world. Each displayed forces striving in
directions almost as diverse as can be manifested in human nature and
human culture. Near the end of the time under consideration a genius like
Chaucer will show this diversity in individuals more acutely than anyone: it
will be the partial encounter and partial confrontation of Christianity and its
'contrasting framing'.[2] In simpler, more conventional terms, the achievements of Greek and Roman antiquity, however imperfectly known, act anew
by their glamour upon the minds of the students of many schools. The much
more recent achievements of Islam with *its* schools — some brilliant — and
ways of life tempt many fighters and readers and travellers in the Orient: the

[2] Cf.: 'Chaucer's ambiguity, irony, and multiple perspectives may reflect his artistic
responses to cultural instabilities of his time', William C. Johnson Jr., 'The Man of Law's
Tale, Aesthetics and Christianity in Chaucer', *Chaucer Review* 16 (1981 – 82) 201 – 21, p.
215.

more evident the failure of the crusades, the more powerful could be the pull of the unconquered Moslem world. What to say of the wide expanses of lands peopled by numerous Germanic tribes and some of other origin, at best half-converted and often hardly able to forget their barbarism? We might thus range over the various overt or 'subterranean' aspects of the pre-Christian or non-Christian world to reach the easy conclusion that this world was likely to develop in agreement with its own dominant ideas and/or traditions (and in disagreement with the teaching of missionaries). There were specific, collective patterns of custom and culture, some certainly noble. There were also in each individual and in several institutions the standard human shortcomings, some petty, some enormous, the immemorial pulls of avarice, envy, pride and, to remain within medieval categories — though familiar later as well — all the standard sevenfold company of Deadly Sins, operating both within and without the Christian structures.³ Our chief interest is the 'cultural consequences' of those variegated pressures that every student knows about. In the field of letters one notes such phenomena as the spread of Ovidian motifs all the way to *remedia amoris*, some radical versions of the Courtly Love texts (those repudiating marriage, like *Cligès* by Chrétien de Troyes or *Lais* by Marie de France); the glorification of tribal revenge in some epics like the *Nibelungenlied*. In the field of factual history we note the ever-recurrent blood-shedding wars to avenge one's 'loss of honour'; there are motifs in the domain of the visual arts, either frankly meant to present the love-urge as all powerful or all-excusing, or displaying total licence 'in actu' (some illuminations and ivoires are unmistakable in this respect: they show, incidentally, how 'natural' it will be for Chaucer to describe reprehensible things without any beating about the bush).⁴ The 'war declared on chastity' on some pages of the *Roman de la Rose* is even more telling.⁵

The above instances are the nearest to something which might be called half-hearted confrontation between Christian and non-Christian thinking and action. There was also any amount of 'incomplete benevolent fusion',

---

³ See M. W. Bloomfield, *The Seven Deadly Sins. An Introduction to the History of a Religious Concept, with Special Reference to Medieval English Literature* (East Lansing, Mi., 1952).

⁴ Cf. the illustrations from 'Taymouth Hours' in the British Museum and the ivory mirror case from Victoria and Albert Museum, reproduced respectively as nos 5 and 59 in *A Preface to Chaucer. Studies in Medieval Perspective* by D. W. Robertson Jr. (Princeton, 1962).

⁵ See Guillaume de Lorris et Jean de Meun, *Le Roman de la Rose*, Daniel Poirion ed. (Paris 1974) ll. 15788 ff, p. 426; 19489 – 90, p. 517. The latter couplet is specially striking: Venus . . .

> Li met ou poing un ardent cierge
> Qui n'estiot pas de cire vierge.

and again, even more sweepingly and unreservedly, ll. 19505 – 20184, pp. 517 – 34.

from whichever side the initiative to it came. We can point to such processes as the gradual Christianization of the ritual of dubbing a knight, originally probably a mere endorsement of the acquisition of military skill. Or we may recall the 'classicization' of sacred art with the growth of Gothic where nature looks more natural and the figures of men and women look more human.[6] The give and take, the mutual exchange of motifs between the sacred and profane spheres of medieval culture is so familiar as to surprise nobody. In the thirteenth century we have the synthesis and near-balance between the two currents, the basic formulation to be found of course in St Thomas. The greatest of theologians is also the author of the sentence that *genus humanum arte et rationibus vivit* as well as, on a more modest scale, of several injunctions emphasizing the importance of courteous behaviour in contact with people.[7] His fundamental defence of the role of 'standard' human, indeed pagan, wisdom is elementary knowledge.

Our excessively swift historical enquiry into the background moves now into the fourteenth century in which whatever synthesis and balance had been outlined began to disintegrate.[8] Naturally, we must not oversimplify by ignoring the various successful constructive efforts and outstanding personalities on the side of Christian culture. Many works of importance were written,[9] many monuments of art were shaped.[10] Moreover, as Duby shows in his renowned *Le Temps des cathédrales, L'art et la Société 980 – 1420*, one can speak of a wider link between the activity of the Church (the mendicants) and the life of the community. The increase in popular (and

---

[6] Cf. my article 'Mediaeval Art and Aesthetics in *The Canterbury Tales*,' *Speculum* 33 (1958) 204 – 21, p. 205 and E. Mâle, *The Gothic Image, Religious Art in France of the Thirteenth Century* (New York, 1958), p. 54: 'These ingenuous artists carved animals as they did flowers, simply to express some aspects of nature which appealed to them'.

[7] Cf. the observations on the importance of civility to one's company, e.g. IIa IIae, q. 114, art 1 and 2. We note, too, the linking of friendship with affability. Eutrapelia, the virtue of cheerful sociability is praised repeatedly, e.g. in Ia IIae, q. 60 art. 5. The point is also educational: the training of youngsters in good manners was recommended by monastic and lay instructors, see *The Matter of Courtesy. Medieval Courtesy Books and the Gawain-Poet* by J. W. Nicholls (Woodbridge, 1985). This good study reports the contribution of the monks but not the analogous activity of the friars.

[8] Cf. *The Evolution of Medieval Thought* by David Knowles (New York, 1962), pp. 311, 317, 340.

[9] To mention, by way of examples, only a few of the most renowned books include such titles as *La Divina Commedia* by Dante, Petrarch's *Rime in Vita e Morte di Madonna Laura*, Boccaccio's *Il Decameron, Piers Plowman* and *Libro de buen amor* in literature, *Opus tripartitum* by Meister Eckhart and Ruÿsbroek's *De vera contemplatione* in mysticism, *Dialogus* of William Ockham, *Tractatus de Primo Principio* of Duns Scotus in philosophy.

[10] In art the Spanish cathedrals of Barcelona or Toledo, the French in Strassbourg and Metz, the choir in the Cologne cathedral in Germany, in England the choirs of York and Canterbury, the perpendicular achievements in Bristol and Gloucester, in Italy the great frescoes in Florence and Siena, the paintings of Simone Martini, etc.

lay!) participation in religious life, particularly in the towns, setting up communities of tertiaries and the like, may have affected the life of someone like Chaucer.[11] On the other hand, in the fairly uniform view of scholars, the time *is* one of crises. The philosophical field is notorious. Historians of scholasticism[12] stress above others the role of William of Ockham as exemplifying the sceptical weakening of a system of thought once unquestioned; now even the principle of causality was scrutinized. Outstanding among others whose names reveal the trend are Pierre d'Ailly, Duns Scotus, Jean Jandun, Nicolas d'Autricourt, Jean de Mirecourt, Jean Rodington, Nicolas d'Oresme and Jean Buridan. Before Gilson, the critical and sceptical currents in Paris and Oxford were traced by the indefatigable manuscript researches of the Cracow Rector Konstanty Michalski.[13] In the universities, even when some fundamentals are reaffirmed in the spirit of piety, the aims assigned to speculation are particularized: the dons now expected to help more in serving their kings or nations, or in promoting *special* political designs. The two jewels of medieval speculation, universalism and objectivism, dwindle. Among other domains, the decline of chivalry calls for attention. Its once crucial function in warfare repeatedly proves a mistaken 'option', beginning with Poitiers in 1346 and ending with Agincourt in 1415. With regard to overall structure, nothing can be more telling than the split in the hierarchical power of the papacy. The consequences for art and letters were bound to prove complex. The student comes across various works: in some, the earlier fusions of heterogenous elements, by no means ubiquitous or invariably perfect, unravel. The bland inclusion of a number of amoral and immoral stories in Boccaccio's *Decameron*, otherwise full of references to Catholic ideas and traditions, seems a relevant case in point. The *Libro de buen amor* by Juan Ruiz is another. It is true that the same century saw some further fascinating, if not always consistent, attempts at synthetic (and yet not necessarily syncretic) combinations of 'lay inspiration' and dogmatic backbone. The unsurpassable example is a number of pages in *La Divina Commedia*, notably the elevation of Dante's *donna gentilissima* to her role of supreme guide through the paradisal realms. Others might be found, none, of course, of comparable rank. One deserves attention, however. I am thinking of course of the oft-discussed plot of *Sir Gawayne and the Greene Knyght* with its basic preservation of chastity coupled with scrupulous observance of

---

[11] Paris, 1976, Cf. the English translation to which I had access, Chicago, 1981, esp. pp. 222 – 3 and 227 – 32. Duby notes also an increase of private devotion, meditation, recourse to the Bible, all centring in the *devotio moderna*.

[12] See E. Gilson, *La Philosophie au Moyen Age. Des Origines Patristiques à la fin du XIVe siècle* (Paris, 1952), chapters I, II, III, IX, pp. 591 – 686.

[13] See K. Michalski, *La Philosophie au XIVe siècle. Six Etudes* (rep. Frankfurt, 1969), esp. pp. 38 – 42, 67.

88   *Religion in the Poetry and Drama of the Late Middle Ages*

courtesy to ladies, even, as the readers remember, in quite drastic circumstances.[14]

Both before and after Dante's *mezzo del camin*, 1300, there were, in many parts of Europe, plenty of samples of two parallel, though different trends in the frame of one topic; there was, for example, the anxious wish to see the clergy orthodox, devoted to their vocation — and at the same time ruthless denunciation of actual conduct where opposed to such a demand. There can be no doubt that the young Chaucer encountered many works of this kind, in Latin as well as in the vernacular, whether English, French, or Italian. The second kind of 'coexistence' will be the rise of the fabliaux — together with the standard praise of virginity and/or exemplary marital conduct; and the third will be sceptical utterances occurring in the same period as expressions of fervent belief. It is a kind of puzzle that there should be found inconsistencies or at least discrepancies of interest in an epoch so ardently logical. The author of *Troilus and Criseyde* learnt to live with both from his boyhood.

III

We shall now take a closer look at the 'case of Chaucer', bearing in mind his gifts, his probable psychology and especially his kind of humour, to some extent his circle of acquaintances, and above all his actual writings. We cannot, except for the already invoked Retraction, have recourse to his direct personal avowals, since no such documents on religious subjects are extant (except for the unconfirmed, if plausible, story of the later deathbed remorse).

I begin by a review of the texts unquestionably expressing the orthodox view. First we have the early paraphrase of the praise of the Virgin, *ABC*, and at the end we find the winding up of the Canterbury pilgrimage with the Parson's lengthy penitential instruction, followed by the just mentioned, baffling, Retraction. In between, the Man of Law comes out with his hagiographical romance, the poet himself with the allegory of the *Tale of Melibee*, the Oxford Clerk with the story of Griselda, and the two Nuns recite respectively the narrative of the murdered little clergeoun and of the martyrdom of St Cecilia. All of these are without doubt to be accepted as examples of a directly religious outlook.

I will deal first with the early piece, the additionally 'rhetoricized' version of Deguileville's poem; concentrating on the doctrinal content, I pass over all the supplementary ornaments. There is the standard assertion of God's

[14] See Th. Silverstein, ed., *Sir Gawain and the Green Knight: A New Critical Edition* (Chicago and London, 1984), ll. 653, 1208 – 90, 1476 – 557, and the notes, pp. 134 – 5, 147 – 8, 152 – 3, and Introduction, p. 11.

scheme of rescue for His criminally ungrateful and thoughtless children through sharing their well-deserved predicament, all the way to ransoming them by His own Son's blood shed on Golgotha, which leads to the New Covenant. The resulting Charter is valid for all the happy-go-lucky bankrupt wretches. Now, in this scheme the role of Christ's Virginal Mother is of course of unique importance. She is the Co-Redemptrix by Her special participation in the Passion which led to Her being the 'Source of Grace' to all people (if duly contrite) and merited for Her the supreme title of the Queen of Heaven and Earth.[15]

The rest of the substance of the poem is taken up by ardent appeal for succour and expression of adoration. Nothing could more neatly conform to accepted medieval worship of Christ's Mother — or be more opposed to future Protestant views — and it looks at more than one point like an earlier, sketchy version of François Villon's widely-known *Ballade*, written for his mother. In the case of Chaucer the lady ordering the writing was, as Speght reports in the 1602 edition, Duchess Blanche of Lancaster. The supposition of the executor's personal emotional engagement is plausible, though must remain short of 'scientific' proof, but we have said that we should be content primarily with formulating the 'immediate' and 'objective' meaning of the given text.

We all know the view that the exchange of motifs between the tradition of courtesy and the doctrinal development of the position of the Virgin went far in the middle ages. The *ABC* poem makes for an example in Chaucer's output of that famous symbiosis: the worship of a lady achieves here its metaphysically enhanced form.

In the much later lines of the Prologue to the *Prioress's Tale* the adoration of Mary is equally plain. The doctrinal claim emphasizes, after Dante's *Paradiso*, the exaltation prepared by humility. In this case the dramatic appropriateness of the message in the case of a nun is entirely obvious. There is also cohesion between literature and edification: the paradox pleases by its appeal to the sense of contrast and at the same time promotes a man spiritually. Here, the hymnic Prologue is commented upon separately because of its form. The turn of the tale itself comes later.

For reasons of substance, let us now look more attentively at the decisive text, that of the *Parson's Tale*. This treatise, based perhaps on Guilielmus Peraldus's *Summa seu Tractatus de Viciis* and *Summa Casuum Poenitentiae* by Raymund de Peñaforte, also possibly on *Somme des Vices et Vertues* of Frère Lorens presupposes in the reader a certain number of dogmatic assumptions as unchanged near the end of the fourteenth century as they had been in the thirteenth. A hundred and thirty years after the works of

---

[15] The visual arts offer continual support: '. . . traditional stories of the life and death of Our Lady are found *everywhere* in the churches'. (E. Mâle, *op. cit.*, p. 232: italics mine).

Peraldus and Peñaforte these 'textbooks' of instruction seem to have been regarded as still outstandingly good, probably recommended by well-orientated ecclesiastics; otherwise Chaucer would not have chosen them for (partial or mixed) translation. It is the final participation in the series of items spoken by the members of the pilgrimage and it completes the execution of the Host's initial scheme.[16] It is also, on the other hand, felt by some critics — not quite rightly — to disrupt the previous practice which from the *Knight's Tale* on consisted in a *literary* competition. The Parson, as we know, does not care for literature (X I 31 – 34) and is content to instruct his fellow pilgrims in the skill of preparing a good confession which is implied in the performance of pilgrimage. Telling this *myrie tale in prose* (46)[17] entails some basic views, apparently not identical with those implied in the previous cases. The right 'mood' for preparing confession, i.e. contrition, presupposes first the consciousness of the total dependence of man, the creature on the Creator; most people in Chaucer's age were still ready to swallow this paradoxical and commonsensical condition for remaining 'merry'. The liberating effect of truth (we may compare the refrain of the *Balade de Bon Conseil: trouthe thee shal delivre, it is no drede*) also includes the truth about man's sinfulness. But other elements of such a situation include the possibility of a wrong moral choice resulting in a new kind of dependence to which man reduces himself by disobeying the Almighty Creator's law and instead obeying his new, tyrannous master to the point of *thraldom* (servitude). This mistaken and treacherous choice of the illegitimate master is also punished by the Right One, the Parson emphasizes, with all the pertaining terrible severity. There is, too, the awareness of all the good that is forfeited, both in the past and in the future life. To this is added the awareness of the paramount charity of Christ manifested, of course, in His redeeming death.

All the above go to make up a regular presentation of the accepted teaching of the Church, regularly opposed to modern man's frequent belief

---

[16] Cf. P. A. Olson's view that the Parson's Tale '. . . is not an "anti-tale" which implicitly rejects tale-telling. Like the other tales, it responds to earlier tales, and comments on them', in *The Canterbury Tales and the Good Society* (Princeton, 1986), p. 276.

[17] Helen Storm Corsa's treatment of this aspect is duly rhetorical whilst basically right: 'Banter and joking, contention and strife, lusty joy and earthy gaiety are stilled, but "mirth" remains, for the Parson's "meditation", though it deals with sin, defines the conditions for forgiveness . . .', in *Chaucer Poet of Mirth and Morality* (Notre Dame, Ind. 1964), p. 235. Paul G. Ruggiers, 'Serious Chaucer: The *Tale of Melibeus* and the Parson's Tale' in *Chaucerian Problems and Perspectives: Essays Presented to Paul E. Beichner*, eds. E. Vasta and Z. P. Thundy (Notre Dame, Ind., 1979), pp. 83 – 94, writes on similar lines that the Parson's Tale 'is not without qualities of vitality, of a theological humor, of high indignation, of fervent love that make for the literature of power', n. 92. Such views strike one as attempts at applications in scholarship of the shrewd amateur opinions of G. K. Chesterton for whom Chaucer's humour grew of his theology(!), in *Chaucer and His Age* (London, 1932): 'The Moral of the Story'.

in his unlimited freedom. Chaucer's alleged sympathy for Wycliffite doctrine, though plausible at times, certainly finds no support in the subsequent directive that oral confession of the sinner's guilt should be made personally to another human being, notably a priest, with no reservations as to the priest's prerogative to grant absolution under any circumstances foreseen by Canon Law.[18]

The Parson, in an unusual way, may be seen as winning a game — as did his Master by His Sacrifice on Golgotha.[19] The Tale contains a vast subsidiary insertion which has no intrinsic link with the doctrine of seeking pardon as such — the Treatise on the Seven Deadly Sins — yet quite striking at times from the literary and psychological point of view. It shares such qualities with some other texts on the *Peccata Capitalia* in which many authors, including some otherwise inconspicuous ones, reveal penetration into human failings with the corresponding inward mechanisms and mutual linking. The effort to convince or shake the reader moves several of them to write with vivacity, introduce striking examples and comparisons, and use well-chosen quotations. This came to Chaucer all the more easily, though not all the time. In fact, the impression of heaviness prevails on many pages of the treatise (as it does every now and then in certain lines of the earlier Tales). But the many 'fortunate touches' match partly — never consistently — the narrative and rhetorical skill of the successful versified stories.[20]

I have reported the main points of the main text. The assumption throughout was of the author's commitment to the content.[21] But there are a few additional premises of another kind which make for finishing touches. First there is the portrait of the teller of the 'tale'. The near-standard observation that the picture of the Parson is one of the rare ones in which the great satirist soberly gave up direct satire strengthens the impression that Chaucer was prepared to 'vouch' for his last speaker. The priest's stern appeal for moral reformation was to be seen as coming from a dedicated, poor preacher of the pure Gospel message; also, the pointing to . . . *Cristes*

---

[18] D. L. Jeffrey specifies: '. . . it is clear that one did not have to identify with Wyclif in the theological arguments: in Brewer's words, "many who might better be described as orthodox evangelical Christians shared the Lollards' general concerns without their extremism" ': 'Chaucer and Wyclif: Biblical Hermeneutic and Literary Theory in the XIVth Century' in D. L. Jeffrey, ed., *Chaucer and Scriptural Tradition* (Ottawa, 1984), pp. 109 – 40, p. 110.

[19] Cf. Michael Olmert's strikingly original article on 'The Parson's Ludic Formula for winning on the road', *Chaucer Review* 20 (1985), in which the Teller is shown as concentrating 'on the rules of the game', Christ being 'the ultimate gameplayer', (pp. 159 and 163).

[20] Alfred David thinks that 'It will never again be possible to ascribe Chaucer's religious or didactic passages to the limitations of his age or to patronize them as dull and conventional.' *op. cit.*, p. 4. Can we be sure what will still be impossible a hundred years from now?

[21] Paul G. Ruggiers is even convinced that '. . . these frankly moral works contain many of the values that Chaucer himself held', *art. cit.*, p. 87.

loore and his apostles twelve in the words and deeds of the Parson is the best
hint out of many of Chaucer's reliance on his frequent Biblical readings,
shown recently in detail by a group of Canadian scholars. The presence of
his brother the Ploughman, humble, hard-working and full of charity,
'makes the assurance doubly sure'.

My plan now makes essential a few words about the Tales between ABC
and the Parson's Tale. First there is the *Tale of Melibee* and the *Man of
Law's Tale*. The former propagates extreme forgiveness and the pursuit of
peace. It thus provides as it were, the counterpart to the profession of arms,
even of the Christian version thereof, apparently in the spirit of the Sermon
on the Mount (Mat 5: 39 – 41) and somewhat like a medieval precedent of
certain modern peace campaigns.[22]

Both tales are strikingly unconventional in two different ways. The *Tale
of Melibee* by its theoretical quality, so much at variance with the realism
and the satirical bent prevalent in several other narratives (the characters
here are abstractions) and by the central idea, distant from the 'facilitating'
approach for 'ordinary' pursuers of principles of decency. For once or
twice, the commonsensical Chaucer is being highly theoretical.

In the case of the *Man of Law's Tale* it is worth observing the bold
application of fictitious material to the edifying purpose, so clearly differing
from the Parson's injunction and revealing Chaucer's broadness even where
the tales of 'strict edification' are concerned. (There will be much of similar
design behind several 'lay' tales.) The plot has its origin in a *märchen*, a
fairy story, assigned by the poet's enigmatic decision to the shrewd lawyer;
in a way, partial unconventionality may reside in another puzzle, that
experienced by the heroically pious lady-protagonist in the face of turns of
events as painful as they seem undeserved — though we may note in this
another convention.

Clearly the same kind of lesson is believed by critics to underlie the
account of the stunning experiences of the supremely patient Griseldis in the
hands of Marquis Walter. For the third time the illustration of a principle
derived from faith is abstract and abstruse.[23]

There are still the Tales of the two Nuns. The narrative of the Prioress
glorifies the mercy and the power of Mary shown to Her juvenile
worshipper in the form of a miracle. The *Second Nun's Tale* provides a

---

[22] Cf. the succinct and precise summary of P. Olson, *op. cit.*: 'The Melibee does not exhibit
the pacifism of the Wycliffites of the 1380s or of the 1395 *conclusions*; rather, it allows for
the possibility of just wars. But it also asserts that repentence, faith, prudence, and the
wisdom of forgiveness can restrain the ruler God's representative', p. 118.

[23] James Sledd detaches the importance of the message of *The Clerk's Tale* (patience matters
supremely) from the question of realistic or successful presentation of the characters: 'The
Clerk's Tale, The Monsters and the Critics', *Modern Philology* 51 (1953 – 4) 73 – 82, p.
77.

translation of a straightforward account of martyrdom. Additionally it eulogizes chastity, as befits a nun. The whole story presupposes a swift and strong action of grace, following the affirmation of the tenets of Christianity.

If we were to put into a few words the gist of the items in Chaucer's writings related to faith, we could say that most of the standard articles of the latter are either included or implied in the texts we have. The term used signifies no humdrum placidity: the demands from the believer are shown as high, indeed, absolute. Two aspects, of different nature, may be perceived: on the one hand the believer is asked to affirm articles transcending his everyday experience, intellectual and sensual, an expectation which is enhanced by the unusual quality of the illustrative stories and also by the contrast, indeed discrepancy, between the content of the Creed and the 'fully secular' tales; on the other hand the sober student notes in the faith features of common sense and common loyalty.

IV

The second major section of this paper is to deal with what has been called the critical spirit. Its range must be very wide. The problem begins with the consideration of the Tales which, in the author's own final assessment 'sownen into synne', being 'translaciouns and enditynges of worldly vanitees'. To use more objective language, I will limit myself to selecting in this survey from the ample body of 'non-religious' or 'not strictly religious' Tales those narratives whose parts or aspects, at least outwardly, seem to contrast most with the Parson's standpoint. I suggest a broad division of the material in question under three headings:

   (a) anticlerical motifs, strictly antifraternal and antimonastic ones, and some
      other satirical portraits and sketches,
   (b) obscenity,
   (c) scepticism.

Before these categories are taken up in some detail, it may prove helpful as an introduction to reflect in one more way upon the origin of the conception of the *Canterbury Tales*. Although conditioned by cultural antedecents, as I have argued, the point has always seemed to me to be something in the nature of a breakthrough. Here was a most perceptive and creative writer intending to show how varied humanity was: he must have heard from his teachers the directive stressing that all things are better perceived through their contraries (*omnis res a suo contrario elucidatur*) — also in writing. Also to give birth to humour or enhance an inborn disposition to it; the importance of the disposition in someone like Chaucer

94   *Religion in the Poetry and Drama of the Late Middle Ages*

cannot be overstated. More comprehensively and philosophically (I suggested exactly thirty years ago in the Harvard *Speculum*, 1958) the inspiration may have descended upon the great observer and admirer of God's Plenty in connection with some such conviction as that revealed in the text of Hugh of St Victor: the beauty which the Creator displays in the reality leaving His hands has the necessary quality of variety (*pulchrum divinum est varificans, id est varie ac multipliciter declarans*). Other ideas perhaps lying at the bottom of Chaucer's dazzlement remain to be discovered. For my part, I have found two more references to diversity. Aquinas goes so far as to say that 'there is beauty in the very diversity'. Again Witelo, known to Chaucer, declares that 'diversity makes for beauty'.[24]

Another likely inspiration and a familiar comparison is one of the greatest achievements of the medieval era: the cathedrals. Whilst the early edifices of that category are by their simplicity, often their bareness, nearer to pure contemplation of the spiritual nature of God, later development allows for more and more presentation of the material marvels of Creation, the reality of the physical side of nature and of man 'realistically' rendered, all the way down to the misericord seats. Generally speaking, religion once more was helping art and art was serving religion. In Chaucer's century part of the role played by cathedrals was now to be taken over by large frescoes. Artists will cover large spaces of walls with actual detailed panoramas of communities.

I have been labouring here a paradox, though an essential one. Broadness and inspiration which as such are *not* manifestations of the critical spirit become, in our poet's case, ways leading to its exercise. We should now imagine the case of a clerk, anxious to write, endowed with an unparalleled sensitivity, for whom everyday encounters are so many psychological revelations. He feels like repeating some stories about them; in fact, he would like to attach to each a characteristic narrative. We should add that thousands of readers and critics have been discovering for generations how such narratives, even when 'non-religious', suggest moral lessons.

At this point the universal, nearly cosmic broadness leaves room for a special company. A concourse of various representatives of mankind, even when a religious custom such as a pilgrimage provides the occasion, brings

---

[24] Cf. Hugh of St Victor, in Edgar de Bruyne, *Études d' esthétique médiévale* (Bruges, 1946), II, 217; St Thomas Aquinas, Opusc. XIII, *Compendium Theologiae* 102, as translated by T. Gilby in his edition of *Philosophical Texts of Aquinas* (Oxford, 1956), no. 437 on p. 157: the opinion is seen as postulated by the notion '. . . that the distinction and multitude of things is established by the intention of the first cause which is God': *op. cit.*, no. 432, p. 150, cf. *Sum. Theol.* Ia XLVII, 1; again Witelo (mentioned by Chaucer in *The Squire's Tale*, V (F) 232) speaks of diversity and beauty in *Optica*, ed. by Baeumker, IV, 148, cf. Alhazen, II, 59, as quoted by W. Tatarkiewicz in his *Historia estetyki*, p. 313.

together individuals not only of different 'shapes and colours', but of *very* different degrees of respectability. Bluntly, as well as 'decent' people, it will draw buffoons and rascals. These deserve particularly to be satirized and our clerk knows he possesses the gift of satirizing.

(a) Thus we will try to consider in more detail the first of the three aspects of the critical spirit in Chaucer, the talent for caricature.

It is difficult to assess the exact intentions of a satirist, especially of a great satirist. But he surely decided to utilize his abilities in ridiculing members of the community who did not live or behave as they should. The 'critical spirit' was unquestionably involved; so too was a kind of scepticism. Whether that specific moral danger for keen satirists, the vindictive urge, was perfectly under control, we will never know precisely. Nor will it be easy in each case to measure how close the caricatured vice was to the actual 'scientific' statistical truth concerning the given social group. It will be less difficult to pin down the writer's targets, by a close look at the text.

Whom then was Chaucer aiming at more particularly? One category comes first in our interests: the members of the monastic and mendicant communities: the Monk, the Prioress and the two Friars (I include figures from the stories with those from the Prologue), plus the marginal ecclesiastical retainers, the Summoner and the Pardoner. There are non-ecclesiastical figures in the satirist's field of vision, too, but we cannot afford the time and attention to deal with them.

One safe general observation is, to introduce a negative formula, the lack of submissive, 'punctilious' obeissance expected by excessively self-assured and pleasure-seeking monks and friars. Chaucer felt as free as any other clerk of his pre-Tridentine epoch[25] to explode their assumption of privileges, when specious and undeserved, and to lay bare their duplicity where undeniable. Since we now know more about his familiarity with the Bible, we may even suppose his finding in the words of Christ an encouraging example of stern intransigence in smashing the false pretences of the clerical class and their hypocrisy. Christ, indeed, could be taken as the union of the supremely sober 'critical spirit' and pure piety and prayer.

One figure has struck most readers as attracting a maximal measure of the writer's 'scathing attention' — that outstanding member of the company of pilgrims, in a negative sense, of course: the Pardoner. Nowhere does the spirit of criticism move nearer to the *sentimiento tragico de la vida*, in Unamuno's oft-quoted title. It is not enough to speak of a 'familiar target',

---

[25] For Chaucer's precedents in the matters of anticlerical satire, see F. J. E. Raby's comprehensive presentation in Vol. II of his *A History of Secular Latin Poetry in the Middle Ages* (Oxford, 1934), pp. 45 – 54, 89 – 102, 190 – 227.

notably pretence or cheating, because what is involved here is the cheating of humanity's deep-seated desire to see its crimes forgiven.[26] We must once again give some thought here to Chaucer's familiar source, Boccaccio. A recent study by Nicholas Havely in the volume edited by our gentle Host shows a striking co-existence in the author of *Il Decameron* of fiercely 'antifraternal' stories with a sincere appreciation of the friars' ideals.[27] If this tangle was possible in the spontaneous Boccaccio, how much more does something like it seem plausible in the shrewd and reflective Chaucer. Strictly speaking, however, we have no evidence.

Another approach that may usefully widen the discussion is the search for a common denominator among the vices described, probably a cross between literary tradition and personal observation, the two concurring in the Seven Deadly Sins, with priority given to avarice, followed by pride and then lechery. There seems little doubt as to the number of servants of Lady Mede under the pen of Langland's courtly Colleague.

The motivation of realism as dutiful truthfulness, which sounds so strikingly modern, is, as we know, by no means absent. The presentation of the Miller's silhouette, of his announcement and the poet's argumentation against exclusive gentility 'give a good deal to think about'. One of the least controvertible conclusions is an immediate dramatic farewell to the direct, sheerly edifying, exclusive appeal to virtue.

We find a different motivation suggested in a recent book by Paul A. Olson of Princeton, *The Canterbury Tales and the Good Society*, a very remarkable, if not always convincing, scholarly achievement. Professor Olson would relate the choice of the obnoxious qualities chosen by the satirist to the danger for the establishment evinced by the outburst of 1381. Chaucer would have been ready, positively, to support the surviving social frame and, negatively, to suppress distruptive rascals of various levels.

Apart from the 'perfect' knight, there are three pilgrims deprived of objectionable features, all of them of modest condition, all of them 'non-revolutionary': the silent, marginal Yeoman, the peasant Ploughman and his brother, the edifying country Parson. In all three cases there is a combination of two things: approval, indeed praise of the 'lower than

[26] My formulation somehow converges with that of Penelope Curtis who says that the Pardoner '. . . tries to make nonsense of any journey of aspiration to any Canterbury'. See her 'The Pardoner's Jape', *Critical Review* II (1968), p. 16.
[27] Nicholas Havely points that out in 'Chaucer, Boccaccio and the Friars', pp. 252, 254 in Piero Boitani, ed., *Chaucer and the Italian Trecento* (Cambridge, 1983) pp. 249 – 68. See also Penn. R. Szittya, 'The Anti-fraternal Tradition in Middle English Literature', *Speculum* 52 (1977) 287 – 313, pp. 287 ff., with his point that ever since Guillaume de St Amour the friars became *symbolical* embodiments of the evils exposed by the secular clergy and by other defenders of the establishment which makes historical enquiry about the former partly immaterial. Arnold Williams also suggests that Chaucer sided in this matter with the powers that be, in 'Chaucer and the Friars', *Speculum* 28 (1953) 499 – 513, p. 513.

genteel' members of the community in the spirit of Christian acceptance of the spiritual dignity of any individual, however inconspicuous — elsewhere, even clear accents of democratic egalitarianism are not missing — and at the same time the humble bread-earners remain humble and will not meddle with the radical preachers of revolt, thus remaining on their level supporters of the 'establishment'.

But it would be a simple-minded interpretation of Chaucer's way of thinking and writing to consider all the portraits that are not rigorously pious only from the angle of the contrast involved. The awareness that this would be an unacceptable narrowness inspired Ruth M. Ames' brisk book, *God's Plenty, Chaucer's Christian Humanism*, published in Chicago in 1984. This is the document of a steady critical effort to appreciate to the full the free artist in the Christian author of the *Canterbury Tales*. It makes for swift and pleasurable reading (no notes!) whilst one feels a good deal of the scholarship and reflection under the 'surface'. Yet, if I may be allowed the remark, there may be just a little too much American optimism in the reconciliation attempted. Something of a mystery and of a dilemma may have remained even (and precisely) in the mind and under the pen of a master of satirical humour. Whatever the differences between the various Tales and the views held by their critics, all are at one in making an abstraction of the Retraction. Yet it is there, immovable, if quite succinct. The Tales are by now equally immovable, Living with a mystery is one more implication of the *Parson's Tale*, if not in quite the same sense.

(b) The problem of 'accepting' and joining the fabliau vein, the second in this selective paper, is different from the problem of satire. Here was a substantial tradition of narratives in the *esprit gaulois* in which the comical point hinged on some kind of sexual transgression. To recognize the frequency of such transgressions was once more a matter of realism, but the basic motivation was not to lay bare a social evil: the motivation was to seek and/or provide fun. The abuse, though one of the most widespread in humanity, would immediately, it was assumed, have most of its sting taken out.

Once such reasoning was accepted as valid, the way was open to another conclusion. If it was legitimate to write a fabliau, the writer-designer became a narrative artist whose duty it was to produce as good a tale of this kind as of any other. Thence, further, the mastery of structure displayed for instance in the *Miller's Tale*, hardly if at all inferior to the preceding *Knight's Tale*, which it parodies otherwise.

This firm reasoning perhaps broke down some time after the text had reached the copyists and left them, already transcribed, and the poet decided that he had gone too far either in the matter of quantity (five tales may be qualified as fabliaux) or quality (the drastic character of some descriptions such as the copulation of May on the pear tree in the *Merchant's Tale* — C IV(E) 2352 – 3, or the equally blunt report of John and Alleyn's demeanour in Symkyn's family bed in the *Reeve's Tale* — I(A) 4230 – 1). This is just one of the various thinkable conjectures as to the motivation of the Retraction, if treated at its face value. For all the equivocality experienced at times by the reader of the *Canterbury Tales*, I would claim for their author a higher probable basic 'unity of thought' than strikes one over some passages of Andreas Capellanus, Jean de Meun, and above all of Juan Ruiz, whose *Libro de Buen Amor* may prove the top monument of ambiguity.

In a way, the coexistence of opposites à propos of the fabliaux in the *Canterbury Tales* is anticipated for the reader by the juxtaposition of two pivotal motifs in *Troilus and Criseyde*. First, contrary to the unimaginative blindness of mere reciters of prohibitions, the poet sings the ecstasy and the splendour of the union of two 'bright young things', eager and beautiful, with their full mutual adoration and commitment. The poet, by now completely mature, seems to choose unhesitatingly the most exquisite touches of his pen to show the glory of the love of man and woman. Has not the Creator Himself made male and female the summits of beauty and supremely attractive to one another, and that through sensual charm as well as through minds and hearts? Then, equally unhesitatingly, he gives full rein to his critical spirit and points to the tragic curtailing of the delirious happiness latent in human matters. As in the story of the Garden of Eden, weakness *will* respond to strong temptation by breakdown and betrayal. Shortsighted believers in accessible bliss refuse to consider this. But it is there; it is as deeply ugly as the delight was previously marvellous and it drives the heretofore enthusiast to suicidal despair. Part of the difficult truth of the matter may still be related to the same Author of Nature who allows the wonders of youth to pass with time to decay and death. But those ready to believe in His message as a merciful Master of Fate, willing to repair the results of the catastrophe (*qui humanae substantiae dignitatem mirabiliter condidisti et mirabilius reformasti*, as Chaucer would find in every missal of the old liturgy) are asked to enter another world, setting at nought the promises of the senses, but providing instead the promise of a lasting fulfilment. In this sense *Troilus and Criseyde* would be compatible with the later lesson by the Parson.

One basic question needs asking: as we come across divergences we strain to find a unifying formula. But must we? If Chaucer has been described as presaging some subsequently noted qualities of the English mentality, why could we not include among such anticipations a distrust of logic?

(c) The third category of texts which may seem to break more perceptibly out of the confines of strict or punctilious orthodoxy are the quasi-sceptical ones. They were probably once regarded as significant for Chaucer's own views. A large section of them adheres to the satirical mode, in the sense that mocking what ought to be, theoretically, a model expresses a scepticism of sorts. Nearer to our interest proper, something in the nature of uncertainty concerning some religious tenets, never final, does occur in a few places. The writer is mildly agnostic in the *Legend of Good Women* for a certain number of lines (F 1 – 9) and then withdraws (F 10 – 16). The narrator in the *Knight's Tale* ignores the fate of Arcitae's soul — I (A) 2809 – 2815; he declares he is 'no divinistre', an understandable avowal from a poet, confirmed in a way by C. S. Lewis in his *Allegory of Love* when he quotes the Dantean distinction that '. . . li teologi questo senso prendono altrimenti che li poeti'. There are above all the bitter doubts about the decrees of providence in the words of Palamon, 'second hand', it is true, in the dramatic scheme — I (A) 1303 – 1325, and a similar challenge by Dorigen, similarly 'slanted' in the *Franklin's Tale* — V (F) 869 – 884. There is also the line in the portrait of the Physician, merely showing the poet's awareness of how other people could feel truly sceptical: 'His Studie was but litel on the Bible' — I (A) 438. In a general way, the author of the *Knight's Tale*, the *Man of Law's Tale*, and the translator of Boethius gave as much space to the questioning of metaphysical assurances as the Bible itself allows in the Book of Job and elsewhere, but the recurrence of the motifs may suggest a preoccupation.[28] The over-all cool assessment, especially against the background of utterances collected by Dr M. E. Thomas some forty years ago in her book on *Medieval Scepticism and Chaucer*[29] would, as I read her, sum up the poet's position as that of a thinking, indeed shrewd educated layman, basically content to accept the requirements of his faith together with his 'non-specialist' status, who also understands the accompanying intellectual difficulties experienced by many in his time but will not voice them aggressively or peremptorily. Could this, apart from philosophy, be also a matter of caution in view of what was probably felt round the court in the atmosphere of the years preceding the 1401 statute *De heretico comburendo*? We must be satisfied to ask the question without knowing the answer.

V

The discrepancy which we finally view here between the rich display of literary portraits of humanity as it actually is and the Parson's sober piece of instruction may be considered in one more way. The portraits and the

---

[28] Cf. *LGW*, 'The Story of Philomela', 2228 – 2243 and *The Complaint of Mars*, 218 – 244.
[29] Dr Thomas ranges both over the opinions doubting Chaucer's orthodoxy (H. Simon, E. C. Maxfield) and those asserting it (Looten, J. S. P. Tatlock). Herself votes for the latter (*op. cit.*, p. 95).

stories, even if they were taken at their best, belong to the world of art, God's granddaughter in St Bonaventure's phrase, whilst the created reality stands for God's daughter, and therefore the medieval sense of hierarchy would always place the latter in a higher position.

European Christianism had not yet gone through the doctrinal development which would one day fully assure the right dignity of lay arts and letters (without either forsaking the conviction of the need of preaching the metaphysical claims and duties, or refusing a legitimate place to man's interests, which the 'moral Chaucer' knew perfectly). Though in point of fact several representatives of those fields (arts and letters) had made their names, in theory there could be stumbles, the best-known case, inspired by intransigence, being that of Savonarola, a hundred years after Chaucer. This is not to say that some kind of theory of what we now call culture did not exist, but it may not have been fully clear or have reached all who had need of it. Whether Chaucer knew the precise formulation of the right kind of intellectual command of a craftsman's material, the *recta ratio factibilium* of Aristotle and Aquinas, is perhaps an open question. I am convinced he was acquainted with the idea in some form, but even if he was, he may not have found all the arguments necessary to defend himself against the charge of the opposite of Savonarola's sermons, the accusation of too much freedom and laxity. He certainly observed, in his special way and in its special place, the postulate of showing the rules of moral conduct, together with its religious warrants. Even a liberal philosopher would consider its presentation by the poet as only fair to all sides. Much more than fairness was assumed in the case of Chaucer; as a minimum the idea of a sound choice of the aim and the best means to attain it: *recta ratio agibilium*, as taught by the same above-mentioned thinkers, but such a minimum would be elevated higher. If there was at times a lack of an unequivocal stand, we should remember that even the universities wavered on certain issues, and so may have a genius who always recognized that writing, not doctrine — however interesting the latter may have been to him — was his primary forte and vocation.

THE AESTHETIC OF CHAUCER'S RELIGIOUS TALES IN RHYME ROYAL

C. DAVID BENSON

Modern readers are often made uneasy by the religious poems in the *Canterbury Tales*. Although there have been excellent studies of individual works, George Keiser accurately notes that the tales of religious pathos are commonly regarded today as 'either a lapse from a truly Chaucerian — that is, an ironic — standard, or . . . as parodic responses to an inferior, popular taste'.[1] Dramatic interpretations of the tellers have taken an especially heavy toll on these poems, allowing critics to dismiss the tales of the Prioress and Man of Law in particular as satiric attacks on their pilgrim narrators. Often the religious tales are simply ignored, as in the *Companion to Chaucer Studies* published by Oxford University Press (an omission rectified in the admirable *Cambridge Chaucer Companion*).[2] Last summer during a National Endowment for the Humanities Institute on the *Canterbury Tales* at the University of Connecticut, a distinguished Chaucerian stated that Chaucer was not an important religious writer and speculated that his works in this mode may have been undertaken only grudgingly at the demand of a powerful patron.

The religious tales are now treated with the disdain that an earlier generation reserved for Chaucer's fabliaux. In 1906 the great scholar Robert K. Root described the tales of the Miller and Reeve as works 'which no sophistry can elevate into true art', and declared that because 'these tales

---

[1] George Keiser, 'The Middle English *Planctus Mariae* and the Rhetoric of Pathos', *The Popular Literature of Medieval England*, ed. Thomas J. Heffernan (Knoxville, 1985), p. 167. See also Derek Pearsall, *The Canterbury Tales* (London, 1985), p. 246: 'The religious tales are generally lacking in the qualities that modern readers expect to find in Chaucer, and their insistent and pervasive doctrinal emphasis makes them uninteresting or even repugnant to many. They are less frequently read than the other tales, and even less frequently enjoyed'.

[2] The *Companion of Chaucer Studies*, ed. Beryl Rowland, rev. ed. (Oxford, 1979) has essays on the romance and fabliaux, but none on the third major Canterbury genre — the religious tales. All three genres are treated in *The Cambridge Chaucer Companion*, ed. Piero Boitani and Jill Mann (Cambridge, 1986). Chaucer's religious tales have been treated most recently by Roger Ellis, *Patterns of Religious Narrative in the Canterbury Tales* (London, 1986), although Ellis finds many of the tales imperfectly realised because of limitations in their tellers.

are by their very nature not true art, I think it unfortunate that Chaucer included them'.[3] Today, it is Chaucer's pious tales that literary ecologists fear may be contaminating the springs of Helicon, as in Robert Burlin's refusal to grant that the *Prioress's Tale*, for all its technical skill, 'satisfies the demands of great art'.[4] Great art, like high seriousness, is more inclusive than sometimes thought. We need to bring the religious tales back into the central Chaucerian canon as the fabliaux have been brought back. Indeed, the fabliaux and religious tales can be seen as the opposite poles of Chaucer's mature art: they mark new departures from his earlier courtly writings and together dominate the *Canterbury Tales*. Chaucer is as much a religious artist as a comic artist, as his earliest readers recognized. Of the three major genres in the *Canterbury Tales* (religious tale, romance, and fabliau), the religious works were the likeliest to be taken out of the collection and anthologized by fifteenth-century scribes (the fabliaux never were), and the tales of the Man of Law and Clerk are the only ones not omitted by one or more of the major manuscripts of the *Canterbury Tales*.[5] To exclude the aesthetic or moral claims of either the fabliaux or the religious tales is to reduce the achievement of the whole.

I shall limit myself here to the religious tales of the Prioress, Second Nun, Man of Law, and Clerk. These four Christian narrative poems define themselves as a coherent group by their use of rhyme royal.[6] Significantly, they are the only Canterbury tales written in this verse form, which, as Charles Muscatine notes, 'is always an implement of seriousness' for the poet.[7] The elegant beauty and flexibility of rhyme royal, the secrets of whose power still await full critical analysis, are crucial to the aesthetic of the religious tales. Chaucer handles rhyme royal with consummate skill in each of the four poems. In contrast to fifteenth-century imitators like Lydgate and Hoccleve, he carefully preserves the integrity of individual stanzas, which are made the unit of narration.[8]

[3] Robert K. Root, *The Poetry of Chaucer* (Boston, 1906), p. 176.

[4] Robert Burlin, *Chaucerian Fiction* (Princeton, 1977), p. 192.

[5] See Ellis, pp. 9 – 10; and E. T. Donaldson, 'The Manuscripts of Chaucer's Works and Their Use', *Geoffrey Chaucer: Writers and Their Background*, ed. Derek Brewer (Athens, Ohio, 1975), p. 95.

[6] For very different treatment of the four religious tales in rhyme royal, see Martin Stevens, 'The Royal Stanza in Early English Literature', *PMLA* 94 (1979) 62 – 76, esp. pp. 67 – 73; and Saul Nathaniel Brody, 'Chaucer's Rhyme Royal Tales and the Secularization of the Saint', *Chaucer Review* 20 (1985) 113 – 31.

[7] Charles Muscatine, *Chaucer and the French Tradition* (Berkeley, 1957), p. 192.

[8] The awkward run-on stanzas in Hoccleve's 'The Monk and Our Lady's Sleeves' and Lydgate's 'The Legend of Dan Joos' — both found in *The Middle English Miracles of the Virgin*, ed. Beverly Boyd (San Marino, Calif., 1964) — also deserve Pearsall's criticism that the handling of the rhyme royal stanza in John Capgrave's *Life of St Katherine* reveals an 'almost total neglect of its inherent structure' ('John Capgrave's *Life of St. Katherine* and Popular Romance Style', *Medievalia et Humanistica* n.s. 5 [1975], p. 124).

Although I am arguing that the religious tales in rhyme royal share a common aesthetic, I would not deny their stylistic variety, which I have analysed in detail elsewhere. Each of the four tales can be seen as an experiment by Chaucer with the potential of a particular kind of religious poetry. Each has its own distinctive way of using such elements as narrative voice, dialogue, and imagery. The affective lyricism of the *Prioress's Tale* differs from the didactic intellectualism of the *Second Nun's Tale*, and the romance adventures of the *Man of Law's Tale* differ from the austere parable of the *Clerk's Tale*. The stylistic variety of the religious tales is strong proof that Chaucer is fully engaged in these works and that he is not working mechanically or under compulsion.

In the discussion that follows, I shall assume that the rhyme royal religious tales are neither parodic nor failures, and I shall concentrate on what they have in common rather than on what distinguishes one from another. Appreciation of their achievement will complicate the standard view of Chaucer and reveal him as deeper than the ironic, detached, relativistic poet our age has created as a reflection of its own values. Although I can only begin to sketch out the aesthetic of the religious tales here, even with the considerable help of previous studies, four elements seem to me central: fidelity, emotion, accessibility, and transcendence.

I

Chaucer's tales of religious faith are appropriately more faithful to their sources than any other kind of narrative the poet ever wrote. He drastically reshapes the romances in the *Canterbury Tales*: Boccaccio's *Teseida* is much reduced, and some of its characterization simplified, to produce the *Knight's Tale*, whereas the *Franklin's Tale* contains themes and episodes not found in any analogue. The fabliaux are similarly made into something quite different by Chaucer, as can be seen in such things as the elaborate character portraits of the *Miller's Tale*, the wide-ranging learning of the *Merchant's Tale*, and the sophisticated dialogue of the *Shipman's Tale*. In the religious tales, by contrast, Chaucer truly achieves what he only claims to practise in works like *Troilus and Criseyde*: 'as myn auctour seyde, so sey I' (II,18).[9]

Although the immediate source for the *Prioress's Tale* has not been discovered, the known analogues suggest Chaucer is following it closely

---

[9] All quotations from Chaucer are taken from *The Riverside Chaucer*, ed. Larry D. Benson et al., 3rd ed. (Boston, 1987). Chaucer's fidelity to his sources indicates neither immaturity nor disengagement, but the sort of respect commonly found in saints' lives; see Alexandra Hennessey Olsen, ' "De Historiis Sanctorum": A Generic Study of Hagiography', *Genre* 13 (1980) 407 – 29.

with only minor, though important additions, such as lowering the little clergeon's age and introducing his friend.[10] The Prologue to the *Second Nun's Tale* promises to reproduce the 'wordes and sentence' of the traditional legend (VIII,78 – 84), and, for at least the first half of the story, it does so slavishly, though critics have often faulted the tale because of this loyalty.[11] More surprising is the fidelity of the *Clerk's Tale*, which is universally regarded, even by those who question its thematic coherence, as one of Chaucer's most ambitious works. Yet until the very end, the tale of patient Griselda is virtually a line-by-line rendering of Petrarch's Latin prose (aided by an anonymous French translation), as the Clerk announces in his Prologue.[12] The tales of the Clerk and Second Nun show that fidelity is no bar to great poetry; to read both along with their Latin sources is to watch a kind of artistic alchemy as Chaucer transforms serviceable prose brick (though Petrarch's is elegant enough) into poetic marble. The *Man of Law's Tale* takes the most liberty with its sources, but it carefully preserves the shape and essential material of the inherited story, and V. A. Kolve stresses that the tale would have been accepted by its original readers as history.[13]

For all their careful fidelity, Chaucer's religious tales are far from mechanical hackwork. Even as the *Second Nun's Tale* closely follows the *Legenda Aurea*, the poet carefully develops imagery of sight, busyness, and fruitfulness suggested by his source, and he gives greater prominence to the

[10] See Carleton Brown in *Sources and Analogues of the Canterbury Tales*, ed. W. F. Bryan and Germaine Dempster (1941; rpt. New York, 1958), pp. 462 – 63. See also Margaret H. Statler, 'The Analogues of Chaucer's *Prioress's Tale*', *PMLA* 65 (1950) 896 – 910.

[11] See G. H. Gerould in *Sources and Analogues*, pp. 664 – 84. In the most recent study, Sherry L. Reames, 'The Sources of Chaucer's "Second Nun's Tale" ', *Modern Philology* 76 (1978) 111 – 35, shows that Chaucer follows the *Legenda Aurea* very closely for the first 250 lines and then either treated his source somewhat more freely or used a source different from any now extant. In the last century Thomas Lounsbury, *Studies in Chaucer*, 3 vols. (New York, 1892), 2, p. 487, dismissed the tale as a feeble translation that 'introduces none of those peculiar touches by which Chaucer usually modified or changed the character of his originals'; a view echoed more recently by E. T. Donaldson's declaration in *Chaucer's Poetry*, 2nd ed. (New York, 1975), that the tale 'does not show the poet at his characteristic Chaucerian best' because 'he exerted no diligence to retell the story subtly' (p. 1108).

[12] See J. Burke Severs, *The Literary Relationships of Chaucer's Clerk's Tale* (1942; rpt. Hamden, Conn., 1972), and his essay in *Sources and Analogues*, pp. 288 – 331.

[13] V. A. Kolve, *Chaucer and the Imagery of Narrative* (Stanford, 1984), pp. 298 – 99. The Man of Law says he learned the story of Constance from a merchant, but the narrator insists on his fidelity to a written record (for instance II,893 – 94, 1094) and usually announces when he is abbreviating his source (for instance, II,232 – 259, 1114 – 17). Although the *Man of Law's Tale* is the most changed of the rhyme royal religious tales, its faithfulness is striking when compared with similar long narratives associated with romance, such as *Troilus and Criseyde* or the *Knight's Tale*.

climactic trial scene between Saint Cecilia and Almachius.[14] Likewise, the *Clerk's Tale* contains small, but significant modifications of its source, such as the narrator's three interventions to blame Walter and more sinister descriptions of the sergeant who takes away Griselda's children. An even subtler change is the surprising pronoun that Griselda uses when she gives the sergeant her baby daughter for what she believes is certain death: 'Have heer agayn youre litel yonge mayde' (IV,567). The unexpected 'youre' fully expresses the absoluteness of Griselda's loss.

The *Man of Law's Tale* shows Chaucer's essential fidelity in these works even when he may seem to be most original. The poet modifies his sources, Nicholas Trivet's Anglo-Norman *Chronicle* and John Gower's *Confessio Amantis*, but his purpose is neither random nor merely literary and humanizing.[15] The story of Constance is trimmed of secondary issues, such as Alla's Scottish wars and other political matters, in order to make it a more purely religious work. Chaucer refines rather than redefines. As the narrator declares at one point, 'Me list nat of the chaf, ne of the stree, / Maken so long a tale as of the corn' (II,701 – 2). Although the additions to the *Man of Law's Tale* have been studied, little attention has been paid to Chaucer's reductions of even highly dramatic scenes in order to remain faithful to the spiritual essence of the story.

At times Trivet and Gower are actually more exciting to read than Chaucer. For example, the slaughter of the Sultan and his followers by his mother is developed into a touching scene of fifteen lines by Gower complete with vivid details describing Constance's dismay amid the flowing blood ('The Dissh forthwith the Coppe and al / Bebled thei weren overal' — II,688 – 703), whereas Chaucer's version is curt and distant: 'The Sowdan and the Cristen everichone / Been al tohewe and stiked at the bord' (II,429 – 30). Similarly, the extensive accounts in Trivet (pp. 38 – 39) and Gower (II,1272 – 1301) of Alla's maddened questioning and execution of his traitorous mother is greatly shortened in the *Man of Law's Tale*, as the narrator indicates: 'Th'effect is this: that Alla, out of drede, / His mooder slow — that may men pleynly rede' (II,893 – 94). Such reductions reveal Chaucer's desire to keep the reader's attention squarely on the religious meaning of the story. Rather than distracting us with garish, but ultimately

---

[14] For studies of the imagery in the *Second Nun's Tale*, see, for example, Russell A. Peck, 'The Ideas of "Entente" and Translation in Chaucer's *Second Nun's Tale*', *Annuale Medievale* 8 (1967) 17 – 37; Carolyn Collette, 'A Closer Look at Seinte Cecile's Special Vision', *Chaucer Review* 10 (1976) 337 – 49; and Trevor Whittock, *A Reading of the Canterbury Tales* (Cambridge, 1968), pp. 251 – 61. For the prominence of the trial scene, see Reames, especially pp. 128 – 29.

[15] Quotations from Trivet are from the edition and facing page translation by Edmund Brock in *Originals and Analogues of Some of the Canterbury Tales*, Chaucer Society 2nd ser., no. 7 (1872; rpt. London, 1887); quotations from Gower from G. C. Macaulay's edition of the *English Works*, 2 vols., EETS ES 81, 82 (1900 – 01; rpt. London, 1957).

secondary episodes, the poet instead develops the providential lessons of Constance's two sea journeys.

The account of the death of Constance's closest friend in Britain, Hermengild, reveals Chaucer's method clearly. A young knight who has been sexually rebuffed by Constance takes his revenge by killing Hermengild and leaving the knife by Constance, who is sleeping next to her. The discovery of the murder by Elda, Hermengild's husband, who has been with the king, is extraordinarily dramatic in Trivet:

> Elda entered the castle, and came in haste to his consort's chamber to tell the news of the king's coming. Constance, who was wakened with the noise, thinking the lady slept, moved her hand to wake her; and when she felt that her body was all wet with blood, in great alarm she cried out, 'My lady is dead!' At which word, Elda and those who were present, greatly amazed at the word, as those who knew naught of the crime, shouting, 'Light! light!' found the throat of Hermingild hideously cut, and her body all covered with blood. And when all exclaimed at the cruelty, asking Constance the truth, this traitor, who had done the crime, . . . leapt about in all directions like a mad man, until he had found the knife where he himself had hidden it; and showing before all the instrument of the crime, with a great cry he accused the maiden of treachery. (pp. 22 – 23)

Chaucer's version is brief and much less colourful:

> Soone after cometh this constable hoom agayn,
> And eek Alla, that kyng was of that lond,
> And saugh his wyf despitously yslayn,
> For which ful ofte he weep and wroong his hond,
> And in the bed the blody knyf he fond
> By Dame Custance. Allas, what myghte she seye?   (II,603 – 08)

As pure narrative, Trivet's version is clearly superior, but Chaucer's fidelity to the deeper meaning of the story makes him downplay this episode in favour of the following scene in which Custance is compared with Christ at the Cruxifiction and is saved by the direct intervention of God (II,617 – 86). The death of Hermengild in Trivet is a wonderful piece of melodrama, but irrelevant to the religious meaning of the story.

II

If Chaucer eliminates melodrama in the *Man of Law's Tale*, that does not mean that the religious tales lack emotion. Although Chaucer, unlike Dante or Langland, does not portray himself on a religious quest nor do we find the thirst for personal salvation that drives later English poets like Donne or Herbert, the tales in rhyme royal are the most emotional group in the

Canterbury collection, an expression of the pathos that was so important to late medieval spirituality.[16] The pious emotion of the religious tales stands in contrast to the amoral cleverness of the fabliaux, nowhere more sharply than when the coolness of the *Shipman's Tale* is immediately followed by the warmth of the *Prioress's Tale*. The pathos of the religious tales has been well analysed by previous critics and need not be discussed here at length, but what may need stressing is the centrality of this quality in Chaucer's work.[17] The modern emphasis on Chaucer's comedy and irony sometimes allows us to overlook the importance of the pathetic for him as early as the *Book of the Duchess* and its dominance in his first masterpiece, *Troilus and Criseyde*.

Insistent narrative voices in the *Man of Law's Tale* and the *Prioress's Tale* directly solicit our sympathy for the sufferings of Constance and the little clergeon, and even the generally austere *Second Nun's Tale* makes us feel that the deep Christian love that unites St Cecilia, her husband, and his brother before they suffer martyrdom. Chaucer does not seem to be working toward a single ideal of affective piety in these tales, as Payne argues, but he instead explores different kinds of pathos. Sympathy is evoked for the royal Constance during her extensive series of adventures as well as for the humble little schoolboy during his one day passion. In contrast to its overt solicitation in the tales of the Prioress and Man of Law, pathos is kept under strong restraint during most of the *Clerk's Tale*, with only a few brief narrative expressions of indignation against Walter, until the powerful release of emotion when Griselda is finally reunited with her children:

> 'O tendre, o deere, o yonge children myne!
> Youre woful mooder wende stedfastly
> That crueel houndes or som foul vermyne
> Hadde eten yow; but God of his mercy
> And youre benyngne fader tendrely
> Hath doon yow kept — and in that same stounde
> Al sodeynly she swapte adoun to grounde.   (IV,1093 – 99)

Some have seen a conflict between the human sympathy added to Chaucer's religious tales and their Christian message, but, in fact, our emotional involvement is not demanded indiscriminately or for its own sake, as in Trivet, but used to teach about the faith.[18] The didactic program

---

[16] See, for example, the second chapter on medieval devotion in Douglas Gray, *Themes and Images in the Medieval English Religious Lyric* (London, 1972).

[17] An important, older example is Robert O. Payne, *The Key of Remembrance* (1963; rpt. Westwood, Conn., 1973), esp. pp. 163 – 170; a recent example is Robert Worth Frank, Jr., 'The *Canterbury Tales* III: Pathos' in *The Cambridge Chaucer Companion*, pp. 143 – 58.

[18] Keiser, 'Middle English *Planctus*', pp. 174 – 77, notes, in contrast to Northrop Frye, the pedagogical purpose of late medieval pathos; see also Thomas H. Bestul, 'The *Man of Law's Tale* and the Rhetorical Foundations of Chaucerian Pathos', *Chaucer Review* 9

of the *Second Nun's Tale* gives more emphasis to St Cecilia's several defences of Christianity, especially her triumphant debate with Almachius, than to her suffering, and even the passionate *Prioress's Tale* contains the child's careful exposition of the mercy of Mary and Christ (VII,649 – 69). Interpretation is demanded by the excruciating emotions raised in the *Clerk's Tale*, as the narrator himself insists at the end, but perhaps the most revealing examples of Chaucer's use of pathos to teach is found in a number of passages in the *Man of Law's Tale* that develop narrative moments in Trivet and Gower.

For example, when Constance must leave her family and friends in Rome to marry the Sultan, the narrator kindles our sympathy for her plight, comparing it with the anguish at the fall of great cities and severely blaming her father's astrological ignorance (especially, II,288 – 315). But Constance's personal unhappiness does not distort her faith. Sorry as she is to be separated from her parents, she notes that her strongest relationship is with 'Crist on-lofte' (II,277), whose own greater suffering and help she invokes ('But Crist, that starf for our redempcioun / So yeve me grace his heestes to fulfille!' — II,282 – 84) and to whom she finally commends those weeping for her: 'Now Jhesu Crist be with yow alle!' (II,318).

The didactic purpose is clearer behind the even more emotional scene during which Constance is exiled from Britain and put into an open boat with her little son (II,806 – 75). Chaucer seems to have taken hints from Gower for Constance's long departure speech on the shore, which has no parallel in Trivet, but he both deepens the emotion of the episode and shapes it to teach a lesson.[19] The injustice of exile is so gross that even the official who must send Constance away cries out: 'Lord Crist . . . how may this world endure / So ful of synne is many a creature' — II,811 – 12). Yet amidst the pathos, Constance's words and actions demonstrate an ideal Christian response to adversity. Her own sorrow is extreme, but entirely for her child, whose eyes, in an exemplary gesture, she carefully covers with her kerchief (II,837 – 38), and pity for whose innocent suffering she arouses in passionate language: 'O litel child, allas! what is thy gilt, / That nevere wroghtest synne as yet, pardee?' (II,855 – 56). Even in misery her faith remains constant. We are told that she 'taketh in good entente / The wyl of Crist' (II,824 – 25), and she begins her speech with 'Lord, ay welcome be thy sonde!' (II,826). Constance then teaches us to trust in God and to put human suffering in perspective. She declares that she continues to trust in Divine Providence despite the apparent hopelessness of her situation (II,827 – 33), and she directly addresses the Virgin Mary, whom she

(1975), p. 220: 'Chaucer pursues to a limit that aspect of medieval poetics which taught that poetry convinces not through logical demonstration, but through the emotions'.
19 Constance's speech in Gower is part of a briefer scene that occurs at sea (II,1051 – 83); compare Trivet, pp. 32 – 33.

obviously resembles, noting that whatever the woes of ordinary mortals they are nothing compared to those of Christ and his mother at the cross (II,841 – 54).[20] The didactic pathos of Chaucer's religious tales challenges the traditional view of Chaucer as a detached, worldly, genial poet, as well as the modern assumption that he is a moral relativist, with no fixed principles or deep beliefs.

III

The solicitation of the reader's emotion in the religious tales is part of their aesthetic of accessibility. By accessibility I mean two things — the open and transparent presentation of these narratives and their appeal to the common experience of a general audience. In contrast to the intricate courtliness in Chaucer's romances and the complex plots and levels of style in his fabliaux, three of the religious tales (the *Man of Law's Tale* is the exception) are skilled experiments in the plain style. The narration of the *Second Nun's Tale* is remarkably spare and ingenuous, and Sumner Ferris praises the 'artful simplicity' of the *Prioress's Tale*, a work that has also been compared to the poetry of Wordsworth.[21] The deliberate plainness of the *Clerk's Tale*, what Ian Robinson has called its 'chastity of style', is set off and confirmed by the stylistic fireworks of the envoy.[22] None of the religious tales has the exuberant physical detail of the fabliaux or concern themselves with a precise realization of physical space. Robert Payne has been the most sympathetic interpreter of this kind of poetry, and Muscatine, who does not much like it, nevertheless describes it well: 'composed with simple characterization, plain diction, spare and humble setting, and reaching for great idealizing power'.[23]

---

[20] Hope Weissman, 'Late Gothic Pathos in *The Man of Law's Tale*,' *Journal of Medieval and Renaissance Studies* 9 (1979) 133 – 53 (esp. pp. 149 – 53), demonstrates the extremes of modern ironic approaches to Chaucer's religious tales. Weissman considers the departure scene a parody, nothing more than an attempt by the Man of Law 'to acquire maximum publicity for his star', (pp. 149 – 50). Accusing Constance of a 'self-conscious performance' by which she ambitiously appropriates the suffering of the Virgin for her own glorification, Weissman fails to note that Constance, who is indeed a type of Mary, fully recognizes how far ordinary mortals like herself are below the Holy Family and thus makes a didactic point about the need for human patience in adversity.

[21] Sumner Ferris, 'The Mariology of *The Prioress's Tale*', *American Benedictine Review* 31 (1981) 232 – 54 (p. 250); Pearsall, *Canterbury Tales*, p. 248, makes the Wordsworth comparison.

[22] Ian Robinson, *Chaucer and the English Tradition* (Cambridge, 1972), p. 159. Robinson finds Wordsworthian echoes in the *Clerk's Tale*.

[23] For Payne, see note 17 above; Charles Muscatine, '*The Canterbury Tales*: Style of the Man and Style of the Work', *Chaucer and Chaucerians*, ed. Derek Brewer (London, 1966), p. 106.

110   *Religion in the Poetry and Drama of the Late Middle Ages*

In a famous essay, Erich Auerbach has explored the pedigree of this religious plain style. Faced with the distressing literary poverty of the New Testament, at least to those trained in classical rhetoric, Augustine in particular extolled a new *sermo humilis*, which would break the traditional link between dignity of style and dignity of subject matter, just as Christ had violated the boundaries between divine and human by humbling himself to become man. The *sermo humilis* was rhetorical, but a rhetoric of plainness, in which 'the highest mysteries of the faith may be set in the simple words of the lowly style which everyone can understand'.[24] Auerbach concludes his essay by quoting the early commentator Benvenuto da Imola on the description in *Inferno* 2,56 of Beatrice's voice as 'soave e piana': 'this is well said, for the divine style is sweet and plain, not lofty and proud as that of Virgil and the poets'.[25]

For all their differences, Chaucer's four religious tales in rhyme royal clearly identify themselves with this humble literary tradition. The Prologue to the *Prioress's Tale* characterizes what is to follow as the song of a child (VII,484 – 87). In her Prologue the Second Nun insists that she will make no attempt to endite her story 'subtilly' (VIII,80), and her later description of Cecilia's preaching as 'open and pleyn' (VIII,284) well describes the tale as a whole. Although the Clerk in his Prologue praises the 'rethorike sweete' (IV,32) of Petrarch, he responds to the Host's demand that he speak 'pleyn at this tyme' (IV,19) by declining to reproduce the 'heigh stile' (IV,41) of the laureate's proem. Even the Man of Law, whose tale is not plain, declares in his Prologue that he spurns the Muses and that he will 'speke in prose' (II,91 – 96).

The plain style in the tales of the Prioress, Second Nun, and Clerk is not threadbare or monotonous. Each poem is an individual working out of the different possibilities within this tradition. The *Prioress's Tale* is a carefully crafted exercise in affective piety, whose 'deceptively easy and simple' verse, as G. H. Russell has shown, is also 'conceptually and emotionally rich and dense'.[26] In contrast, the more austere and intellectual *Second*

---

[24] Erich Auerbach, *'Sermo Humilis'*, *Literary Language and Its Public in Late Latin Antiquity and in the Middle Ages*, trans. Ralph Manheim, Bollingen Series 74 (New York, 1965), p. 37.

[25] Auerbach, p. 66.

[26] G. H. Russell, 'Chaucer: The Prioress's Tale', *Medieval Literature and Civilization: Studies in Memory of G. N. Garmonsway*, ed. D. A. Pearsall and R. A. Waldron (London, 1969), p. 226; see also Payne, p. 169. The ability of the *Prioress's Tale* to employ great poetic skill in the service of a piety accessible to general lay readers is clearest when we compare the tale with the contemporary Middle English miracles of the Virgin collected by Beverly Boyd (see note 8 above). The simplicity of early fourteenth-century poems such as 'The Clerk Who Would See Our Lady' or 'How Chartres Was Saved' constantly degenerates into prosy doggerel. In contrast, Lydgate's fifteenth-century 'The Legend of Dan Joos', heavily influenced by Chaucer, chokes on its aureate diction and rhetorical

Nun's Tale develops the imagery and didactic speeches of its source. Undoubtedly, the most challenging of the three is the *Clerk's Tale*, whose chaste and restrained style is capable, like the Bible itself, of raising the most profound and troubling questions. One example of what can be accomplished within this aesthetic is the speech from the *Clerk's Tale* by an unnamed respresentative of the people, who calls on Walter to marry and produce an heir. Addresses to medieval rulers were supposed to be in the high style, as the Host reminds the Clerk (IV,18), and David Burnley has recently discussed a contemporary example of this, an elaborate letter from the citizens of London to Henry V.[27] The speech to Walter begins with some rhetorical flattery, but its dominant tone is elegant simplicity. The haunting warning about death introduces a major theme in the tale, yet it achieves a spiritual resonance without ever sacrificing concrete imagery or the sound of a speaking voice:

> And thenketh, lord, among youre thoghtes wyse
> How that oure dayes passe in sondry wyse,
> For thogh we slepe, or wake, or rome, or ryde,
> Ay fleeth the tyme; it nyl no man abyde.
>
> And thogh youre grene youthe floure as yit,
> In crepeth age alwey, as stille as stoon,
> And deeth manaceth every age, and smyt
> In ech estaat, for ther escapeth noon;
> And al so certein as we knowe echoon
> That we shul deye, as uncerteyn we alle
> Been of that day whan deeth shal on us falle.   (IV,116 – 26)

The *Man of Law's Tale* is the obvious exception to the plainness of Chaucer's religious tales. Although we are told the tale will be in prose and the narrative itself is generally simple and direct, Chaucer has supplemented his sources with several passages of moralistic and emotional rhetoric containing wide-ranging allusions that demonstrate, in Kolve's words, 'what poetry can do at its fullest dignity, in the service not of fable but of Christian truth'.[28] As Kolve suggests, this kind of rhetorical decoration has a broad didactic appeal. Although often dismissed as obvious and unsophisticated by modern readers, such additions as the five-stanza explanations of God's protection of Constance on land and sea (II,470 – 504) or the one-stanza demonstration of the wages of lust (II,925 – 31) are careful expositions of standard Christian doctrine that would be accessible to a general audience. Moreover, as if to appeal to a taste for popular secular

display. Chaucer keeps the simplicity of the earlier miracles, while adding a poetic elegance and narrative intensity unequalled in Middle English religious poetry.
[27] David Burnley, *A Guide to Chaucer's Language* (Norman, Oklahoma, 1983), pp. 186 – 88.
[28] Kolve, p. 299.

romance in that audience, Chaucer somewhat underplays the piety of the tale at the beginning. The narrator gives early emphasis to the enterprising 'chapmen' from Syria and their inquisitive Sultan, whose passion for Constance is described in courtly terms (II,204 – 10). Constance herself is less of an active Christian evangelist in Chaucer than in Trivet or Gower and is initially celebrated as much for her high birth as for her holiness: 'O my Custance, ful of benignytee,/ O Emperoures yonge doghter deere' (II,446 – 47).

The pattern of learned allusions that Chaucer has added to the *Man of Law's Tale* further suggests a deliberate movement from secular to Christian romance. The first such passage refers to the deaths of seven classical (and one Biblical) figures (II,197 – 203), and the second to the fall of Troy, Thebes, and pagan Rome (II,288 – 94; see also II,400 – 01). After these opening references to pagan heroes and events, however, all other passages of allusions in the tale are Biblical or Christian (II,470 – 504, 639 – 44, 932 – 45). But if these additions increase the dignity of the tale, they do not limit its accessibility. The allusions appear in groups, often with brief explanation, and their didactic significance is clear. Their careful and straightforward presentation has none of the elusiveness and sophistication of the learning in other Chaucerian works like the *Merchant's Tale* or the *Wife of Bath's Tale*. The classical figures in these passages include Pompey, Julius Caesar, Hercules, Turnus, and Socrates, whereas Daniel, Jonah, David, Judith, and Saint Anne are among the Biblical ones (along with the popular Christian legend of Egyptian Mary). These are quite conventional references, so generally known even today that an American college graduate might be able to identify some.[29]

Chaucer is the most ostentatiously bookish of Middle English poets, but a striking quality in all the religious tales is the restraint and accessibility of their learned references. In the *Man of Law's Tale* there are several such references, though they are not exotic; in the other religious tales they are much less frequent than elsewhere in the *Canterbury Tales*. We may not be surprised that the few allusions in the childlike *Prioress's Tale* are to popular religious figures like Saint Nicholas (VII,514), Herod (VII,574), and Rachel (VII,627), but more revealing is the almost complete absence of learning in the *Clerk's Tale*. Despite the evocation of Petrarch in the Prologue and the academic teller, the only explicit mention of another literary work in the course of the narrative is a single, significant citation of Job (IV,932).

---

[29] Another rhetoric addition, the astrological passage early in the tale (II,295 – 308), seems obscure to us today, but it has elements that in Chaucer's day would have been 'accessible to one moderately versed in the subject', as argued by J. C. Eade, ' "We ben to lewed or to slowe': Chaucer's Astronomy and Audience Participation', *Studies in the Age of Chaucer* 4 (1982) 53 – 85, p. 82.

Like the frescos of Giotto, the religious tales do not limit themselves to an educated elite or courtly coterie — they address common people and use the experiences of everyday life. Domesticity, for instance, is central to their aesthetic. The marriages they describe can not simply be turned into allegories of Christ and his Church, for they suggest some of the strains and joys of real relationships. Even the ascetic St Cecilia[30] gets married, which is unusual for a female saint, and makes first her husband and then his brother her 'allies'. Pearsall notes that the anguish of the child's mother in the *Prioress's Tale* speaks directly to all parents: 'Chaucer has caught both the homeliness of the experience and the grandeur of the mother's emotion in language of the greatest simplicity'.[31] The Virgin Mary, simultaneously wife, mother, and maiden, who is the special protector of ordinary sinners, is constantly evoked in these tales. Heiko Obermann has recently suggested that study of religious thought in the fourteenth century can no longer be described only in terms of philosophy and academic theology: 'Lay thought and lay piety now begin to occupy the center of the stage'.[32] Chaucer's religious tales are built on the experiences, fears, and hopes of ordinary secular life — relations between children and parents, fear of death and the unknown, hopes of marriage. These feelings ought to be as accessible to modern, post-Romantic readers as they were to a general audience in the Middle Ages.

IV

If Chaucer's religious tales draw on the experiences of everyday life, they nevertheless present a pessimistic view of this world that sees hope only in a transcendent faith. Here again Chaucer differs from other great medieval religious poets, such as Dante, who never ignores the activities of current Italian society, or Langland, who carefully examines how daily life is lived, and how it should be lived, in Malvern, London, and Westminster. In contrast, Chaucer's religious tales do not address the contemporary English world at all, but are set instead in a distant time or place where Christian values are under threat from the established power. In addition to direct persecutions by Romans, Jews, or Moslems, there are the crueller tortures of Walter in the *Clerk's Tale*. Even in the Christian world of the *Man of Law's Tale*, earthly joy lasts but a little while (II,1132 – 33). Chaucer's vision in these tales is less that of Dante than that of Innocent III, whose *De Contemptu Mundi* he had apparently once translated and knew well.

---

[30] Ellis, p. 92, notes the many traditional religious symbols in Cecilia's life.
[31] Pearsall, *Canterbury Tales*, p. 248.
[32] Heiko A. Oberman, 'Fourteenth-Century Religious Thought: A Premature Profile', *Speculum* 53 (1978), p. 93.

Deeply pessimistic about this world, the religious tales instead look to (though, unlike the *Divine Comedy* or *Pearl*, they are never set in) a divine realm that transcends the temporal, as expressed most clearly in the *Second Nun's Tale*: 'ther is bettre lif in oother place, / That nevere shal be lost' (VII,323 – 24). Indeed, the impossibility of true satisfaction in this life and the delusions of materialism are constant themes throughout Chaucer's work, in poems as diverse as *Troilus and Criseyde* and the tales of the Knight, the Pardoner, and the Wife of Bath. Such Christian pessimism might be seen as the other side of Chaucer's comedy, for in their different ways both the religious tales and the fabliaux suggest the foolishness of the secular world.

In the *Second Nun's Tale*, worldly power does nothing except oppress and kill the good, whereas the *Clerk's Tale* shows the vanity of both wealth and birth, as well as of popular opinion, whose fickleness turns against Griselda despite her benevolent governance (IV,981 – 1001). Mothers cannot even be trusted not to murder their sons in the *Man of Law's Tale*, which frequently stresses human inadequacy: 'mennes wittes ben so dulle' (II,202; see also 315 and 481 – 83). There is little scope for effective human action in either the *Man of Law's Tale* or the *Prioress's Tale*. The most significant events in both are accomplished by supernatural forces, whether it be Satan inspiring murders by the Sultaness (II,365 – 71), a knight (II,582, 598), and the Jews (VII,558 – 64) or God protecting Constance on land and sea and, with Mary, rescuing the little clergeon after his death.

As these last examples of divine mercy show, Chaucer's religious tales are pessimistic only about earthly life, not about Christian faith. In an important study of the *Man of Law's Tale*, Morton Bloomfield notes that in the *contemptus mundi* tradition the 'tragedy of the world is the comedy of God', because the tears we shed here will be washed away when 'we shall enter into our final home' and 'laugh from a divine perspective'.[33] All of the religious tales end happily from a Christian point of view with the main characters close to God. If earthly power, like Walter's sergeant, is suspect, salvation is accessible to any who are open to it. Moslems and pagan Britains are converted to Christianity in the *Man of Law's Tale*, and ancient Romans take instruction in the faith in the *Second Nun's Tale*. Even Walter changes. Lack of intelligence is no barrier, for a small boy, despite his ignorance of exactly what his song to Mary says, wins grace in the *Prioress's Tale*. Although the central characters often find themselves alone and vulnerable to secular power, they are not isolated from God. Satan operates in this world, but he is finally no match for Mary and Christ.[34]

---

[33] Morton W. Bloomfield, 'The Man of Law's Tale: A Tragedy of Victimization and a Christian Comedy', *PMLA* 87 (1972), p. 388.

[34] The isolation of the religious heroines has been noted by Frank, p. 151, and by Keiser, p. 184.

Chaucer's celebrations of transcendent faith in the religious tales are not as politically conservative and reassuring to the established power as some critics believe. The female heroines who dominate these works create what might be called a Christian feminism, in which Chaucer uses the historical marginality of women (and a child) to criticize the operation of the secular world, which is run entirely by men.[35] I call what Chaucer is doing here *Christian* feminism advisedly, for the special favour of the weak (including women) in God's eyes has always been an important Christian theme. Recent critics, however, especially those whose primary interest is in political power, fail to appreciate the validity in these tales of spiritual power. David Aers, for instance, begins his discussion of the *Second Nun's Tale* thus: 'Saint Cecilie is an upper-class lady whose sole vocation is "to kepe hir maydenhede" '.[36] The judgment is unpleasantly reductive (note also the sarcastic use of 'lady') and exposes the dangers of a materialistic criticism that thinks only in terms of social hierarchies ('upper-class') and the physical ('maydenhede'). In fact, Cecilia quickly gives up the privileges and protection of her high rank, referring to it only as a joke to disconcert Almachius at the beginning of his inquisition (VIII,425), just as she quickly passes beyond defense of her virginity to an evangelical fruitfulness. In contrast to the deaths of so many other Roman and Christian famous women, Cecilia's martyrdom has nothing to do with preserving her maidenhead. Her concern is elsewhere: after reversing the traditional male sway in marriage that would treat her as a commodity, she defeats the full political might of the Roman state, showing it to be no more than a 'bladdre ful of wynd' (VIII,439). Along with Almachius, critics such as Aers are unable to recognize Cecilia's spiritual power, which, with only faith and words for weapons, redefines woman's place in both private and public life.

David Burnley offers a medieval explanation for why Chaucer's saints and martyrs are invariably women and children. Because both were

---

[35] As the adjective Christian in Christian feminism suggests, my argument differs from many modern approaches to these questions. For example, I would only partially accept the view of Marxist critics like Sheila Delany, 'Womanliness in the *Man of Law's Tale*', *Chaucer Review* 9 (1974) 63 – 72, and Stephen Knight, *Geoffrey Chaucer* (Oxford, 1986), pp. 95 – 97, 108 – 12, that the *Man of Law's Tale* and the *Clerk's Tale* are essentially conservative works meant to comfort Chaucer's traditional establishment audience. If Chaucer is conservative, he is neither smug nor easily reassuring, but like the conservative Dr Johnson who could toast the next slave revolt in Jamaica. I would agree with another Marxist critic, David Aers, *Chaucer* (Brighton, 1986), esp. pp. 34 – 36, 59 – 61, that Chaucer's religious tales often undermine the political authority of the late medieval world, but disagree that this makes Chaucer a stoic or proto-bourgeois individualist. Chaucer's radically pessimistic religious vision looks for no amelioration in this world from any secular ideology. For an argument that the *Man of Law's Tale* questions worldly authority, see Eugene Clasby, 'Chaucer's Constance: Womanly Virtue and the Heroic Life', *Chaucer Review* 13 (1979) 221 – 31.

[36] Aers, p. 52.

considered 'irrational creatures', lacking 'prudence, resolution, [and] emotional stability', they make especially dramatic religious ideals: 'What better way to demonstrate the power of the Holy Spirit in a human vessel than by picturing it in the weakest possible vessel, suspending the alleged laws of nature'.[37] I would suggest that Chaucer is even more radical. His holy women do not just equal men, they surpass them. They reveal the limits of reason and prudence, which are practical virtues that Almachius would claim and which are futilely practised by those parodies of male aggression, Constance's two mothers-in-law. Against such worldly virtues, Chaucer's holy women and child offer faith. Class, age, and patriarchy all lack privilege in Chaucer's religious tales where the first shall be last and the last first.

Christian feminism so dominates Chaucer's religious tales that men are viewed with approval only when they begin to act like women — the message, of course, of the long prose *Melibee*. The most obvious instances of men following the example of a woman are in the *Second Nun's Tale*, whose saintly heroine teaches the truth of Christianity to her husband, his brother, the Roman troops sent to arrest her, and the community as a whole. Those men, including Valerian, Tiburce, and Maximus, who imitate Cecilia become 'Cristes owene knyghtes leeve and deere' (VIII,383); those who do not, especially Almachius, are lost. A similar celebration of men who act like women occurs in the *Man of Law's Tale*. When Alla is told that Constance has born him a monster, his surprisingly patient response, which has no source in either Trivet or Gower, anticipates Constance's own words when she is sent into exile from Britain (II,826):

> 'Welcome the sonde of Crist for everemoore
> To me that am now lerned in his loore!
> Lord, welcome be thy lust and thy plesaunce;
> My lust I putte al in thyn ordinaunce'.   (II,760 – 63)

These hardly sound like the words of a fierce military commander; Alla has begun to learn the lessons of Constance.

At the end of the *Prioress's Tale* men are also shown acting like women (specifically like the child's mother), as the abbot leads his monks in lying on the ground and weeping over the little corpse while praising the mother of God (VII,673 – 78). Perhaps the most remarkably male conversion occurs in the *Clerk's Tale*. Walter is such an extreme example of male oppression that his final reunion with Griselda has seemed unconvincing, if not repellent, to many. Although I do not wish to simplify the *Clerk's Tale*, the most convincing reading of this demanding work argues that Griselda's obedience suggests the obedience, even unto humiliation and death, of

---

[37] J. David Burnley, *Chaucer's Language and the Philosophers' Tradition* (Cambridge, 1979), p. 85.

The Aesthetic of Chaucer's Religious Tales in Rhyme Royal

Christ.[38] Griselda is Jesus as wife and mother. Instead of revolting against
Walter, as many modern critics desperately want her to, Griselda does
something even more astonishing when Walter mocks and reviles her, she
loves him. Her patience is God's with humankind and thus Walter's final
willingness to accept her love is a model for us all.

A more politically subversive expression of Christian feminism occurs
late in the *Man of Law's Tale*. Chaucer introduces a scene in which
Constance, who has been cruelly set adrift for years in a rudderless boat, is
met by the Roman fleet sent by her father the emperor, which is returning
from destroying the Sultaness and her followers (II, 967 – 73). This brief
encounter between a warship and a ship of suffering is generally
overlooked, but Chaucer seems to be setting up an opposition between two
different kinds of power and two different kinds of Christianity, what we
might call the conflict between Constance and Constantine. The victorious
Roman fleet, which is described as 'saillynge ful roially', represents a
militant, imperial Christianity that uses the full violence of the masculine
State to impose his will. In contrast, the little boat in which Constance sits
'ful pitously', whose symbolic importance Kolve has recently explored,
represents a faith that rejects force and instead trusts completely in God's
will. The clear suggestion of this meeting at sea is that even a nominally
Christian state falls short of the transcendent faith celebrated in Chaucer's
religious tales.

The aesthetic of Chaucer's religious tales depends on literary qualities not
always prized today; fidelity, emotion, and accessibility, which together
produce a transcendent pessimism about this world. Although these works
are different from the dominant conception of Chaucerian poetry, we need
to recognize their contribution to the total achievement of the *Canterbury
Tales*. The religious tales are not ironic, parodic, or bad; instead they show
Chaucer working in a genre of great potential beauty that is capable of
addressing a wide general audience while questioning established earthly
power in the name of a secure faith. Constance's boat is a modest but
powerful craft.

---

[38] See, for example, Edward I. Condron, 'The *Clerk's Tale* of Man Tempting God', *Criticism*
26 (1984) 99 – 114.

THE PARDONER'S TALE: AN EARLY MORAL PLAY?

†PAULA NEUSS

The purpose of this paper is to discuss and illustrate how Chaucer's *Pardoner's Tale* anticipates, and/or possibly draws on, the techniques and devices of the English moral plays. I say *perhaps* draws on, because the earliest known complete English moral play, *The Castle of Perseverance*, is usually dated about 1425, and even the fragment *The Pride of Life*, though earlier, is normally dated about 1405, five years after Chaucer's death. However, tantalising references to a York Paternoster play, in a tract by John Wyclif as well as in the early York records themselves, suggest that there were plays resembling moral plays, which dramatised the activities of the Seven Deadly Sins at least by the late fourteenth century.

> Confirmation for this assumption comes from records of the nearby Yorkshire town of Beverly where, on 1 August 1469, were performed 'the different pageants of Pater Noster'. Eight pageants were listed, together with the guilds responsible for them. The first of these was 'the pageant of viciose'; the remaining seven were 'superbie . . . luxurie . . . accidie . . . gule . . . invidie . . . ire'. In a summary of players ('lusores') the seven deadly sins are once again given, followed by 'vicious'.[1]

This is important as showing the existence of the vice ('vicious'), a central figure especially of later moral plays, in pageants which focussed on particular deadly sins in turn. The earlier moral plays do seem to centre on the examination of one vice in particular: *The Castle of Perseverance* on avarice, *Mankind* on sloth, and *The Pride of Life* on pride. Thus it is very central to my argument that the theme of *The Pardoner's Tale* is Covetousness stated by him explicitly in the Latin form

> *Radix malorum est Cupiditas* (334)[2]

and that the figure who represents Covetousness (i.e. the vice) is the Pardoner himself:

---

[1] Robert Potter, *The English Morality Play* (London, 1975), p. 23.
[2] All quotations from Chaucer are from *The Riverside Chaucer*, 3rd edn., gen. ed. L. D. Benson (Boston, 1987).

> I preche of no thyng but for *coveityse*.
> Therfore my theme is yet, and evere was,
> *Radix malorum est Cupiditas*.   (424 – 6, my italics)

and

> For though myself be a ful *vicious* man,
> A moral tale yet I yow telle kan,
> Which I am wont to preche for to wynne.   (459 – 61, my italics)

In both these quotations from his prologue the Pardoner identifies himself with the vice of Covetousness; in the second example actually calling himself 'vicious', the exact word used of the dramatic figure in the pageants at Beverley.

Now, it has long been suggested that the *Pardoner's Tale* has affinities with the morality play genre, perhaps most recently and clearly by Helen Cooper in her book on *The Structure of the Canterbury Tales*:

> . . . both stories [she is also discussing *The Physicians Tale*] have not only an examplary but something approaching an allegorical quality.
>   None of the characters is a moral personification [I disagree with her about the Pardoner here]; but the handling of both stories has similarities with the allegorical mode of the morality play. The Physician's Tale was indeed turned into one in the later sixteenth century, as *Apius and Virginia*, 'wherein is lively expressed a rare example of the vertue of Chastity' . . .
>   The Pardoner's Tale, by contrast, gains much of its morality-like quality from its lack of proper names.[3]

I do not agree with all Helen Cooper's reasons for drawing a parallel between these tales and the moral plays: the Pardoner to me is clearly a personification of Covetousness (though of course that is not *all* that he is, only one facet of his personality). Similarly the lack of proper names does not necessarily make a work into a 'morality', or rather, conversely, there are many moral plays, especially later ones, where the characters *have* proper names but are still treated allegorically and concerned with the discussion of virtue and vice, as a moral play must be, (such as *Fulgens and Lucrece*, which disputes at length about the virtues of gentleness and nobility and their opposite, churlishness). However it is interesting that even though Helen Cooper uses slightly different criteria it is clear to her as well as to me that *The Pardoner's Tale* is in the moral play mode.[4]

---

[3] Helen Cooper, *The Structure of the Canterbury Tales* (London, 1983), pp. 156 – 7.
[4] A critic of the early drama has to make many difficult decisions about terminology: the choice between 'morality play' and 'moral play' is a case in point. Helen Cooper prefers the term invented by nineteenth-century critics by analogy with the French 'moralite'. This is convenient because it has been in general use for a long time, but the contemporary (late

I would wish to go considerably further than she does, however, and suggest that *The Pardoner's Tale* is in effect an early moral play. I am not just talking about the dramatic qualities of Chaucer's writing though of course these are extremely important. The point is twofold, partly that all *The Canterbury Tales* are a kind of 'play' or game, but also that within this game *The Pardoner's Tale* is a play or game of a particular kind, i.e. a play on a moral, which I have already mentioned he has stated as '*Radix malorum est Cupiditas*'.

There are numerous references throughout *The Canterbury Tales* to the idea of the whole work as a 'play' or game. We may pick out two for convenience. The Host tells the pilgrims as they set out on their journey:

> And wel I woot, as ye goon by the weye,
> Ye shapen yow to talen and to *pleye*;   (A,771 – 2, my italics)

Then, when the pilgrims are some way along on their journey, the Host chides the Clerk for being too serious, and invites him, since he is part of the 'play' or 'game' to tell a 'myrie tale'

> For Goddes sake, as beth of bettre cheere!
> It is no tyme for to studien heere.
> Telle us som myrie tale, by youre fey!
> For what man that is entred in a *pley*
> He nedes moot unto the *pley* assente.   (E, 7 – 11, my italics)

It will of course be objected that these uses of 'pley' or game in Chaucer refer only to light-hearted entertainment in general and not to the kind of dramatic activity that we usually understand by the word 'play' now. There are two points to be made here. Firstly these terms of 'pley' and 'game' were exactly the same ones that were used of contemporary drama, as V. A. Kolve makes clear in his excellent study of the mystery plays *The Play called Corpus Christi*. He deals especially in his second chapter, 'The Drama as Play and Game' with the various terms for dramatic representations in the early period, and points out how the Latin word '*ludus*' proves by its 'very ambiguity':

> an entrance into the medieval idea of theater, for it is this word *ludus*, in its English equivalents 'play' and 'game', that becomes the ubiquitous generic term for the vernacular drama.[5]

And he adds in a note that:

medieval) term was 'moral', and I prefer this term because it gives a clearer idea of the plays' form and mode.
[5] V. A. Kolve, *The Play Called Corpus Christi* (Stanford, 1966), p. 12.

Similarly, the vernacular drama in France called itself *jeu*, and in Germany *spiel*.[6]

Kolve has discovered many examples which restore the original force of the 'game' element in the word 'pley'. His work is so valuable, but there is time to quote just a couple of pertinent examples. Firstly from the Chester Banns:

> you bakers, see that the same words you utter,
> as Christ hym selfe spake them, to be A memoriall
> of that death and passion which in *play* ensue after shall.[7]

And then from the Proclamation to the *Ludus Coventriae*:

> In the xxiij[ti] pagent palme Sunday
> In *pley* we purpose ffor to shewe.[8]

The Corpus Christi pageants then, were called 'pleys' or 'games' in exactly the same way that *The Canterbury Tales* was. Kolve does not discuss the moral plays in this book, but they were sometimes termed 'plays' too, though 'interlude' is a more common term for a later moral play. The printer's introduction to *Everyman* tells us:

> Here begynneth a treatyse how the hye Fader
> of heuen sendeth Dethe to somon euery
> creature to come and gyue a-counte
> of theyr lyues in this worlde/ *and*
> *is in maner of a morall playe.*[9]

I shall have more to say about this introduction in a moment.

Meanwhile there is a second point I would like to make about *The Canterbury Tales* and the idea of 'pley'.

I would argue that the response of Chaucer's audience to the way he presented his work is very close to that of the audience of an early play. We note the meaning of the word 'audience' — those who listen — and bear in mind the famous picture of Chaucer reading his poetry aloud to a courtly audience from the manuscript in Corpus Christi College Cambridge (MS 61, fol 16).

Of this miniature, Kolve, whose recent work on Chaucer is of great relevance to my study of *The Pardoner's Tale*, writes:

> . . . we cannot speak of readers only. The well-known miniature . . . that shows Chaucer reciting to a courtly company in the grounds of a castle reminds us that he had another audience simultaneously in mind. Here we see

---

[6] *Ibid.*
[7] *Ibid.* p. 13, my italics.
[8] *Ibid.* p. 14, my italics.
[9] *Everyman*, ed. A. C. Cawley (Manchester, 1961), p. 1, my italics.

him concerned not with the transmission of his work to a predicted posterity, but with its publication to his own contemporaries: the poem as process, as literary event, in a social setting.[10]

Kolve had earlier discussed the process by which a medieval reader could be shown in the act of reading and simultaneously seeing the described events in his mind's eye, and he quotes from a translation of Richard de Fournivall's fourteenth-century *Li Bestiairs d'amours*:

> When one hears a tale read, one perceives the wondrous deeds as if one were to see them taking place.[11]

Thus the 'pleys' in *The Canterbury Tales* are 'perceived' in the minds of the audience in a manner which is not far away, especially in a tale as rich in dialogue and description of setting as *The Pardoner's Tale* is, from the perceptions of an audience at a fully realised dramatic event, what the anonymous author of *A Tretise of Miraclis Pleyinge* would have called a 'quick' book:

> sithen it is leveful to han the miraclis of God peintid, why is not as wel leveful to han the miraclis of God *pleyed*, sithen men mowen bettere reden the wille of God and his mervelous werkis in the *pleyinge* of hem than in the peintinge? And betere they ben holden in mennus mind and oftere rehersid by the *pleyinge* of hem than by the peintinge, for this is a deed bok, the tother a quick.[12]

In my view, *The Canterbury Tales* is presented as such a 'quick bok', more dramatically than is often assumed.

The Pardoner's Tale, then, can reasonably be termed a 'pley', and would have been understood as such by its listening audience.

I now want to consider the aspects of the tale which relate it specifically to the *moral* play. These seem to fall into two categories: its overall structure, and its use of individual devices and images which are common in other moral plays. For what I have to say about the shape and structure of the moral play I am drawing on work of my own, both published and unpublished, and because of the shortness of time I have to ask you to take my word on one or two points which are argued and explained more fully elsewhere. Much more work has been done by other critics on images and

[10] V. A. Kolve, *Chaucer and the Imagery of Narrative* (London, 1984), p. 12.
[11] *Ibid.*, p. 10.
[12] Clifford Davidson, ed. *A Middle English Treatise on the Playing of Miracles* (Washington, 1981), p. 40.

124   *Religion in the Poetry and Drama of the Late Middle Ages*

devices in the plays, especially by Glynne Wickham in *Early English Stages Vol. III: Plays and their Makers to 1576.*

Firstly then, the structure of *The Pardoner's Tale* in relation to that of the moral play. There seem to be two points to be made here; one relatively simple, the other more complicated.

It has long been assumed, after the pioneering work of Owst in *Literature and Pulpit in Medieval England*, that moral plays 'developed' from sermons, beginning by being small *exempla* used by the preacher to reinforce his point, like one who

> suddenly displayed the skull of a dead man which he had been carrying under his cloak[13]

thereby reminding the audience of the nearness of Death. They made abstract words concrete by using visual images, and sometimes these images were translated into actions.

In my article 'Active and Idle Language: Dramatic Images in *Mankind*'[14] I showed how the theme implicit in Mercy's opening sermon against idleness, which could be summed up in the proverb 'The Devil finds work for the idle', was made concrete in the actions of the play between Mankind and the vices Newguise, Nowadays and Nought, with the later intervention of Mischief and Titivillus. The words of the sermon were elaborated on in the play and reinforced in a manner that would bring them home to the audience, and indeed would make the audience see that they themselves were (and are) Mankind.

Now we can see the same structure operating in *The Pardoner's Tale*, and this, as I say, is my relatively simple first point. Like the play *Mankind*, the tale begins with a sermon — the Pardoner is at pains to tell his audience how he preaches in church, and what his theme always is:

> 'Lordynges', quod he, 'in chirches whan I preche,
> I peyne me to han an hauteyn speche,
> And rynge it out as round as gooth a belle,
> For I kan al by rote that I telle.
> My theme is alwey oon, and evere was —
> *Radix malorum est Cupiditas.*   (C,329 – 334)

The audience are in fact in a tavern rather than in church, and I shall return to this when discussing moral play images and devices. The Pardoner chooses to 'forget' this and sets himself up to give a sermon on his favourite theme, of which the main exemplum is a powerful dramatic tale. Just as the antics of Mankind and the vices illustrate the theme of idleness in *Mankind*, so the behaviour of the rioters in search of Death illustrates the theme of

[13] G. R. Owst, *Preaching in Medieval England* (Cambridge, 1926), p. 351.
[14] *Stratford-upon-Avon Studies*, XVI (London, 1973) 40 – 67.

Covetousness. But it does this in a much less immediately obvious way than the action of *Mankind*, and this is where I come on to my second, much more difficult, point. *Mankind* is a relatively simple play — it makes a point and sticks to it. The Pardoner, on the other hand, has a clear idea of the very complex implications of a 'moral' work, which is, as I shall show, one with more than one level of meaning. He responds absolutely to the 'gentils' insistence that he should tell 'som moral thyng', and says:

> Youre likyng is that I shall telle a tale.
> Now have I dronke a draughte of corny ale,
> By God, I hope I shal yow telle a thyng
> That shal by reson been at youre likyng.
> For though myself be a ful *vicious* man
> A *moral* tale yet I yow telle kan,
> Which I am wont to preche for to wynne.   (C,455 – 461, my italics)

I have already mentioned the significance of identifying the Pardoner as 'vicious': I would now like to spend some time examining the meaning of the term 'moral', as it is clear to me that it is used in a technical sense, here, and that this has implications for *The Pardoner's Tale* as a whole.

Although I have been deliberately speaking of 'moral plays', the term 'moral' is actually in much wider general use in medieval writing and in fact in the early period only one play, *Everyman*, is actually labelled a moral play.

Some later plays, however, were called 'moralls', and lists of dramatic works mention the term, as Alan Dessen has shown:

> In the Induction to Marston's *What you Will* (1601) Doricus asks if the play is '*Commedy, Tragedy, Pastorall, Morall, Nocturnal* or *Historie*?'. The second edition of *The Malcontent* (1604) presents the play as revised for the King's Men; in Webster's Induction, Condell describes the word as 'neither Satyre nor Morall, but the meane passage of a historie'.[15]

Both as substantive and adjectivally, moral has, and always has had, a wide range of meanings. It is however in *Everyman* clearly used as a technical term.

> I pray you all give your audience,
> And hear this *matter* with reverence,
> *By figure* a *moral play*.
> The Summoning of Everyman called it is,
> That of our lives and ending shows
> How transitory we be all day.
> This *matter* is wonders precious;

---

[15] Alan C. Dessen, 'The Morall, as an Elizabethan Dramatic Kind: An Exploratory Essay', *Comparative Drama* 5 (1971), pp. 143 – 4.

> But the *entent* of it is more gracious,
> And sweet to bear away.
> The *story* sayth: Man, in the beginning
> Look well, and take good heed to the ending,
> Be you never so gay!   (*Everyman*, 1 – 12)

As well as this statement in the prologue, there is support from the printer, who uses the term 'moral play' twice, at the beginning and the end of the text. The first has already been quoted, but it will be useful to repeat it.

> Here beginneth a treatise how the high Father of heaven sendeth Death to summon every creature to come and give account of their lives in this world/ and is in manner of a *moral play*.

> Thus endeth this *moral play* of Everyman.

As well as these uses of the adjective, the substantive occurs in the Doctor's concluding speech, which comments on the remarks made by the Angel who takes Everyman to Jesus:

> Now shalt thou in to the heavenly sphere,
> Unto the which all ye shall come
> That liveth well before the day of doom.
> *Doctor.*   This *moral* men may have in mind.   (*Everyman*, 899 – 902)

In his edition of *Everyman*, A. C. Cawley notes of lines 2 – 3 that:

> The distinction between matter 'mater' and form 'fygure' is a familiar one in scholastic theology. The 'matter' referred to here is the doctrine which Everyman has in common with medieval treatises on the art of holy dying and the allegorical exemplum it borrows from sermons on true and false friendship . . .; the 'form' is the visual and dramatic presentation of both doctrine and exemplum in the play[16]

'The matter' means 'the subject matter' or theme and is a common technical term in early drama as of course in other sorts of writing. An amusing example of its use occurs in *Gammer Gurton's Needle*:

> Here is a *matter* worthy *glosynge*
> Of Gammer Gurton's nedle losing
> And a foul piece of work.
> A man I think might *make a play*
> And need no word to this they say
> Being but half a clerk.

[16] *Everyman*, p. 29.

Soft, let me alone, I will take the charge
This *matter further to enlarge*
Within a time short. (*Gammer Gurton's Needle*, II ii 6 – 18, my italics)

The 'matter' in *Gammer Gurton's Needle* is worthy *glosynge*, i.e. of being given a moral application, and having a play made out of it, in a comic variation of what is done more seriously in *Everyman*, and in *The Pardoner's Tale*.

In *Everyman* the 'matter' is the same thing as 'the story' mentioned in line 10. It is distinguished from the 'figure' or form. But 'figure' has another, technical, meaning too, as we see from the following passages from *Respublica* and *The Life and Repentance of Mary Magdalen*:

First, health and success, with many a good new year,
Wished unto all this most noble presence here.
I have more to entreat you of gentle sufferance,
That this our *matter* may have quiet utterance.
We that are the actors have ourselves dedicate,
With some Christmas *device* your spirits to recreate,
And our poet trusteth the thing we shall recite
May without offence the hearer's minds delight.

But now of the *argument* — to touch a word or twain,
The name of our play is *Respublica*, certain;
Our meaning is (I say not as by *plain story*,
But, as it were, *in figure*, by *an allegory*)
To show . . .   (*Respublica*, 1 – 8; 15 – 19)

We desire no man in this point to be offended,
In that virtues and vice we shall introduce;
For in men and women they have depended:
And therefore *figuratively* to speak, it is the use.
          (Prologue to *The Life and Repentance of Mary Magdalen*)

Udall, the author of *Respublica*, tells us that 'in figure' means 'by an allegory', and Lewis Wager says in his play that it is customary to speak 'figuratively', that is, to introduce 'virtues and vice' as well as 'men and women'. So it seems that line 3 of *Everyman* can have two possible meanings; firstly, as Cawley suggests, 'a moral play in form', and secondly, 'through the use of allegory (or figures), a moral play'. (Here we observe the economical use of a term that conveys several layers of meaning by its density, one of the distinguishing features of moral plays).

The prologue to *Everyman* also distinguishes between 'the matter' and the 'entent', between, that is, the 'story', what in *Respublica* is termed the 'plain story' and the purpose or message or 'moral', between the literal story and what the story 'sayth' or 'means'.

This technical terminology is both parodied *and* taken seriously in *The Pardoner's Tale*:

For myn *entente* is nat but for to wynne,
And nothyng for correcioun of synne.   (C, 403 – 4, my italics)

But shortly myn *entente* I wol devyse:
I preche of no thyng but for coveityse.   (C, 423 – 4, my italics)

The Pardoner claims his purpose is to get money, but the ambiguity of 'for coveityse', which can mean both 'out of covetousness' and '*against* covetousness', shows that there is an ambiguity in his own comprehension of his purpose. His purpose may be to get money, but there is a moral *entente* too.

In *Everyman*, 'the story' is of a man, any man or 'every/man' who is suddenly asked to make a reckoning and show his account book in good order (it might now best be dramatised as a visit to one of us by a representative of H.M. Inspector of Taxes). What this story *says* ('sayth') is or implies a general message or warning:

The *story* sayth: Man, in the beginning
Look well, and take good heed to the ending
Be you never so gay!   (*Everyman*, 10 – 12)

This message is proverbial, deriving from Ecclesiasticus 7:36: 'Whatsoever thou takest in hand, remember the end, and thou shalt never do amiss'. It is cited in Tilley's *Dictionary of Proverbs* as 'Think on the end before you begin' (Tilley, E 128). This then is the *moral* which the Doctor exhorts us to have in mind as he begins his Epilogue, and this parallels the Pardoner's theme of 'Radix malorum est Cupiditas'. *All* moral plays have a central theme, often a proverb, which their actions dramatise.

So in one sense, in line 3 of *Everyman* 'moral play' means 'a play with a moral', or perhaps more precisely a play *on* a moral. But 'moral' had another sense which is relevant here too, and which relates closely to the use of 'in figure' in *Everyman*, line 3.

This technical sense of moral is found in passages which treat of the fourfold interpretation of scripture or other allegorical writing, for example, in the well-known passage in Dante's *Letter to Can Grande*:

The meaning of this work is not simple . . . for we obtain one meaning from the letter of it, and another from that which the letter signifies; and the first is called literal, but the other allegorical or mystical. And to make this matter of treatment clearer, it may be studied in the verse:
'When Israel came out of Egypt and the House of Jacob from among a strange people, Judah was his sanctuary and Israel his dominion'.
For if we regard the letter alone, what is set before us is the exodus of the Children of Israel from Egypt in the days of Moses; if the allegory, our redemption wrought by Christ, if the *moral sense*, we are shown the conversion of the soul from the grief and wretchedness of sin to the state of grace; if the anagogical, we are shown the departure of the holy soul from the

thraldom of this corruption to the liberty of eternal glory. And although these mystical meanings are called various names, they may all be called in general allegorical, since they differ from the literal and historical.

The subject of the whole work, then, taken merely in the literal sense is 'the state of the soul after death straight-forwardly affirmed', for the development of the whole work hinges on and about that. But if, indeed, the work is taken allegorically, its subject is: 'Man, as by good or ill deserts, in the exercise of his free choice, he becomes liable to rewarding or punishing Justice'.[17]

While Boccaccio writes:

It is to be understood in regard to these fictions that they are not to be thought of as having only one sense but may rather be said to be polysemous; that is multiple in sense. For the first sense is to be understood from the cortex or rind and this is called literal; other senses are to be understood through those things signified through the cortex and these are called allegorical. And that our intention be more readily grasped, we will give an example. Perseus, the son of Jupiter, by a poetic fiction, killed the Gorgon and, victorious, flew away into the air. If this is read literally, the historical sense appears; *if its moral sense is sought, the victory of the prudent man against vice is demonstrated and his approach to virtue.* If, however, we wish to adopt an *allegorical* sense, the elevation of the pious mind above those mundane delights which it despises, to celestial things, is designated. Further, anagogically it might be said to prefigure by a fable Christ's ascent to the Father, having overcome the prince of this world; which senses, however, although they may be called by various names can equally all be designated allegorical; which is often done. For 'allegoria' is derived from 'allon' which, in Latin, signifies 'other' or 'diverse'; and thus, whatever deviates from the literal or historical sense may, as is said, properly be called allegorical.[18]

Again, in his *Literature and Pulpit in Medieval England*, G. R. Owst writes:

. . . it is clear that Holy Scripture is not merely to be understood according to its literal or grammatical sense, but with equal truth according to the mystical or *moral sense* . . . It is to be observed . . . that, according to the doctors, there are four senses of Holy Scripture, namely, the literal or Historical; the allegorical, or Allegory; the tropological or Tropology, that is *the moral*; the anagogical, or Anagogy. Concerning these senses there are two such verses as the following (and he quotes from a sermon of Robert Rypon, c. 1400):
    'Littera gesta docet; quid credas, allegoria;
    Moralis, quid agas; quo tendas, anagogia'.[19]

---

[17] From Dante's *Letter to Can Grande*, trans. Dorothy L. Sayers, *The Divine Comedy*, (Harmondsworth, 1949), pp. 14 – 15, my italics.

[18] Boccaccio *Genealogie*, I iii p. 19, translated in Pamela Gradon, *Form and Style in Early English Literature* (London, 1971), pp. 47 – 8, my italics.

[19] G. R. Owst, *Literature and Pulpit in Medieval England* (Cambridge, 1933), p. 59, my italics.

In all such accounts of how a text may be read or understood on four different levels, the *moral* level (also called tropological) is always used of the level treating of vices and virtues, the figures or characters of a moral play, and also 'quid agas' (what we act or do). Here, then, *moral* is a technical term describing one of the 'levels of meaning' in scriptural exposition:

> that mode of interpreting a passage of Holy Scripture which treats of the events recorded as typical of something in the life of the Christian soul   (*OED* 9a)

This definition actually omits any mention of the 'vices and virtues' which are an integral part of this way of reading allegorically, but we may compare a sense cited separately in *OED*:

> treating of or concerned with virtue and vice, or the rules or right conduct, as a subject of study   (*OED* 2)

This sense of 'moral', a technical one deriving from the discipline of four-fold scriptural interpretation, is normally applied to a level of reading a text or story where there may also be other possible levels (allegorical, anagogical) that need not detain us here. All the writers quoted stress that the allegorical senses may be grouped together 'since they differ from the literal and historical' as Dante says.

The 'story' can, indeed must, be read literally and also tropologically or morally, and *both* levels have weight. In figural writing there is a literal story which can be read on a moral level — a story and a moral, which of course are closely tied together. *Everyman* has a literal, story-level, that of a man caught out, say, by the Tax Inspector, though it functions as an *exemplum* too. Similarly, Chaucer's *Pardoner's Tale*, is a 'moral tale' on the theme or moral 'Radix malorum est Cupiditas', in which the story of the three rioters is both a literal narrative, firmly fixed in place and time, and an *exemplum* of the theme. In the frequently quoted passage in which Shakespeare's Richard III compares himself to the vice of the moral plays, he says:

> Thus like the formal vice, Iniquity,
> I moralise two meanings in one word.   (*Richard III*, III. i. 82 – 3)

'Moralising' means finding *two* meanings — this is an essential part of the technique of writing a moral play. The Pardoner, also 'vicious' like the vice Iniquity, found 'two meanings' in preaching 'for coveityse' — both *for* gain and against it.

The 'two meanings' of a moral play are held together by various devices or images which cross the literal and moral levels of the narrative or drama. To quote Glynne Wickham:

As the literal narrative or debate advanced horizontally, so to speak, in terms of story-line, so the moral argument, whether ethical, political or social, must advance vertically in terms of added, emblematic texture.[20]

In his book *Plays and their Makers to 1576* (*Early English Stages*, Vol. III) Wickham has made a definitive study of the use of device in early drama. He finds 'device' very difficult to define, in just the way Kolve finds it hard to choose a suitable word for the narrative images he describes in his book *Chaucer and the Imagery of Narrative*. In my view, and this is the most important point I want to make in this paper, Wickham's dramatic 'devices' and Kolve's narrative images have precisely the same function — they are the imaginative embodiments or concrete representations of the ideas or themes central to early English poetry (which of course includes drama). The best statement about how such images or devices actually come about is made, unsurprisingly, by Shakespeare, in Theseus' famous speech on imagination (image-making) at the opening of Act V of *A Midsummer Night's Dream*. Speaking of poets (having dealt with lunatics and lovers) he says:

And as imagination *bodies forth*
The forms of things unknown, the poet's pen
Turns them to *shapes*, and gives to airy nothing
A *local habitation* and a name.
Such tricks hath strong imagination
That if it would but apprehend some joy
It comprehends some bringer of that joy.   (V. i. 14 – 20, my italics)

Thus if Chaucer, in *The Pardoner's Tale*, wishes to 'apprehend' the idea of Covetousness, his imagination 'comprehends' a bringer of covetousness, and gives that bringer a suitable 'local habitation', in a tavern. I have already referred to the appropriateness of the tavern setting for *The Pardoner's Tale*, and we may note that 'the tavern' is the third visual device studied by Glynne Wickham in detail.[21] Tavern scenes are almost legion in early moral plays, being good places for meeting Lechery, Gluttony, Sloth, and any other Deadly Sins one cares to name. The tavern is an obvious setting for the arrival of corrupting influences, whether they be the vices Newguise, Nowadays and Nought in *Mankind* or the revellers of Eastcheap in *Henry IV pt I*. The story of the three rioters in the tavern in *The Pardoner's Tale* is a localised, literal narrative, but the very idea of Riot is itself a device from the moral plays, as Dover Wilson has shown so well in his book *The Fortunes of Falstaff*. Discussing *Henry IV pt I* in moral play

[20] Glynne Wickham, *Early English Stages 1300 to 1660, Vol. III: Plays and their Makers to 1576* (London, 1981), p. 70.
[21] *Ibid.*, pp. 94 – 99.

terms, he shows the parallel between the character Riot in the moral play
Youth, and Falstaff.[22]

There is much here that we can see 'prefigured' in *The Pardoner's Tale*.
The wanton youths, revelling and caring nothing for the future, are
cautioned by a good counsellor (indeed two, the boy and the old man),
choose to ignore their good advice, go out and fall prey to the very sin that
their inventor has been warning against.

What we apparently do not have in *The Pardoner's Tale* (and any drama
specialists in the audience are probably shifting in their seats wondering
how I am going to get out of this) is any central 'mankind' figure who is
ultimately saved from the consequences of his sin by the intervention of
grace. But this is where we come back to the ambiguity of the Pardoner and
his preaching. Like Mercy in *Mankind*, the Pardoner involves his audience
in his drama — they (and we) are mankind, and it is *they* who will be saved
by offering to his relics. In their excesses of *coveityse* (or other sins, for
covetousness is the root of *all* evil) he will intercede for them, as Mercy did
for *Mankind* just as he was about to hang himself. By turning upon the
audience at the end, in a manner which all critics find difficult, the Pardoner
almost succeeds in bringing us into his moral drama. Almost but not quite,
for the Host's rebuff:

> . . . I wol no lenger *pleye*
> With thee, . . .   (C, 958 – 9, my italics)

shows that he is ultimately refusing the role of sinful mankind. The Knight,
however, wants the play or game to continue:

> And Pardoner, I prey thee, drawe thee neer,
> And as we diden, lat us laughe and *pleye*.   (C, 966 – 7, my italics)

The drama of *The Canterbury Tales* will go on, then, but the moral play
on the theme of Covetousness is concluded.

---

[22] J. Dover Wilson, *The Fortunes of Falstaff* (Cambridge, 1964), pp. 17 ff.

TROILUS AND CRISEYDE AND THE NUN'S PRIEST'S TALE: THE DRAWING AND UNDRAWING OF MORALS

SAUL N. BRODY

> How so it be that som men hem delite
> With subtyl art hire tales for to endite,
> Yet for al that, in hir entencioun
> Hir tale is al for som conclusioun.
> (*Troilus and Criseyde*, II, 256 – 9)[1]

Chaucer's poetry is filled with questions. By this I do not mean simply the many questions that his characters raise, though these are everywhere, fascinating in themselves, and worth studying on their own. It would be tempting, I must admit, to undertake a consideration of how and when Chaucer puts questions — questions such as the Monk's 'How shal the world be served?' (*CT* A, 187), to take but one example. However, my purpose is something else. I want to pursue a broader problem with you, the matter of Chaucer's feeling for the openness of questions, his distrust of final answers. In other words, it is not so much Chaucer's questions that interest me here, but the kinds of responses he offers, for if he delighted in asking questions, he also took pleasure in clouding the answers.

How Chaucer came to distrust authoritative pronouncements is another interesting problem, but one that could not conceivably be worked through here. Still, it can be said that he must have come to it in part through the influence of his reading and of ideas that were in the air. The work of Abelard, Boetius of Dacia, and Siger of Brabant may well have helped shape Chaucer's sensitivity to the value of competing truths. These were philosophers who contributed to a tradition of what has been called 'skeptical fideism', a tradition 'rooted in the awareness of coexistent contradictory truths and resulting in the suspension of final rational judgment', a tradition, moreover, 'found in cosmology, metaphysics,

---

[1] All Chaucer quotations follow Larry D. Benson, ed., *The Riverside Chaucer*, 3rd ed. (Boston, 1987).

encyclopedic compilations, poetry, and popular treatises'.[2] In addition, one might keep in mind the strong influence of Boethius on Chaucer's development of a sense of irony, 'a way of saying opposite things simultaneously without either being undermined by the other',[3] and of Dante, who may have contributed to Chaucer's 'unwillingness to render final judgments on his characters and to determine fine morals . . .'.[4]

In accounting for Chaucer's skeptical view of dogmatic teachings, I would be remiss not to suggest one other probable shaping force. Let me propose that had Chaucer not become a writer, the slipperiness of experience and the uncertainty of authoritative pronouncements would not have come to occupy him as they did. As a writer, he surely felt a responsibility — common enough among his contemporaries, common enough at any time — to write about the truth, or if not the truth exactly, at least the truth as he saw it. As a writer, he was undoubtedly inclined to articulate the truth, whatever it was, by making it real, by giving it life, by fixing it with the telling detail. Perhaps a truth he wanted to fix for his audience was the commonplace that sin is deadly to the soul, and what better way to do this than to make a character not only recognizably iconographic, but also recognizably alive. One thinks, for example, of the Summoner's fire-red cherub's face, or of the ulcer on the Cook's shin. As he particularized a character with a charged detail, what Chaucer found, I suspect, is what many another writer has found: that the character could come to write itself, to take on an independent reality, a separate existence. In other words, his creation could become complex and elusive and irreducible. It could become not it, but he or she, not simply Lust or Wrath or whatever, but someone he could deprecate and love by turns, or even simultaneously. If the artist set out to produce a moral type, he could make that person so real that moral condemnation could become not so much wrong as incomplete.

However it was that he came to it, the point is that from a very early stage in his career, Chaucer was preoccupied with the aesthetic and moral problems that flowed from his exquisite awareness of the complexity of human experience. I would like to illustrate this proposition by looking briefly at the *Parlement of Foules*, and then moving on to *Troilus* and the *Nun's Priest's Tale*.

---

[2] Sheila Delany, *Chaucer's House of Fame: The Poetics of Skeptical Fideism* (Chicago, 1972), p. 1.

[3] Peter Elbow, *Oppositions in Chaucer* (Middletown, CN., 1975), p. 14. See also Ida L. Gordon, *The Double Sorrow of Troilus: A Study of Ambiguities in 'Troilus and Criseyde'* (Oxford, 1970), pp. 24 – 60.

[4] Bonnie Wheeler, 'Dante, Chaucer, and the Ending of *Troilus and Criseyde*', *Philological Quarterly* 61 (1982) 105 – 23, p. 113.

The *Parlement* begins with the narrator's telling us that when he thinks about Love, he moves into uncharted territory, a world without boundaries, a place with no fixed mark.

> . . . whan I on hym thynke
> Nat wot I wel wher that I flete or synke. (6 – 7)

He needs help in learning 'a certeyn thing' (20), and so he turns to a book. As it happens, the book is so absorbing that he loses himself in it, or (to be more exact) he loses touch with thinking, the thinking that caused his confusion in the first place:

> To rede forth hit gan me so delite
> That al that day me thoughte but a lyte. (27 – 28)

The summary of Macrobius that follows is brief and as true to the text as something so brief can be. What the narrator has somehow gleaned from the book is the message that the world is mutable, deceptive, and full of hard grace; to achieve the bliss of heaven one must recognize one's immortal soul, follow the law, avoid lechery, and work for the common profit. The cool asceticism of the lesson is familiar and orthodox enough, although, looking to learn a certain thing about Love, the narrator seems not to have exactly the thing he wanted:

> For bothe I hadde thyng which that I nolde,
> And ek I ne hadde that thyng that I wolde. (90 – 91)

I would offer this observation about the first part of the *Parlement*. The narrator, like an artist, like Chaucer himself, is seeking to make some sense out of the complexity and confusion of the human situation, or if that seems too sweeping a statement, out of love merely. He turns to what medieval writers (including Chaucer) regularly turned to, a book, and the work provides the refuge that so many of us find in books — refuge in imagination as distinct from bewildering and confusing thought. What he finally learns from the book is what books, especially medieval ones, are prone to offer: rules and dogma.

He next falls asleep and dreams, and as he dreams, the narrator, the artist, slips away from books and into a world purely imagined. In his dream, he is brought by Scipio to an enclosed park or garden, a garden that is not Paradise itself but what human beings were left with after the Fall: this world. And what the narrator finds are two alternatives to Scipio's hard message.

The first is in the Temple of Venus, and it is lechery and the pain and suffering and sterility that follow from it. The temple is artful and artificial, like a stage set, and appropriately for a place so carefully crafted, the last thing the narrator sees in it are wall paintings of the stories of lovers who died for love.

The other alternative to Scipio's asceticism is encountered in Nature's assembly of birds. If Venus' temple seems artificial, the parliament has the feel of the real thing, and it is the reality of the birds — which is only to say, their resemblance to humans — that threatens to keep Nature from carrying out God's plan for the regeneration of the species. Nature calls on the birds to procreate, but four of them (the three aristocratic male eagles and the female they hope to gain) are unable to choose mates. The debate on the matter threatens to dissolve into utter chaos and confusion, which Nature barely succeeds in averting. The poem ends as the narrator awakens from his dream, saying that he will continue his search for something better in other books.

The *Parlement of Foules* thus pivots on a single undefined and unanswered question having something to do with love. In the course of the poem, Chaucer unfolds three major visions of love, two of them worldly, one other-worldly, two of them sacred, one profane, and none capable of answering whatever it is that the narrator wants to have answered.

The structure of the *Parlement* reveals the philosophical underpinnings of Chaucer's canon taken as a whole. The poem's narrator addresses the one great topic that Chaucer was never to abandon or, in my view, ever to successfully resolve. The problem raised is presumably the Monk's problem of how to serve the world, or — put just a little differently — it is the problem of discovering (and then pursuing) the proper object of love. In the *Parlement*, the narrator finds his answers in three competing arenas: theology (as communicated by Scipio), art (as encountered in Venus' temple), and life (as experienced in the confusion of Nature's gathering of birds). Each answer, partial as it must be, is at once attractive and unsatisfying, leaving the great question which begins the poem still open at the end.

The tension among theology, art, and life remained fundamental to Chaucer's poetry, and the strength of the claims made by each brought the poet to develop an aesthetic built on unresolved claims that permeates his work. Although I might have explored this approach in any number of Chaucer's poems — for instance, the *House of Fame* and the *Franklin's Tale* make good candidates — in what follows, I want to restrict myself to tracing a line that can be discovered moving out of the *Parlement*, through the *Troilus*, and into the *Nun's Priest's Tale*.[5]

Readers have often observed that the pagan world of *Troilus and Criseyde* offers its hero all that he needs to overcome its seductions but for one crucial

---

[5] For a general study of narrative inconclusiveness in Chaucer, see Larry Sklute, *Virtue of Necessity: Inconclusiveness and Narrative Form in Chaucer's Poetry* (Columbus, 1984).

thing: the light of Christian revelation. In other words, the world of the poem is given to us as almost perfectly self-contained and in many ways beautiful. A young man in such a world might imagine, for example, that he had seen a woman's face that was 'lik of Paradys the ymage' (IV, 864), and he could come to worship that woman as if she were Paradise itself. What the poet does is to present that woman so fully, as so complex a joining of beauty, seductiveness, frailty and danger, that we fall in love with her along with the young man, though probably without his utter abandonment. The poet will not let us be so single-minded, and he is careful to have us see Criseyde in ways that Troilus does and perhaps can not. The catalogue of her faults is easy to produce, for Chaucer is at pains to give us Criseyde in a variety of lights, not all of them complimentary. She may be frightened and vulnerable, for example, but she is also experienced, aware, calculating, and manipulative. The point is brought home to us from very early in the narrative, and surely no later than the scene near the beginning of Book II, in which Pandarus announces to Criseyde that Troilus is in love with her. Criseyde plays the role expected of her: she sighs when necessary (e.g., 428), stops weeping when the moment is right (469), and all with the awareness that she must 'felen what he [Pandarus] meneth, ywis' (387). 'It nedeth me ful sleighly for to pleie' (462), she says. In other words, if one aspect of Criseyde is that Venus-Citheria, 'the wel-willy planete' (III,1257), is to be found in her, also in her is the other Venus, Venus-Luxuria, the Venus who is discovered in a corner of the temple in the *Parlement*.[6]

In the figure of Criseyde we find a paradigm for all the characters in the story and beyond that of the city that is the setting for the poem. She is a combination of virtues and faults, of perfections and imperfections, just as Pandarus is, just as Troilus is, just as Troy is. We must feel about Criseyde exactly as we must about the others: many things at once, many inconsistent things, so that we feel some of our feelings with great reasonableness (Criseyde is not a woman to be trusted) and others in spite of ourselves (she is to be pitied and, more than pitied, she is to be loved).

In short, the world of *Troilus and Criseyde* is confusing, deceptive, attractive — it is the world, after all. It lays its hold on us, much in the way that the world of the *Parlement of Foules* does: by asserting the competing claims of three lives — one devoted to sensual pleasure and self-gratification; another also lived in this world, also in pursuit of Love, but lived ethically and virtuously; and a third that looks beyond this world toward salvation in the next.

---

[6] On the role of the two Venuses in *Troilus and Criseyde*, see George D. Economou, 'The Two Venuses and Courtly Love', in *In Pursuit of Perfection: Courtly Love in Medieval Literature*, ed. Joan M. Ferrante and George D. Economou (Port Washington, 1975) 17 – 50, pp. 39 – 47.

The dual opposition between the call to a life in this world, however conceived, and the call to a life beyond this one already is present in the opening lines of *Troilus*, with the narrator's appeal to 'ye loveres, that bathen in gladnesse' (I,22) to pray for those who suffer through love:

> And preieth for hem that ben in the cas
> Of Troilus, as ye may after here,
> That Love hem brynge in hevene to solas;
> . . .
> Thus biddeth God, for his benignite,
> So graunte hem soone owt of this world to pace,
> That ben despeired out of Loves grace.   (I,29 – 31, 40 – 42)

The narrator may not at this point realize the full implications of what he is saying, but never mind. If we have read the *Parlement*, we know what he is about. Like the narrator of the *Parlement*, he is not a lover himself, as he admits (I,15 – 18), and like the other narrator he has not thought through the problem of finding a proper object for human love. He imagines that successful lovers have obtained full bliss, and his concern is not for their happiness or welfare (they, he must imagine, have passed through the gate into 'that blysful place / Of hertes hele and dedly woundes cure' [*PF*, 126 – 27]); what he is concerned about is unhappy lovers, and if they cannot find their paradise in this world, let them at least have it in the next.

As the poem unfolds, its world becomes more complex and, in fact, more like the one in the *Parlement*, at least insofar as it represents more than a mere opposition between this world as profane and the other one as sacred. We find that this-worldly love can be profane, as it is under Pandarus' direction, but it can also be ennobling, as it is when Troilus and Criseyde, for a moment at the end of Book III, come to feel the perfect love embodied by the Venus who is invoked at the beginning of Book III. Not many among us are so single-minded in our disdain for this world that we can lightly dismiss either 'this hevene blisse' (III,1322) that Troilus and Criseyde enter into, or the straightforward eroticism that Pandarus is after. Precisely the reverse. Just as the narrator in the *Parlement* is drawn in three directions at once, just in fact as the narrator of *Troilus* is also pulled in three directions, so are we.

Chaucer's unsettling ability to make every alternative attractive, even clearly sinful ones, is what prevents him from constructing a closed text, not alone in the *Parlement of Foules*, but also in *Troilus and Criseyde*. To be sure, the ending of *Troilus* — and I am now referring to the last portion of Book V, beginning at about line 1765[7] — does seem to be a definitive

---

[7] A critical consensus on the extent of the poem's close does not exist (John M. Steadman, *Disembodied Laughter: 'Troilus' and the Apotheosis Tradition: A Reexamination of Narrative and Thematic Contexts* [Berkeley, 1972], pp. 149 – 52). Steadman's judgment

ending, one that puts everything in place, one that offers a final and authoritative perspective on the action. If there is a lesson to be learned, a moral to be drawn, that lesson would appear to be contained in the poem's epilogue.

How far that is from being true, or more exactly, how little agreement exists over how the moral is to be taken, can be seen in the numerous interpretations of the epilogue that have been offered by readers.[8] Most

strikes me as sensible: 'The epilogue does not (it would seem) constitute a clearly defined or strictly differentiated section of the poem, and there is room for doubt as to whether Chaucer actually regarded the conclusion of the poem as a formal epilogue' (p. 152).

8 See, for example, E. T. Donaldson, 'The Ending of Chaucer's *Troilus*' in *Early English and Norse Studies, presented to Hugh Smith . . .* Eds. A. Brown and P. Foote (London, 1963), pp. 26 – 45; Rpt. in Donaldson, *Speaking of Chaucer* (New York, 1972), pp. 84 – 101; P. Dronke, 'The Conclusion of *Troilus and Criseyde*', *Medium Ævum* 33 (1964) 47 – 52; M. J. Evans, ' "Making Strange": The Narrator (?), the Ending (?), and Chaucer's *Troilus*', *Neuphilologische Mitteilungen* 87 (1986) 218 – 28; A. E. Farnham, 'Chaucerian Irony and the Ending of the *Troilus*', *Chaucer Review* 1 (1967) 207 – 16; A. T. Gaylord, 'Chaucer's Tender Trap: The Troilus and the "Yonge, Fresshe Folkes" ', *English Miscellany* 15 (1964) 24 – 45; Sr. A. B. Gill, *Paradoxical Patterns in Chaucer's 'Troilus': An Explanation of the Palinode* (Folcroft, 1960); A. R. Kaminski, *Chaucer's "Troilus and Criseyde" and the Critics* (Athens, Ohio, 1980); W. Kamowski, 'A Suggestion for Emending the Epilogue of *Troilus and Criseyde*', *Chaucer Review* 21 (1987) 405 – 517; P. M. Kean, 'Chaucer's Dealings with a Stanza of *Il Filostrato* and the Epilogue of *Troilus and Criseyde*', *Medium Ævum* 33 (1964) 36 – 46; E. D. Kirk, 'Paradis Stood Formed in Hire Yen: Courtly Love and Chaucer's Re-vision of Dante', in *Acts of Interpretation: The Text in Its Contexts, 700 – 1600. Essays on Medieval and Renaissance Literature in Honor of E. Talbot Donaldson.* Ed. Mary J. Carruthers and Elizabeth D. Kirk (Norman, 1982), pp. 257 – 77; M. F. Markland, '*Troilus and Criseyde*: The Inviolability of the Ending', *Modern Language Quarterly* 31 (1970) 147 – 59; G. Morgan, 'The Ending of *Troilus and Criseyde*', *Modern Language Review* 77 (1982) 257 – 71; C. Muscatine, *Chaucer and the French Tradition: A Study in Style and Meaning* (Berkeley, 1966), pp. 161 – 5; S. Nagarajan, 'The Conclusion to Chaucer's *Troilus and Criseyde*', *Essays in Criticism* 13 (1963) 1 – 8; R. H. Osberg, 'Between the Motion and the Act: Intentions and Ends in Chaucer's *Troilus*', *ELH* 48 (1981) 257 – 70; E. Reiss, 'Troilus and the Failure of Understanding', *Modern Language Quarterly* 29 (1968) 131 – 44; H. L. Rogers, 'The Beginning (and Ending) of Chaucer's *Troilus and Criseyde*' in *Festschrift for Ralph Farrell*, eds. A. Stephens, H. L. Rogers, and B. Coghlan (Bern, 1977), pp. 185 – 200; L. Sklute, *Virtue of Necessity: Inconclusiveness and Narrative Form in Chaucer's Poetry* (Columbus, Ohio, 1984); J. M. Steadman, *Disembodied Laughter: 'Troilus' and the Apotheosis Tradition: A Reexamination of Narrative and Thematic Contexts* (Berkeley, 1972); J. S. P. Tatlock, 'The Epilog of Chaucer's *Troilus*', *Modern Philology* 18 (1920 – 21) 625 – 59; B. Wheeler, 'Dante, Chaucer, and the Ending of *Troilus and Criseyde*', *Philological Quarterly* 61 (1982) 105 – 23; K. Young, 'Chaucer's Renunciation of Love in *Troilus*', *Modern Language Notes* 40 (1925) 270 – 76. For two surveys of criticism on the epilogue, see Gill, *op. cit.*, pp. ix – xvii and Kaminski, *op. cit.*, pp. 41 – 43, 49 – 51, *et passim*.

critics fall into one of two camps. The first sees the poem as divided
into two parts that clash: all that leads up to the epilogue is to be read
ironically, as pagan and hence insufficient, and the epilogue itself is to
be taken as the poet's considered and Christian rejection of the poem's
pagan world. The other camp, and it is by far the larger one, finds no
clash at all between the poem and its epilogue, but views the *Troilus* as
philosophically and stylistically coherent: the lesson at the end grows
naturally and inevitably out of the narrative. I do not wish to enter
here into a comparison of readings such as these, all of which find one
or another *moralite* at the poem's close, much less to offer a view on
which readings are more persuasive. Rather, my sense of the *Troilus* is
that these kinds of interpretations cannot satisfy fully, and exactly
because the poem is crafted so that the ending only appears to bring
the text to a neat conclusion.[9]

For 8,174 lines, Chaucer gives us a story of love and betrayal and
works it so that we experience that tale not only through his narrator's
eyes and mind, but also through the eyes and minds of the three major
players. Our engagement with the story is thus made to proceed on a
variety of levels and to be considered from a variety of points of view.
And we perceive the action simultaneously not just from the four
dominant points of view (the narrator's, Pandarus', Troilus', and
Criseyde's); the point of view of a single figure — not least of all the
narrator — is likely to shift as the story proceeds. The world of
Troilus, as a post-lapsarian world, is nothing if not *slydynge*. For the
reader, then, Troy is recognizable, not remote, and like the reader's
world, the world of Troy is absorbing, confusing, and frightening.

At line 1765 of Book V, the narrator interposes himself between his
tragedy and the audience, suspending for a moment the awful confrontation between Troilus and Diomede:

> And if I hadde ytaken for to write
> The armes of this ilke worthi man,
> Than wolde ich of his batailles endite.   (1765 – 7)

He says, however, that his purpose is not to describe Troilus in battle
but Troilus in love. Having interrupted himself, the narrator allows
himself a further aside. He tells us that he writes of Troilus' love,

[9] In my reading of the poem, I follow those who see its meaning in not one but multiple
truths, especially E. Talbot Donaldson, 'The Ending of Chaucer's *Troilus*'; Evans,
'Making Strange'; Farnham, 'Chaucerian Irony'; and Wheeler, 'Dante, Chaucer and
the Ending of *Troilus and Criseyde*'.

Byseching every lady bright of hewe,
And every gentil womman, what she be,
That al be that Criseyde was untrewe,
That for hire gilt she be nat wroth with me.   (1772 – 5)

He asks that noble women not blame *him* for Criseyde's infidelity — the story, after all, is in books and is not of his own making: 'Ye may hire gilt in other bokes se' (1776). In any case, the real point is not for the audience to feel sympathy for men who have been betrayed by women, but the reverse: the noble women he addresses should beware men, men who 'with hire grete wit and subtilte / Bytraise yow' (1782 – 3).

The digression is extraordinary. Book V has shown us Criseyde unfaithful and untrustworthy, like the world itself (1748 – 9), but just as the narrator says at the beginning of Book IV that he is forced by his sources to describe her betrayal of Troilus (15 – 21), so here he cannot bring himself to condemn his heroine with his own voice; more than that, he warns against men's treachery, an admonition that at first glance seems gratuitous, though of course it is not.

The narrator, as Donaldson tells us ('The Ending', pp. 91 – 101), is searching for a way to end his poem. He has tried unsuccessfully to invest Troilus with dignity by describing him in epic style, and having failed at that, he has attempted (with little more success) to find a moral for his tragedy in the unstable relations between men and women. The effect on us, I think, is to put us off balance, to warn us that easy teachings can be wrong. He underlines the point in the envoy to his tragedy, which ends with the prayer that it be properly understood:

And red wherso thow be, or elles songe
That thow be understonde, God I biseche!   (1797 – 8)

Having thus put us on our guard against reductive conclusions, he returns to the narrative and in a single stanza (1800 – 6) tells us how Troilus became a slaughterer of Greeks (second only to Hector); in the last line of the stanza, we learn of Troilus' death at Achilles' hands, almost as if that death were an afterthought.

The narrator is by now headed for larger issues than the mere question of how Troilus died, and what he might have said and felt. His object at this point is moral and philosophical: he wants his audience to abandon the sympathies he has cultivated in them for more than 8,000 lines and to view the earth as Scipio did in the *Parlement* — as a little spot, a wretched world to be fully despised. He wants to bring his audience up short, to accuse it of assigning its sympathies to the wrong things, to remind it of the truth that salvation is not to be found in 'payens corsed olde rites' (1849) or in 'thise wrecched worldes appetites' (1851), but in God. Still, he should have known that just as he, moments earlier, could not entirely abandon his sympathy for Criseyde, neither could the audience abruptly deny its sympathy for her and for the world.

In assessing my own response to the epilogue, I am inclined to extend to it Muscatine's judgment of Criseyde: 'Her ambiguity is her meaning' (p. 164). The epilogue offers us at least three explicit lessons: men, beware women (1779); women, beware men (1780 – 6); young folk, turn to God (1835 – 48). Implicit in the epilogue are several other lessons, including the one to be learned by observing Troilus' fate. However, even his fate is uncertain, both as to the exact sphere to which he moves and even more significantly as to where 'Mercurye sorted hym to dwelle' (1827; see Benson, p. 1057, nn. 1809 and 1827). What is more, if Muscatine's judgment of Criseyde suits the epilogue, it suits the entire poem just as easily. As Muscatine says, 'the poem's texture is dense with the interlacing of a wide range of alternative values, tested in themselves and by each other' (p. 165). I should like to suggest that the point of the interlacing is not so much to present one set of values as complementary or superior to another — though hierarchies of values do exist in the poem — as it is to illustrate how difficult it is to choose God over either Venus-Luxuria or Venus-Citheria. Anthony E. Farnham proposes that the poem offers a 'dialectical presentation of alternatives which, despite a categorical opposition to each other, share equally in the truth of experience' (p. 208). Commenting on the question the narrator asks in the course of the epilogue (and does not answer),

> And syn he [Jesus] best to love is, and most meke,
> What nedeth feynede loves for to seke?   (V,1847 – 8)

Farnham offers an apt observation: 'From one point of view, the question Chaucer asks is rhetorical; it implies a moral of which the poem is an *exemplum*. From another point of view, however, the poem as a whole is in vigorous revolt against any such implied moral' (p. 208). Exactly. It is precisely in this sense that the meaning of *Troilus* is contained not in the epilogue, but in the tension between the epilogue and the rest of the poem, not in a neatly phrased moral, but in the problem of making moral choices, which is only to say, of first being able to understand correctly and next of taking a moral to heart.

As I observed at the outset, the struggle in human beings to make a right choice was a preoccupation of the poet Geoffrey Chaucer, and it was the struggle that fascinated him as a poet far more than moral alternatives themselves. The evidence has suggested that the struggle he explored in the *Parlement* became as well the theme of *Troilus*, and the evidence indicates further that he returned to the theme of *Troilus* when he began work on the *Nun's Priest's Tale*, the story of a cock whose failure to understand nearly costs him his life.

The connection between *Troilus* and the *Nun's Priest's Tale* has not received a great deal of attention among Chaucer scholars. In fact, apart from Lynn Staley Johnson's 1985 article, subtitled 'Chauntecleer, Son of Troy,'[10] I am unfamiliar with any extended comparisons of the two works. Fortunately, Johnson offers a helpful analysis of how the *Nun's Priest's Tale* mirrors the structure, characterization, and themes of *Troilus and Criseyde*.

He points out, for example, that the Nun's Priest mentions Troy's fall three times (in the references to Hector's refusal to take heed of Andromache's dream of his death, Sinon's betrayal of Troy, and Priam's death), and he observes further that each time the allusion calls attention to how the Trojans bring about their own tragedy. He notes how alike Troilus and Chauntecleer are: both serve Venus, both 'are inspired to assume a martial air because of love' (p. 230), both have dreams of coming disaster, 'both give a fatalistic credence to these dreams' (p. 232) and both then put the dreams out of mind. Both poems invoke the role of Fortune in human events and its relationship to a tragic downfall, and the presence of Fortune in both invites a comparison of *Troilus'* tragic movement with the comic movement of the *Nun's Priest's Tale*.

The point of all this, Johnson would have us understand, is to provide in the *Nun's Priest's Tale* a remedy for the tragic pattern of *Troilus and Criseyde*. The difference between Chauntecleer and Troilus is in this respect everything, for where Troilus seems trapped in a tragic event, Chauntecleer uses his reason to break free of one. 'In relation to *Troilus and Criseyde*, Chaucer offers us in his rooster an alternative to Troilus, for Chauntecleer's potential tragedy is averted, not by an outside force, but by his ability to use his own wits to save himself' (p. 241).

To the many parallels between the two poems that Johnson adduces, one other needs to be added, namely, the business of drawing a moral from the action.[11] As the Nun's Priest brings his tale to a close, he advises the audience that his story, a seemingly foolish triviality, ought not to be lightly dismissed. It contains a lesson, a *moralite*, some *fruyt* that has been provided for our edification:

---

[10] ' "To Make in Som Comedye": Chauntecleer, Son of Troy', *Chaucer Review* 19 (1985) 225 – 44.

[11] In what follows, I make substantial use of my own article 'Truth and Fiction in the *Nun's Priest's Tale*', *Chaucer Review* 14 (1980) 33 – 47. Reprinted by permission of the Pennsylvania State University Press.

But ye that holden this tale a folye,
As of a fox, or of a cok and hen,
Taketh the moralite, goode men.
For Seint Paul seith that al that writen is,
To our doctrine it is ywrite, ywis;
Taketh the fruyt, and lat the chaf be stille.   (B² 4628 – 33)

The next three lines of the poem (that is, the last three lines), with their prayer for the souls of the audience, imply that our salvation may hinge on our ability to discover the lesson:

Now goode God, if that it be thy wille,
As seith my lord, so make us alle goode men,
And brynge us to his heighe blisse! Amen.   (B² 4634 – 6)

The language of these three lines is reminiscent of other endings in Chaucer's *Canterbury Tales*, all those endings in which the narrator hopes that the audience will win paradise.[12] But given the *Nun's Priest's Tale*'s continual echoing of *Troilus and Criseyde*, the ending of the *Nun's Priest's Tale* — and here I mean not just the last three, but the last nine lines — must also and perhaps especially call the conclusion of *Troilus* to mind.

The careers of both Troilus and Chauntecleer are offered to us as examples, and the narrators of both stories appear to offer clear lessons at the end of each. The rhetoric of the *Troilus* narrator, his use, for instance, of *conduplicatio* (V,1828 – 32, 1849 – 55), lends a particularly authoritative tone to the last sixty-three lines of the poem, just as does the Nun's Priest's call to find the lesson, with the corollary implication that the lesson will be easy to find. But exactly as the question at lines 1847 – 8 of Book V of *Troilus* ('And syn he best to love is, and most meke,/ What nedeth feynede loves for to seke?') is not a definitive pronouncement, but an open, unresolved query, and one with ironic implications (Farnham, pp. 214 – 6), so too is the Nun's Priest's injunction to find the lesson in his tale less authoritative and definitive than it seems.

For what, after all, is the story's moral? Is it Chauntecleer's realization of the peril of being wilfully blind to danger (B² 4621 – 2)? Is it the fox's against chattering when it is better to be silent (B² 4623 – 5)? Or is it the narrator's against being heedless, negligent, and trustful of flattery (B²

---

[12] Cf. the endings of the *Knight's Tale*, *Miller's Tale*, *Reeve's Tale*, *Man of Law's Tale*, *Merchant's Tale*, *Physician's Tale*, *Pardoner's Tale* (C 916 – 918), *Prioress's Tale*, *Canon's Yeoman's Tale*, and *Parson's Tale*, as well as Chaucer's *Melibee*. The idea of separating the fruit from the chaff is also conventional, of course, and appears in three other places in Chaucer (*Man of Law's Tale*, B¹ 701 – 2; Prologue to the *Parson's Tale*, I 35 – 6; and the Prologue to the *Legend of Good Women*, G 312, G 529).

4626 – 7)? These three lessons, offered one after the other, can be taken separately or together. On the other hand, other lessons may be implicit in the text, such as warnings against lechery or complacency, or against wrongdoings revealed through allegorization, or against listening to wives, or against not listening to them.

We are, you see, back in the quicksand of the epilogue to *Troilus*. And how are we to extricate ourselves from it?

Some readers, responding to the tale's comedy and to its lack of a precise moral, warn against reading it too seriously, or pinpointing its lesson too exactly, or finding a lesson at all.[13] Indeed, in the face of the varied lessons that have been discovered on and beneath the surface of the Nun's Priest's narrative — and rejected — a safe course would appear to be the last one suggested, namely, to avoid defining the lesson at all. On the other hand, the very presence of besetting ambiguity in the tale[14] may indicate that if the work does contain a moral, that moral has to do with ambiguity itself.

Consider the lesson that Chauntecleer draws. The rooster is the embodiment of the broad uncertainty in the tale over what is true and not true generally. Though a rooster who scratches for corn, he is nevertheless capable of speaking, and what is more, of speaking truth, the truth about dreams, a truth he demonstrates by recourse to stories. A fantastical talking rooster, he appears in the middle of a piece of fiction that poses as truth, tells a series of *exempla* taken largely (though not entirely) from authoritative sources, and then ignores the truth contained in them. The consequence is that he suffers a reversal of fortune, leading the narrator to remark that the story is as true as the story of Lancelot, itself an acknowledged work of fiction. Like the story about him, Chauntecleer

---

[13] Compare the various readings of C. B. Hieatt, 'The Moral of the *Nun's Priest's Tale*', *Studia Neophilologica* 42 (1970) 3 – 8; R. T. Lenaghan, 'The Nun's Priest's Fable', *PMLA* 68 (1963) 300 – 7; R. M. Lumiansky, *Of Sondry Folk: The Dramatic Principle in the Canterbury Tales* (Austin, 1955), pp. 114 – 5; J. Mann, 'The *Speculum Stultorum* and the *Nun's Priest's Tale*', *Chaucer Review* 9 (1975) 262 – 82; S. Manning, 'The Nun's Priest's Morality and the Medieval Attitude Toward Fables', *Journal of English and Germanic Philology* 59 (1960) 403 – 16; C. Muscatine, *Chaucer and the French Tradition*, pp. 237 – 243; D. E. Myers, 'Focus and "Moralite" in the *Nun's Priest's Tale*', *Chaucer Review* 7 (1973) 210 – 20; D. W. Robertson, *A Preface to Chaucer: Studies in Medieval Perspective* (Princeton, 1962), pp. 274, 376; J. M. Steadman, 'Flattery and the *Moralitas* of "The Nonne Preestes Tale" ', *Medium Ævum* 28 (1959) 172 – 9.

[14] Three ready examples of ambiguity in the *Nun's Priest's Tale* are the reference to the book of Lancelot (4402 – 4403), Chauntecleer's translation of Latin (4353 – 4356), and the narrator's statement, 'I kan no harm of no womman divyne' (4456). See Brody, pp. 41 – 42 and Lawrence L. Besserman, 'Chaucerian Wordplay: The Nun's Priest and his *womman divyne*', *Chaucer Review* 12 (1977 – 78) 68 – 73.

himself has a dual nature. He is true and fictive, rational and irrational, magnificent and trivial, human and animal. Accordingly, when he moralizes on what has happened to him, he draws a lesson that is not so straightforwardly moral as it seems. Chauntecleer warns against being blind, presumably to flattery, but it is only by using flattery that he manages to escape from the fox; hence, while he does seem to have come to a realization about the danger of pride, he has been able to survive only by appealing to pride in someone else.

Moreover, the lessons drawn by the fox and the narrator are similarly ambiguous. Although the fox warns against speaking foolishly, one can only suppose that if he again had the opportunity to capture and eat Chauntecleer he would do so. And while the narrator's warning against heedlessness and flattery is morally sound from one point of view, from another and more cynical one it can be taken as a recommendation to villains (such as the fox) to keep their own interests firmly in view.[15] In brief, all the lessons drawn at the close of the story are ambiguous, and for the very good reason that the human heart is ambiguous.

What the *Nun's Priest's Tale* is doing is grappling with the problem of interpreting experience that also is posed in Troilus. Perhaps the strongest of the lessons *Troilus* concludes with is the advice to scorn the world, but that lesson is relativized or even possibly subverted by the power of the story that precedes it and that exists on an emotional plane largely independent of it. The issue the poet deals with in the *Troilus* — the complexity of experience and the resulting inadequacy of reductive pronouncements about it — is once again the issue in the *Nun's Priest's Tale*. It is precisely for this reason that the tale will not easily support one meaning, that it is confused and ambiguous, that its moral is elusive, and that it can be seen from a variety of angles. The tale's lesson, its *fruyt*, is not to avoid, say, flattery, but to recognize that difficult moral choices are everywhere. The narrator, in raising all sorts of possibilities of meaning, compels the audience to confront the ambiguities raised in the tale, and he thus creates in his fiction a mirror of what individuals regularly confront in life. What moral meaning they extract from or impose upon life, or the story, presumably depends upon their ethical predispositions, and their burden is to make the right choices, if they can figure them out.

In other words, the tale echoes experience, as all stories do, and echoes it convincingly by presenting elusive truths. The story itself is offered as both true and untrue (Brody, pp. 33 – 34), Chauntecleer is said both to be and not to be responsible for what happens to him (Brody, pp. 39 – 40), and the

---

[15] For an admirable treatment of the ambiguities inherent in the *Nun's Priest's Tale* generally, and its *fruyt* in particular, see Mann, pp. 271 – 82.

morals drawn at the end are both edifying and reconcilable with principles of pure self-interest. In the special sense in which the point of the poem is to be found in its confusion, the remark that its *fruyt* is its *chaf* is highly pertinent,[16] as is the observation that the work's 'shifting of focus . . . itself virtually constitutes the theme' (Muscatine, p. 239). For all these reasons, to appropriate one more critic's words, 'the narrator cannot offer a guarantee that he has a moral by which he has shaped it; he can only offer St Paul's guarantee that everything that has been written has a moral in it somewhere' (Mann, p. 277). The function of that assurance, I take it, is much like the function of the prayer in *Troilus* that the poem be understood: it is there to remind us of how difficult it is to achieve certainty.

The line I have been tracing from the *Parlement*, through *Troilus*, and into the *Nun's Priest's Tale* shows Chaucer as a writer preoccupied with the vagaries of the human heart. In all three works he is intensely interested in the problem of conflicting human desires, and less concerned with showing how people should think than he is with showing how they do think. In the *Parlement*, the focus is on the narrator as he searches unsuccessfully for a form of love that will satisfy him. In *Troilus*, the issue is made more complicated, for if the problem is still the one of choosing among the two Venuses and Jesus, the conflict is offered to us through a variety of perspectives, and in particular through the sensibilities of characters represented as complex human beings. We are not being called upon by the narrator to reject Venus and Nature, but Pandarus and Criseyde and perhaps even Troilus. One suspects that the moral drawn by the narrator at the end of *Troilus* was as problematic for Chaucer as it has been for generations of his readers; if not, how then can one explain his return to *Troilus* in the *Nun's Priest's Tale*?

His little animal fable, with its many reminiscences of the earlier tragedy, does not only offer an alternative picture of the hero. The point is not merely to suggest that if Troilus had behaved like Chauntecleer he could have shaped his destiny to something other than a tragic end. More profoundly, the object of the *Nun's Priest's Tale* is to drive home an idea that has its beginning in the *Troilus*, the idea that assuming control over one's life by finding meaning in experience will be complicated by the inevitable ambiguities that surround experience. We should like to be able to extract easy moral lessons from experience, but an exploration of its intricacies alongside the intricacies of human desire reveals how difficult that is to do.

---

[16] Donaldson, 'Patristic Exegesis in the Criticism of Medieval Literature: The Opposition', in *Critical Approaches to Medieval Literature: Selected Papers from the English Institute, 1958–1959*, ed. Dorothy Bethurum (New York, 1960), p. 150. Rpt. in Donaldson, *Speaking of Chaucer* (New York, 1972), pp. 134–53.

For readers of the *Nun's Priest's Tale*, then, there is a striking analogy between Chauntecleer's predicament and their own, for both must try to find meaning in the disorder and confusion of experience — in what they read or hear as well in what happens to them. What Chaucer presses on us is that like Chauntecleer, we are driven by animal passions that can subvert reason and that reason in any case barely is able to make sense of the confusions that assault us. Every moral that our higher sensibilities would draw is likely to be undrawn by another, unregenerate part of our being, and that perception, I would urge, is what lies behind the confusions and uncertainties that are at the heart of both *Troilus and Criseyde* and the *Nun's Priest's Tale*.

A WILL WITH A REASON:
THEOLOGICAL DEVELOPMENTS IN THE C-REVISION
OF *PIERS PLOWMAN*

BRUCE HARBERT

Early in the Vita de Dowel the dreamer learns that the human soul, Anima, lives in the castle of Flesh under the protection of Inwit (A X 1 ff.; B IX 1 ff.; C X 127ff.).[1] The scholastics tended to see the soul as composed of two parts, reason and will.[2] Inwit belongs to the reason: it is the faculty by which we know good from evil. Since Inwit is a power of the soul, it is initially surprising to find him thus distinguished from Anima, who represents the soul itself. The reason for this apparent anomaly becomes clear as the B-text proceeds and we learn that for Langland the will is a more important part of the soul than the reason, because it is with our will that we love. The central problem with which the poem is concerned is the salvation of the dreamer's soul, and for this love is more important than knowledge. The dreamer himself is called Will, and there is considerable overlap in significance between the B-text's concepts of the will and of the soul.

When Anima meets the dreamer several Passus later in B (having, by a process that Langland characteristically leaves unexplained, been turned into a man) he is little concerned with knowing but much with loving. He makes a speech on charity which, he says, can be known only through the will, and defines charity, the highest of the virtues, as *a fre liberal will* (XV 150).

In the Castle of Flesh in A and B Anima lives in the heart and Inwit in the head, an arrangement of accommodation that reflects the division of the soul into reason and will, but Anima's wider significance is recognised in that she is also called Life, and wanders all over man's body. The relationship between Inwit and Anima differs subtly between the A, B and C versions. In A (X 47) Inwit is the help that Anima desires: that is, the intellectual faculty

---

[1] References are to the edition of the A-Text by George Kane (London, 1960), that of the B-Text by George Kane and E. T. Donaldson (London, 1975) and that of the C-Text by Derek Pearsall (London, 1978).

[2] E.g. Bonaventure *Breviloquium* II 9, 7.

is at the service of the will, though necessary to it. In B (IX 59) Inwit has more authority: in accordance with his own wishes he permits Anima to indulge her likes and dislikes. In C (X 170 – 3) she is made more dependent still on Inwit, being said to live by him,[3] and her movements are more restricted: we hear no more of her wandering throughout the body, but are told simply that Inwit is in the head and Anima in the heart.

This giving of greater importance to the reason and comparatively less to the will, which is characteristic of the C-revision, is the subject of this paper. It concentrates on the Vita de Dowel, the section of the poem most concerned with man's inner life. I do not wish to suggest that C takes a position diametrically opposed to that of B. The changes between the two versions are often small and subtle, and some of C's changes merely strengthen tendencies already present in B. That C is a more 'intellectual' poem than B is already widely recognised. I hope merely to shed some light on the nature of this difference and on its relationship to other developments observable in the C-version. Langland was no professional theologian, but I do not believe his poem can be understood unless it is recognised that he had had a thorough theological education and was securely grounded in the western theological tradition, whose agenda were set for the later Middle Ages by the *Sentences* of Peter Lombard.

One well-known characteristic of C is its greater concern for theological accuracy. This probably occasioned the removal of two episodes that could be interpreted as incompatible with orthodox teaching, the tearing of the pardon (B VII 121) and the throwing by Piers of the prop representing the Son of God (B XVI 81f.). In the Banquet-scene of the fourth dream theology is shown in a bad light with the disedifying behaviour of a gluttonous doctor of divinity in both B and C (B XIII 25ff.; C XV 30ff.), but after the banquet C has altered the episode where Conscience and Patience take their leave of Clergy as they set off like pilgrims in search of greater perfection. What becomes of Clergy is not clear — this is one of the loose ends of the C-revision — but the decisive abandonment of Clergy in B, which represents a rejection of learning as useless beyond a certain stage in Christian life, no longer takes place.

Langland's characteristic reserve about the value of theological learning is expressed by Dame Study when she says, in both B and C

> Ac Teologie hath tened me ten score tymes;
> Þe more y muse þeron the mystiloker hit semeth.
>
> (B X 185f.; C XI 129f.)

---

[3] I am assuming that Anima and Life are equivalent at C X 172 in accordance with C XVI 182 and B IX 55.

In C, however, Study goes on to speak with more respect for theology than she had shown in B:

> Ac for hit lereth men to louie y bileue þeron þe bettere (C XI 133)

B had recommended many means by which love can be taught, but theology was not one of them. In the corresponding line in B all she had been able to say for theology was that it *leteþ best bi loue* (B X 190). The reputation of the teaching profession is so improved in C that a few lines later Study speaks of love itself as a doctor, the teacher of Dobet and Dobest, where in B she had merely said that Dobet and Dobest were of love's kin. By thus bringing love and learning into a closer relationship, Study sets in a new context the final piece of advice the dreamer receives at the very end of the poem, 'Learn to love' (B XX 208; C XXII 208). When we come to the end of reading B we have been made aware of various ways in which love may be learnt, Patient Poverty being the chief, but learning, in the sense of academic study, has been allotted a very insignificant place among them. C is more ready to acknowledge that scholarly learning can be part of learning to love.

Not all Christians are scholars, but the reason has a role in the life of every Christian to the extent that Christianity involves belief, an assent to propositions grasped by the reason. This too is given a higher value in C. Where Holy Church has reminded the dreamer of his duty to love her all his life, in C he is urged to love her and believe in her as well (B I 78; C I 75). Mary Magdalen was said by B to have lived in the desert by meditation and keeping God in mind (B XV 295), but C says that *loue and lele byleue* held her life and soul together (C XVII 22). C says (XIX 189) that *loue and bileue* must blow to awaken the fire of the Holy Spirit, whereas B only says that *lele loue* is necessary (B XVII 228). *Sothfaste bileue* is even given as the name of the Holy Spirit (C XVIII 51). There are also places where C introduces a mention of love that had not been there in B (X 79; 91; 269): the point is not that C emphasises belief at the expense of love, but that it seeks to hold them in balance.

The relative claims of love and belief are pondered on by the dreamer after his meeting with Faith and Hope (B XVI 172ff.; C XVIII 182ff.). In B Faith was concerned with belief, explaining the Trinity, and Hope with love, handing on the ten commandments. The dreamer in B was more attracted by what he heard from Faith, saying that belief in the Trinity is easier than love and generosity (B XVII 44ff.). The Good Samaritan replied that he should both set fast his faith after Abraham and love as he was bidden by hope. C does not separate love and belief in this way. C's dreamer says it is easy both to love and believe in one Lord, and that it is only when three persons are involved that both belief and love become difficult (XIX 40ff.). Hope is said not merely to have bidden him to love but to have taught him as well (XIX 98ff.), love and teaching being brought closer together again. The Good Samaritan instructs him both to love and to believe as Abraham has taught (XIX 107f.).[4]

The bond between love and belief had been indicated by Langland as early as the A-text in his use of the words truth and true. It is beyond the scope both of this paper and of my own competence to investigate fully the many senses of this word in *Piers Plowman*, let alone in ME as a whole. They originally denoted the moral quality of loyalty or trustworthiness, and are used frequently in this sense in all the versions of *Piers Plowman*. In the fourteenth century new senses developed profusely denoting objective factual reality, the truth that is grasped by the reason. That Langland was aware of the development of such new 'cognitive' senses during his own lifetime is indicated by his introduction of truth and true in such senses into C at points where they had not been so used in B (e.g. C XI 277; XII 232; XVII 5; XVII 15).

These new senses seem to have presented Langland with a problem when he revised the sections of the third dream concerned with the emperor Trajan (B XI 140ff.; C XII 73ff.). When Trajan appears in B he claims to have been saved *By loue and by lernyng of my lyuynge in truþe*, but in C this changed to *Loue withoute lele bileue* (C XII 85). Similarly, C removes B's assertion that Trajan was saved for his *pure truþe* (B XI 156), although allowing him to call himself a true knight (B XI 141; C XII 74), and speaking like B of Trajan's truth (B XI 157; C XII 89). That is, C only credits Trajan with truth in a limited sense: he was trustworthy, and he was a genuine knight, but his religious beliefs were not true. At the end of the third dream (B XII 283ff.; C XIV 205ff.), Imaginatif recalls Trajan's appearance, acknowledges (in both B and C) that he was a true knight, and then ends his speech with a passage in praise of Truth in man, for which man can hope to be rewarded by God. C has a new ending, which explains that the reward of Truth is

> . . . loue and large huyre if þe lord be trewe,
> And a cortesye more þen couenant was . . .   (C XIV 215f.)

Langland here seems to be avoiding any implication that Trajan's truth in the very limited sense in which he can be said to have possessed it established a right to divine reward, and to be implying instead that it is God's truth, his fidelity to the generosity of his nature, that has saved Trajan by a courtesy that transcends the strict demands of the covenant from which Trajan, not being a Jew, was excluded, for all comes about as God wills and not, we are to understand, as man deserves. To sum up, Langland appears to fear lest in crediting Trajan with truth he be thought to imply that Trajan's

---

[4] Cf. C XI 142ff.

religious beliefs were true; he shows in C a new reluctance to attribute the name or the reward of truth to a life that does not include Christian belief. The semantic development of *truth* also created problems for him when revising Holy Church's speech in Passus I. Already in A (I 131f.) she had spoken of truth as a form of knowledge that operates in the heart (not the head) and teaches a person to love: truth straddles the division between reason and will. B reinforces this with a piece of wordplay which C retains: in the heart is *þe hed and þe heye welle* of love (B I 164; C I 160). But Langland may have felt that, as the cognitive connotations of truth became stronger, the moral ones were weakening, for twice where B has the line which acts as a refrain in Holy Church's speech, *Whenne alle tresores ben tried, treuthe is þe beste*, C introduces a mention of love as well: *Loue hit*, she cries when she has been speaking of truth, *lette may y no lengore / To lere the what loue is* (C I 203f.), and *Than treuthe and trewe loue is no tresor bettre* (C I 135). C's new phrase will be heard again much later in the poem when the dreamer asks Liberum Arbitrium the name of the tree that grows in the country of man's heart and receives the reply that the tree is called True Love (C XVIII 9).

Some of the changes we have been considering are minute, but taken together and with other changes that we shall consider soon they make up a pattern that indicates that between writing the B and the C text Langland had moved away from a voluntarist view of the soul towards an intellectualist one. The classic exponents of these two views are Saint Bonaventure and Saint Thomas Aquinas respectively, and it is interesting to note that when Bonaventure and Aquinas appear in Dante's *Paradiso* each opens his speech with a mention of love, but for Bonaventure it is love pure and simple, *l'amor che mi fa bella* (XII 31), while Thomas speaks of True Love, enkindled by grace, *lo raggio della grazia, onde s'accende / verace amore* (X 81f.).

The difference between these two saints is not simply a difference between two schools of academic theology but between two religious mentalities, between the exuberant spirit of the poetry of Saint Francis and the lyricists inspired by his order, many of whom composed in Middle English, and the more sober, restrained temper of the eucharistic hymns of Thomas Aquinas or of the paintings of Fra Angelico. We can be assisted in understanding the religious mentality of the C-text by a fourteenth-century English author who has much in common with it, Walter Hilton. Although Hilton was an Augustinian canon, and Augustine was the fountain of voluntarist inspiration, Hilton himself is no voluntarist, but an eclectic thinker: among authorities on religious life he gives a high place to Aquinas.[5] Hilton was concerned lest people who read the accounts of

---

[5] See J. P. H. Clark, 'Walter Hilton in defence of the religious life and the veneration of images', *Downside Review* 103 (1985) 1 – 25.

154   *Religion in the Poetry and Drama of the Late Middle Ages*

mystical experience found in writings such as those of Richard Rolle might be led into seeking such experiences for their own sake, and he wrote his treaties *Of Angel's Song* to warn of this danger, He warns his reader:

> For wit thou well that a naked mind or a naked imagination of Jesu or of any ghostly thing, without sweetness of love in affection, or without light of knowing in reason, it is but a blindness and a way to deceit, if a man hold it in his own sight more than it is. For I hold it sekyr that he be meek in his own feeling and hold his mind in regard nought till he may by custom and using of his mind feel the fire of love in his affection and the light of knowing in his reason.[6]

We see here the balance between reason and will that we have found in the C-text, but also a value attached to feeling which is alien to Langland and which Hilton himself was also later to modify. In the treatise on *Mixed Life* he offers consolation to those who cannot feel affection in their devotions:

> . . . me thinketh hit is good to the that when thou disposest the for to thenke on god . . . yif thin herte be dul and merk and thou felest nouthur wit ne sauour ne deuocion for to god, but thou can nought: but than I hope that hit is good to the that thou strive not ouver-muche with thiself, as yif thou woulde be thin owne might overcome thiself, for thou might lightly so falle in to more merknes, but yif thou were sleih in thi worchynge.[7]

By the time he came to write the second book of the *Scale of Perfection*, Hilton had developed a more systematic presentation of his views. That book is largely concerned with his teaching that reformation in faith precedes reformation in feeling, and reformation in faith by itself is sufficient for salvation. It takes the text from the Song of Songs *nigra sum sed formosa* (I 5) to show how a soul can be simultaneously both fair and foul, which should not be a cause for discouragement:

> ffoul withouten as it were a best ffayre with inne lyke to an aungel ffoul in felynge of the sensuality ffayr in trowþe of the resoun ffoul for þe fleschly appetyte ffayr for þe good wille þus fayre & þus foul is a chosen soule . . .
> *(Scale* II 12)[8]

Hilton compares the soul that is granted knowledge of God with the soul that is not:

> ffor þis soule knoweþ sum what of þe kynde of ihu god þurgh þis gratyous sy3t, bot þat oþer knoweþ it not, bot only troweþ that þis is soth.
> *(Scale* II 32)

[6] Ed. C. Horstman, *Yorkshire Writers* (London, 1895), p. 182.
[7] Ed. C. Horstman, *ibid.*, p. 289.
[8] Quotations from the *Scale* are taken from MS London British Library Harley 2387.

and yet this mere trowing is, he goes on to assure us, enough for salvation. At one point, having spoken of love, he takes care to assure the reader that he is not giving love undue prominence:

> lufe comith oute of knowynge and not knowynge oute of luf, therfor it is seid that knowing and insight principally of God with lufe is the blis of a soule, and the more he is knowen the better is he lufed. Bot for as mikel as to this knowynge or to this luf that comith of it may not the soule come withoute luf, ther-fore seide I that thu schuldest only coueite luf . . .   (*Scale* II 34)

Langland never recommends an over-enthusiastic religiosity of the kind against which Hilton warns, but it may be that he had had experience of the teaching of the B-text being unwisely applied. Rash attempts to imitate Piers could be as harmful as rash attempts to imitate Rolle, and the world needs its active ploughmen. In B, love had been the paramount virtue: Augustine's formula for Christian life, *ama et quod vis fac*, could be said to sum up the message of the B-text. Langland writes in C as though he has found this formula insufficient for a balanced view, and that love can be recommended only with qualifications. *Leute* and its corresponding adjective *leel* are often coupled with *love*: they are close in meaning to the moral senses of *truth* and *true*, and their increased use in C may be due to a feeling on Langland's part that *truth* and *true* no longer conveyed these senses satisfactorily.

Where Patience in B had said that Piers Plowman has set all sciences at a sop save love alone (B XIII 125), in C she says that he has impugned all knowledge and skill save *loue and leute and lowenesse of herte*, and proved imperfect all things except *lele loue and treuthe* (C XV 130ff.). *Bileue, leute and loue*, says Clergy, make men Dowel Dobet and Dobest (C XI 161f.); the purpose of Christ's coming to earth, says the Devil, was *to lere men to be lele and vch man to louye oper* (C XX 338; cf. B XVIII 306). The dreamer is urged to begin the life that is *louable and leele to thy soule* (C V 103), and the lark with its beautiful voice, sweet taste and swift flight is compared to Christians who are *lele and lyf-holy pat louyeth alle treuthe* (C XIV 188). Another frequent companion of love in C is law: *Ho-so lyueth in lawe and in loue doth wel* (C X 202).

As we have seen already in the Castle of Flesh, this reduction in the relative importance of love is matched by a demotion of the will. Some passages where B had stressed the dignity of the will are altered. Where in B Charity had been said to be known not through words and works but through will alone, C does not mention the will, but says Charity might be discovered through works, and omits a reference to Piers Plowman seeing more deeply than works and works to the will (B XV 209ff.; C XVI 338f.). The definition of Charity as a *fre liberal wille* (B XV 150) is removed. Several lines are omitted towards the end of the banquet scene where Conscience speaks about the will, including his assertion that there is no treasure to compare to a true will (B XIII 193). The balance between will and reason is observed also in the teaching on the Trinity offered in Passus XVIII of C, where the three persons are twice said to be of one wit and one will (28; 190).

One of the most important changes Langland made in writing the C-text was the introduction of a new character, Liberum Arbitrium, who replaces both Anima and Piers in his appearance at the Tree of Charity. According to the classic definition of Peter Lombard,[9] Liberum Arbitrium is a *facultas rationis et voluntatis*, a title that Liberum Arbitrium translates in the poem when he calls himself *a will with a resoun* (C XVI 176). His speech continues the pattern of balancing reason and will that we have been observing elsewhere in the poem.

Before we consider his speech, however, one problem must be considered. When explaining his names, Liberum Arbitrium says *when y wol do or do nat gode dedes or ille / Thenne am y Liberum Arbitrium* (C XVI 192f.). This could be taken to mean 'when I will do good deeds or will not do evil ones . . .' in which case it is in accord with the Latin definition Liberum Arbitrium gives a few lines later, *dum declinat de malo ad bonum, Liberum Arbitrium est* — when it inclines away from evil towards good it, that is, the soul, is called Liberum Arbitrium. But the more natural interpretation of the English words is 'when I will or will not do good deeds or ill . . .', that is, Liberum Arbitrium does not incline towards the good, but is able to choose either good or evil.

According to Saint Bernard, there are three kinds of Liberum Arbitrium in man: (i) a natural freedom of the will which is never lost and is always free to choose good or evil, called in Latin *libertas naturae*, (ii) the freedom given to the will by God's grace which frees it from its attraction to evil and helps it choose good, *libertas gratiae*, and (iii) a total freedom from inclination towards evil which renders the soul incapable of sin, *libertas gloriae*, which is found only after death in the souls of the redeemed.[10]

Langland's Latin definition of Liberum Arbitrium as inclining towards good corresponds to *libertas gratiae*, but his English definition (according to the more natural interpretation) corresponds to *libertas naturae*. It is highly probable that this discrepancy is deliberate: it certainly corresponds to experience. Though a person with the help of divine grace may incline more and more towards good and away from evil, he never reaches before death a state when he is unable to sin. The pattern of most human lives is a mottled one, with virtue predominating at some times and mediocrity or even vice at others. On this showing, Liberum Arbitrium is, like Meed and Recklessness earlier in the poem, an authority of uncertain value. As

---

[9] *Sentences* II d. 24 c.3.
[10] *De Gratia et Libero Arbitrio* III.

Conscience had said to the King in the B-text 'Ther are two manere of Medes' (B III 231), we might now say that there are two kinds of Liberum Arbitrium.

The dreamer reacts to the ambivalent status of Liberum Arbitrium when, on hearing that Liberum Arbitrium cannot be without a body, he takes him to be inferior to the body and ceases to address him with the respectful plural *ʒe*, adopting the familiar, and in this case even contemptuous *thou*, like Chauntecleer, who calls the fox *ye* while trapped in his mouth, but *thou* once he has escaped and is looking down on him from a tree.[11] When Liberum Arbitrium has explained his nature more fully the dreamer returns to the respectful form, but jokingly: *'ʒe beth as a bischop!' quod y, al bourdynge þat tyme* (C XVI 201) and from then on treats him with a friendly respect, calling him at one point *chere frende* (C XVII 125), while Liberum Arbitrium calls him *thou*, implying superior authority. The rest of Liberum Arbitrium's speech and actions show him to have been established as an authoritative figure, which implies that, assisted by divine grace, he is *libertas gratiae*. The statement that Liberum Arbitrium cannot be without a body perhaps means that we are concerned only with Liberum Arbitrium in this life, not with *libertas gloriae* which, being unable to sin, is free from the ambiguities of terrestrial existence.

Early in his speech Liberum Arbitrium, like B's Anima, rebukes the dreamer for being too hungry for knowledge. However, it soon becomes apparent that he is not so unsympathetic to learning as B's Anima had been. Langland alters an attack on the preaching of friars, which in B had been said to lead astray the unlearned (B XV 72), to say that it causes *bothe lewed and lered* to doubt their belief (C XVI 232). The implication is that only some of the learned are being attacked as corrupt, if others of them are being corrupted. Liberum Arbitrium soon takes it upon himself to warn both learned and lewd of the abuses of avaricious clerks (279ff.) and to include both clerks and lewd among those guilty of covetousness (290ff.). This is to say that Liberum Arbitrium is less inclined than B's Anima had been to see society as divided into the vicious learned and the virtuous lewd: intellectual activity can be good. When speaking of Charity, C adds preaching to the other good works that he does for prisoners (323) and commends those who *lelelyche lyuen and louen and byleuon* (356) with the now familiar collocation of love, *leute* and *bileue* newly introduced.

When speaking of love, Liberum Arbitrium explains that the love he means is not any kind of love: Jews, Saracens, lechers and thieves all love in a sense, but the love he has in mind is that which arises from law and is directed towards God, a person's enemies and his own soul (C XVII 132ff.). The rest of Liberum Arbitrium's speech is chiefly concerned with

[11] Chaucer, *Nun's Priest's Tale* 639ff.

the problems posed by Saracens, whose love is genuine and does proceed from a law, but only *lawe of kynde* (152), natural law rather than the law revealed by God. Liberum Arbitrium expresses a desire that Saracens and Jews be converted to Christian belief, but in a gentler tone than in the corresponding passage in B (XV 459ff.), where Anima had attacked both the heathen, comparing them to wild beasts, and contemporary preachers whose lax lives prevent their work from having any effect. Liberum Arbitrium introduces a more positive note, looking in particular to the Pope to bring all lands into love through his prayers and his patience. Belief and love together are seen as the key to a harmonious society.

A similarly hopeful vision had been offered by Conscience in Passus III 343ff. of a society sharing a common belief and united in law, love and loyalty, the commons and the king standing in right relation to one another and all men in right relation to God. Belief in holy church is one element in this right relation, and Conscience looks forward to the day when the Saracens will sing *credo in spiritum sanctum* — in B their song had been merely *gloria in excelsis Deo*, which can be sung without Christian faith.

Liberum Arbitrium says (C XVII 119) that faith alone suffices to save Christians, thus echoing and confirming the view put forward earlier in the mouth of Recklessness that the poor are bound only to love and believe as the law teaches (XIII 86) and dispensed from the fasts and penances binding on other Christians. By insisting in C less on the limitless demands of love and more on a mere faithfulness in belief that is all that is within the grasp of some people, Langland, like Hilton, is putting forward a religious ideal that is more, not less, generous. What he has lost in loftiness of ideals he has gained in breadth of compassion.

If Langland does not set his sights as high in C as in B, it may be objected that he does not set his sights high enough. The autobiographical passage in Passus V, new to C, suggests that Langland himself was aware of the dangers of too lax a life. Later, in a passage common to B and C the dreamer is troubled by the question of whether or not he is predestined to salvation (B XI 115ff.; C XII 48ff.). He is inclined to the view that his baptism guarantees his salvation, and Scripture encourages him to believe what the theology books teach, that whatever his sins they cannot impede God's mercy. But then Trajan breaks into the scene with contempt for books, one who was saved without baptism or repentance (C XII 73). He is followed (87ff.) by Recklessness, an aspect of the dreamer's own character, who shares Trajan's contempt for learning. The effect of this confusing sequence is to leave the reader wondering whether there is anything that can assure salvation, and whether recklessness might not be the appropriate response to the inscrutability of God's ways.

Antinomianism is always a danger within Christianity, and in Langland's own time was found among the Brethren of the Free Spirit, whose abuses may be alluded to in the writings of Rolle and Hilton and the *Cloud*.[12] The Lollards too were showing disrespect for the ordinary patterns of Christian life. Augustine himself had been accused of antinomian tendencies towards the end of his life by some monks who objected to his teaching on grace on the ground that if salvation is entirely due to grace, any efforts proceeding from human free will, including the rigours of monastic life, must be useless. Augustine's reply in *De Libero Arbitrio* is a classic treatment of the problem. He maintained that grace does not destroy the freedom of the will, and that there remains a role to be played by free will in cooperation with grace in bringing about a man's salvation, even though we cannot see how they can coexist. Langland is within theological tradition, then, in introducing Liberum Arbitrium into a debate about the means of salvation. Liberum Arbitrium confirms the minimalist suggestion of Recklessness that faith alone suffices, but goes on to sketch his higher ideal of a society united in faith and love.

When in the next Passus we see Liberum Arbitrium standing beside the tree of True Love (C XVIII 8ff.), we are surely invited to see a comparison with Adam beside the forbidden tree in the garden of Eden. It was Adam's free will, his *libertas naturae*, that enabled him to choose evil and so introduce sin into the world, and a reformed free will in man, assisted by grace, that can undo this disaster. Liberum Arbitrium's active behaviour beside the tree shows that he is not passive under the influence of divine grace but, in accordance with Augustine's teaching, truly cooperant with it as he wields the props representing the persons of the Trinity (25ff.). This is of a piece with the revaluation of the active life earlier in the poem: if B had tended towards quietism, suggesting that patient poverty is enough, C moves away from that position and attributes greater value to human action, although ultimately it is divine action that matters, as we see when the poem's focus shifts away from Liberum Arbitrium toward Libera Voluntas Dei in preparation for the Incarnation (118ff.).

A positive assessment of the active life is also implied in the sympathetic presentation of the three characters who excuse themselves from taking part in the pilgrimage to Truth in the Visio because one has bought a house, one must plough with his oxen and one, named Actif, has married a jealous wife (C VII 292ff.). They offer their excuses in respectful language, and are not criticised for not joining the pilgrimage. Contemplation ends the Passus by expressing determination to follow Piers to Truth despite the difficulties: the implication is that not all are called to contemplation.

Piers himself does not reject the active life after learning the text of Truth's pardon as he had done in B VII 119ff.: his resolve to be no more

---

[12] See J. P. H. Clark, 'Walter Hilton and "Liberty of Spirit" ', *Downside Review* 96 (1978) 61 – 78.

busy about his belly-joy and to make prayer and penance his plough is omitted. Haukyn the sinful wafer-seller, whose appearance in B XIII had been a revelation of the sins that beset the active life, is removed and replaced in C XV 190ff. by Activa Vita or Actif, whom we may be intended to recognise as one of those who had earlier excused themselves from the pilgrimage to Truth, and who again is not presented as sinful but as a provider of bread and pleasure for rich and for poor: so respectable is he that he is closely associated with Liberum Arbitrium, one of the poem's highest authorities, who is introduced as Actif's leader (C XVI 157).

A sense of the solidarity and interdependence of all members of society is one of the marks of the C-text. It informs the passage on the plight of the poor in Passus IX 70ff., one of the best known and loved of the C-additions, which reminds us that those that most need are our neighbours. It is also to be found in the prayer of Patience for the poor at the beginning of Passus XVI (17ff.) which, though shorter than its counterpart in B, is no less compassionate. Where Patience in B had prayed that Christ would comfort the careful in his kingdom after their death (B XIV 165; 179), in C he prays that God will send them summer sometime, implying that he hopes for relief from their plight in this world (C XVI 17). In B Patience had gone on to speak of baptism as the way to God's kingdom, with confession as a remedy for those who sin after baptism (B XIV 186ff.), but in C he dwells on the need for all alike to repent, *lewed and lered, hey and lowe* (C XVI 34). C has a stronger sense here that society can be improved, that there is hope for the poor if all will accept their responsibilities.

Langland's hopes for the unity of mankind through love and belief are expressed by Liberum Arbitrium in passage new to C where he is asked by the dreamer 'what is Holy church?' and replies:

> 'Charite,' he saide;
> Lief and loue and leutee in o byleue and lawe,
> A loue-knotte of leutee and of lele byleue,
> Alle kyne cristene cleuynge on o will,
> Withoute gyle and gabbyng gyue and sulle and lene.
> (C XVII 125 – 9)

These lines bring together many of the key concepts of the C-revision. The values of the B-text had been those of the spiritual élite, who withdraw from ordinary life in search of the love of God. In making the C-revision Langland was moving towards making *Piers Plowman* more a poem of the common man. It is also becoming a happier poem: the sounds of laughter and song are heard more often in C, and new imagery is introduced from an idealised, almost pastoral view of the countryside that relieves the ennui of city life evoked elsewhere.[13] Langland's sympathies have become more inclusive, his idealism less headstrong: the C-text is the work of a maturer mind, of one who has made some progress in response to his own poem's final command, 'learn to love'.

[13] C XV 200; XVI 300; XVIII 3 (laughter); XIII 16; XIII 58; XIV 185 (song); III 380; XIII 32ff.; XIII 178ff. (countryside).

'LUNATYK LOLLARES' IN *PIERS PLOWMAN*

DEREK PEARSALL

And ȝut ar ther oþere beggares, in hele, as hit semeth,
Ac hem wanteth wyt, men and women bothe,
The whiche aren lunatyk lollares and lepares aboute,
And madden as þe mone sit, more other lasse.
Careth they for no colde ne counteth of non hete
And aren meuynge aftur þe mone; moneyeles þey walke,
With a good will, witteles, mony wyde contreyes,
Riht as Peter dede and Poul, saue þat þey preche nat
Ne none muracles maken — ac many tymes hem happeth
To profecye of þe peple, pleyinge, as hit were.
And to oure syhte, as hit semeth, seth god hath þe myhte
To ȝeue vch a wyht wyt, welthe, and his hele,
And suffreth suche go so, it semeth, to myn inwyt,
Hit aren as his postles, suche peple, or as his priue disciples.
For a sent hem forth seluerles in a somur garnement
Withoute bagge and bred, as þe book telleth:
  Quando misi vos sine pane et pera.
Barfoot and bredles, beggeth they of no man.
And thauh a mete with the mayre ameddes þe strete,
A reuerenseth hym ryht nauht, no rather then another.
  Neminem salutaueritis per viam.
Suche manere men, Matheu vs techeth.
We sholde haue hem to house and helpe hem when they come.
  Et egenos vagosque induc in domum tuam.
For hit aren merye-mouthed men, munstrals of heuene,
And godes boys, bourdyors, as the book telleth.
  Si quis videtur sapiens, fiet stultus vt sit sapiens.
  And alle manere munstrals, me woet wel þe sothe,
To vnderfongen hem fayre byfalleth for þe ryche,
For þe lordes loue or þe ladyes þat they with longen.
Me suffreth al þat suche sayen and in solace taketh,
And ȝut more to suche men me doth ar they passe;
Men gyueth hem giftes and gold for grete lordes sake.

163

Ryht so, ʒe ryche, ʒut rather ʒe sholde
Welcomen and worshipen and with ʒoure goed helpen
Godes munstrals and his mesagers and his mery bordiours,
The whiche arn lunatyk loreles and lepares aboute,
For vnder godes secret seal here synnes ben keuered.
For they bereth none bagges ne boteles vnder clokes,
The whiche is lollarne lyf and lewede ermytes . . .
                                    (*Piers Plowman*, C IX 105 – 40)[1]

In Passus IX of the C-text of *Piers Plowman*, after the apparent failure of
Piers' plan to put the world to work before leading it out on the pilgrimage
to Truth, Truth sends Piers a pardon. The terms of this pardon are specified
in relation to the different estates of society — kings and knights, bishops,
merchants, lawyers, labourers — and some particular attention is given to
beggars. Their place in the scheme of salvation seems, at first, quite clear:

Beggares and biddares beth nat in þat bulle
Bote the sugestioun be soth that shapeth hym to begge.   (C IX 61 – 2)

But determining whether the 'sugestioun' be 'soth' is as always for
Langland a difficult and painful and even harrowing problem.

He had made an approach to the problem, from a socio-economic point of
view, in the ploughing-scene of C VIII, where Piers asks Hunger,

Of beggares and biddares what beste be to done?   (C VIII 210)

Langland echoes here an acute contemporary preoccupation with the
problem of beggars, and of able-bodied beggars in particular. A petition
was presented to the Commons in 1376 which speaks of the itinerant
labourers who drift into beggary as motivated not by need but by a desire to
lead idle lives: they are able-bodied and could well serve the common good
through their labour if they wanted so to serve.[2] Many of them become
criminal vagrants, says the petition, which concludes that the problem can
only be solved by putting them all in prison. The cruel and impractical
stupidity of this kind of solution is one of the things that prompts Langland
to investigate the problem more closely, and he has Piers express the
dilemma in which the thoughtful members of a Christian community —
indeed, of any community — find themselves. On the one hand there is the
clear injunction of the Gospels, of Christ's words in the Sermon on the

---

[1] Reference throughout is to *Piers Plowman by William Langland: An Edition of the C-text*,
by Derek Pearsall, York Medieval Texts, second series (London, 1978). The B-text is
quoted from William Langland, *The Vision of Piers Plowman: A Complete Edition of the B-
Text*, ed. A. V. C. Schmidt, Everyman's Library (London, 1978).

[2] The petition is printed in the *Rotuli Parliamentorum* (6 vols., London, 1783), vol. II, p.
340. There is a translation in *The Peasants' Revolt of 1381*, ed. R. B. Dobson (London,
1970), pp. 72 – 4.

Mount: 'Give to every man that asketh of thee' (Luke 6:30), reiterated and strengthened in the first Epistle of John 3:17:

> But whoso hath this world's good, and seeth his brother have need, and shutteth up his bowels of compassion from him, how dwelleth the love of God in him?

Piers rephrases this in his own terms:

> . . . hit are my blody bretherne, for god bouhte vs alle.
> Treuthe tauhte me ones to louye hem vchone
> And to helpe hem of alle thynges ay as hem nedeth. (C VIII 217 – 19)

Any questions as to who is worthy to have are to be left to God, whilst the individual Christian answers this imperative of compassion. On the other hand there is the equally clear biblical exhortation to labour, 'If any would not work, neither should he eat' (2 Thess 3:10), which of course has the advantage of being in accord with the demands of economic realism.

The traditional pattern of personal almsgiving and of organised welfare provision by religious and civic authorities had in the past fitted in with the general exhortation to charity, but the growth of a larger, more unruly, more conspicuous class of poor people in the 13th and 14th centuries, as a result of agricultural depression, movement to the towns, itinerancy, and the loosening of the traditional structures of charity, increased the pressure to make discrimination in charity.[3] The acceleration of these changes, after the bad harvests of 1315 – 17 and again after the Black Death, exacerbated the problem, especially in creating a new class of the chronic urban poor, more prominent and more visible, more of a threat to what was perceived as the traditional order of society, as well as more importunate in its demands upon that society's compassion. Problems that had always existed were now, therefore, becoming more acute, and Langland, as always, shows himself keenly aware of them. The answer to his question that Piers gets from Hunger argues for a form of discrimination. Hunger says that Piers, as manager of the economy (or, as we should say, the state), has an obligation to ensure that no-one should starve, though no responsibility to maintain life

---

[3] The fullest treatment of these changes in the nature and perception of poverty is given, mostly from continental sources, by Michel Mollat, in his general study, *Les Pauvres au Moyen Age: Etude Sociale* (Paris, 1978), and in the collaborative volume of essays by his followers and pupils, *Etudes sur l'Histoire de la Pauvreté*, ed. M. Mollat, Publications de la Sorbonne, Etudes 8, 2 vols. (Paris, 1974). For a wider survey, see Catharina Lis and Hugo Soly, *Poverty and Capitalism in Pre-Industrial Europe* (Brighton, 1979). For discussion of poverty as a theme in *Piers Plowman*, see David Aers, '*Piers Plowman* and Problems in the Perception of Poverty: A Culture in Transition', in *Leeds Studies in English*, new series 14: Essays in Memory of Elizabeth Salter (1983) 5 – 25; Geoffrey Shepherd, 'Poverty in *Piers Plowman*', in *Social Relations and Ideas: Essays in Honour of R. H. Hilton*, ed. T. H. Aston, P. R. Coss, Christopher Dyer, Joan Thirsk (Cambridge, 1983), pp. 169 – 89.

beyond the meanest level. The similarity between Hunger's recommenda-
tions and the criteria established for poor relief in the Elizabethan Poor Law
cannot help but come to mind, though we must remember too that it is
Hunger who is speaking, and he is spokesman for a limited kind of
economic pragmatism: Piers himself, and presumably Langland too, are
more inclined to accept the traditional obligation to general charity.

Langland returns to these questions in the pardon-passus, expanding on
the treatment of beggary in B with a long interpolation in C, a powerful and
prolonged meditation upon the opposed injunctions of the Gospels and of
texts like Cato (*Cui des videto*) in relation to almsgiving. Langland had
spoken earlier, through Hunger, of discrimination in charity. He now
admits, in this new and more urgent context, which concerns salvation —
are beggars to be saved? — rather than programmes of social security and
welfare provision, that the criteria for discrimination are not easy to define:

> Woet no man, as y wene, who is worthy to haue.   (C IX 70)

What man can see, if he pays attention, is a need among our neighbours that
urges charity, and in a remarkable passage (IX 70 – 97) Langland turns
aside from the traditional 'safe' deserving poor — the old, the sick, the
lame, widows, lepers — to the new class of what I have called the chronic
urban poor, and describes in precise and minute detail the lives of those who
are employed in the most menial part-time and piece-work jobs — scraping
flax, peeling rushes, carding and combing, patching and washing clothes —
and who, though employed, can barely scrape together a living. This is a
new phenomenon, a class of poor people who are in employment, especially
in the textile industries, but who nevertheless live below the poverty line,
exploited on the one hand by their employers and on the other hand by those
retailers who 'han no pite on the peple þat parselmele mot begge' (C III 86),
who take advantage, that is, of those who have to buy in small quantities to
take a proportionately greater profit, and who have no scruples about giving
such customers short measure, short weight, and goods of poor quality.

Langland introduces his meditation on these, the 'new poor', as follows:

> Ac þat most neden aren oure neyhebores, and we nyme gode hede,
> As prisones in puttes and pore folk in cotes,
> Charged with childrene and chief lordes rente.   (C IX 71 – 3)

The association of prisoners in pits — one of the seven groups of recipients
of the traditional works of corporal mercy — with the poor folk is something
more than fortuitous, given that the new poor are in a way the prisoners of
the new money economy, with none of the access to the forms of mitigation
and relief offered in the old world of contractual and charitable obligation.
Langland shows signs in this important passage of slipping at times into a
more comfortable mode of perception in which this new poor can be

identified with the 'safe' traditional deserving class of widows (83, but cf. 84), as well as with prisoners and 'crokede men and blynde' (C IX 97), but this does not subtract much from the extraordinary keenness of response to social distress — a response which is in conflict with traditional orthodoxies of belief to which Langland was equally passionately committed. What seems to come out of this conflict is an assertion of love of one's neighbour — notice how neighbours, our view of them (71), their view of us (87), frame the passage — and of how charity, so far from seeking to discriminate between those who beg, must positively seek out the truly needy in order to fulfil the promise that God will provide whilst maintaining the ban on beggary. Those who have must give so that those who have not need not ask.

Characteristically, as Langland's meditation on poverty and begging continues, this deep compassion, with all its minute observation of the indignities to which poor people are subject, gives way to anger, as Langland thinks again about professional beggars — 'beggares with bagges, þe whiche brewhous ben here churches' (98) — and the way they defraud the truly needy as well as the giver. For such 'lollares' he wishes nothing other than that they should starve to death, unless they are blind or maimed or sick. The idea of professional beggars is to Langland an offence against God and the Church, as well as a hateful act of self-degradation. Later he will describe how such professional beggars break the limbs of their children so as to make them more effective instruments to beg with. Langland is particularly incensed by the idea of beggars with bags, that is, beggars who ask for more than they need for the moment. It is worth recalling that the debate about mendicant poverty had as a particular target of abuse the friars who went about with bags: they were identified with Judas, who 'was a thief and had the bag' (John 12:6).[4] It is worth recalling too how careful the dreamer is in C V to remind Reason and Conscience, his interrogators, that although he goes around begging for food he asks for no more than the needs of the moment:

> . . . on this wyse y begge
> Withoute bagge or botel but my wombe one.   (C V 51 – 2)

What it was that prompted Langland to move from the condemnation of beggary to the rhapsodic celebration of the 'lunatyk lollares and lepares aboute' (C IX 107) which is the subject of the present paper, and quoted in full at the head of it, I am not sure. One impulse is the ruminative rather than dialectic habit of mind which leads him constantly to chew over things, to return to matters that he might be thought to have treated already — here picking up the word 'lollares', and recognising that not all the able-bodied

---

[4] See M. D. Lambert, *Franciscan Poverty* (London, 1961), p. 63.

who do not win their food are to be condemned. There is also the way in
which, in this process of rumination, questions that seemed to be related to
the practical and economic life of society turn out to be questions to do with
the spiritual life of the individual.[5] Langland is anticipating that later
development in the poem in which material poverty will be transcended in
spiritual poverty, in which the voluntary and patient acceptance of poverty
will make of it an instrument of spiritual purification: the difference is
analogous to that between the version of the first beatitude in Luke 6:20
('Blessed are the poor') and that in Matthew 5:3 ('Blessed are the poor in
spirit'). The 'lunatyk lollares' are the heralds of this spiritual metamorpho-
sis.

But I think what chiefly gave him the suggestion was a desire to find the
most striking and dramatic contrast he could find to professional beggary, to
what might be called mendicant exploitation, extraction of the charitable
surplus. He found it in evoking a picture of those beggars who are able-
bodied but feeble-minded, who wander the countryside, careless of weather
or raiment or food or money, literally lunatic in that their state of mind is
affected by the phases of the moon (110). Since they are God's creatures and
exist by his will, they must be serving God's purposes (115): they are in fact
his secret apostles (118), capable of uttering hidden wisdom in their
foolishness (114). Above all, they are the exemplars of a truly spiritual
beggary, as Langland concludes:

> For they bereth none bagges ne boteles vnder clokes.   (139)

They have that divine carelessness of the world which truly manifests the
faith that God will provide.

But it is not only the debate about beggary and poverty that is transformed
in the picture of these men and women. They act also, through a powerful
series of contrasts and paradoxes, as the agents of a new and unworldly
spirituality in Langland's vision of the life of society. An important
influence here is the association with the biblical texts in which Christ
recommends that the disciples should go forth with neither bread nor bag,
nor money, nor more than one coat (Luke 9:3), with no concern for the
morrow (cf. Luke 12:22) and no concern for those niceties of behaviour
(*Neminem salutaueritis* . . .) that mark a man as of the world (Luke 10:4).
The disciples are to be the exemplars of that love of God and desire for
perfection which goes beyond the commandments of the law and answers
the demand that Christ made of the young man:

---

[5] As R. H. Tawney puts it, 'The distinctive feature of medieval thought is that contrasts which
later were to be presented as irreconcilable antitheses appear in it as differences within a
larger unity, and that the world of social organization, originating in physical necessities,
passes by insensible gradations into that of the spirit' (*Religion and the Rise of Capitalism*,
New York, 1926, p. 20).

Go and sell that thou hast, and give to the poor . . . and come and follow me. (Luke 19:21)

The obliviousness of the world recommended here is in striking contrast to the concern for the world and the needs of material man that have dominated the *Visio* up to this point: it is this obliviousness of the world that legitimises their begging and makes their demand for food and lodging an imperative that may not be resisted. There is no need to ask the question, Who is worthy to have? Likewise, the lack of care of the world of the 'lunatyk lollares' makes them powerful if enigmatic exemplars of the same spirituality, imitators of Christ's disciples and in some measure of Christ himself.

It is possible to associate the power of these 'lunatyk lollares' to call forth charity (see lines 124 – 5) with Wordsworth's poem of *The Old Cumberland Beggar* and the familiar argument that the old and enfeebled and socially useless are morally useful in engendering charity in others, in evoking those 'little nameless, unremembered acts / Of kindness and of love' (*Tintern Abbey*, lines 34 – 5), but this is more a kind of moral utilitarianism which, though it is not alien to Langland, is not relevant here. These witless wanderers are not merely a stimulus to charity in others but an imitation in themselves of the life of the spirit which makes them specially dear to God. They are indeed God's 'priue disciples' (118) and, as to their lives, under God's special protection:

> For vnder godes secret seal here synnes ben keuered. (138)

Wordsworth, who is very much in one's mind here, is much closer to Langland, in that reverence for God's purposes mysteriously worked out, in one of his early letters, written in reference to his poem of *The Idiot Boy*, where he says,

> I have often applied to idiots, in my own mind, that sublime expression of Scripture, that *their life is hidden with God*.[6]

Wordsworth's text here, and Langland's too, is Colossians 3:1 – 3:

> If ye then be risen with Christ . . . Set your affection on things above, not on things on the earth. For ye are dead, and your life is hid with Christ in God.

Langland reinforces the power of this assertion of the essentially unworldly nature — indeed the lunacy — of spirituality by appropriating a language of spiritual paradox that is first used in the gospels, as in Christ's words, 'Except ye be converted and become as little children, ye shall not enter into the kingdom of heaven' (Matthew 18:3), and then amplified and extended by Paul in an elaborate fugue on the terms wisdom and foolishness

---

[6] Wordsworth, *Early Letters*, ed. Ernest de Selincourt (Oxford, 1935), pp. 296 – 7.

in the first Epistle to the Corinthians. 'God makes foolish the wisdom of the world' (1:20); and elsewhere, 'The wisdom of this world is foolishness with God' (3:19). What the world regards as foolishness, namely the gospel of Christ crucified, is the wisdom that his apostles preach for the salvation of them that believe (1:21). 'If any man among you seem to be wise in this world', he says, in a verse that is quoted in Langland's recommendation of the lunatic lollers (127a), 'let him become a fool, that he may be wise' (3:18). 'We are fools for Christ's sake', says Paul elsewhere (4:10), in a passage that Langland remembered much later, in the last Passus of the poem, where it is only fools who resist the temptations of Antichrist (C XXII 61). Sir John Clanvowe remembered the passage too, in his treatise on *The Two Ways*:

> The world clepeth hem fooles that goon Goddis weyes, and men clepeth hem 'goode felawes' and worshipful that goon in the fendes weyes.[7]

Clanvowe was a member of Richard II's household, a Knight of the Chamber, and a Chaucerian poet of some merit: his own embracing of 'foolishness' is manifest in this treatise, and in his own subsequent pilgrimage to the Holy Land, on the way to which he died.

Clanvowe goes further, and in another passage (line 512) associates himself with those who are called 'lolleres and loseles', with those meek folk of simple life, that is, who are given these names by men of the world. Clanvowe, of course, had Lollard affiliations, and may be deliberately embracing to himself, in proud humility, a term of abuse already being applied to the radical group that was subsequently declared heretical. Langland uses the same terms — note the variation of lines 107 and 137 — maybe with some similar purpose (though the question of Langland's association with Lollardy is a vexed one), but he also extends the vocabulary of spiritual paradox much further, and in a remarkable way. He takes over all sorts of words of pejorative connotation, and, in applying them to his lunatic lollers, confronts the traditional values of society and institutional-ised religion which are embodied in those words. In talking of them, for instance, as 'lepares aboute', who wander the world aimlessly, Langland is echoing, for the purposes of paradox, phrases in which orthodox preachers condemned pardoners and itinerant priests, phrases such as 'lepers over londe', 'ronners over contreys'[8] — phrases and language similar to those which he himself had used in offering condemnation of the religious who leave the cloister and become 'renaboutes' (B VI 148) or 'outryderes' (C IV 116, C V 157), or of the wandering hermits of the Prologue (31) who traipse

---

[7] Clanvowe, *The Two Ways*, lines 601–4, in *Works*, ed. V. J. Scattergood (Cambridge, 1975).

[8] See G. R. Owst, *Literature and Pulpit in Medieval England* (Cambridge, 1933; 2nd edn. Oxford, 1961), p. 373.

about the country and do not hold to their cells. Langland is conscious here and in many other passages of the *gyrovagi* or wandering monks who violated the Benedictine rule of stability,[9] though he may not be conscious of the historical context into which this attitude towards wandering needs to be set. There was a time when the life of the wanderer, the *peregrinus*, the spiritual nomad who set aside home and family and threw himself upon God, or at God, was the purest type of spiritual dedication; but by the thirteenth century, as Brian Stock describes it in *The Implications of Literacy*,[10] unauthorised wandering was frowned upon, and wandering monks, pilgrims (who, like the Wife of Bath, knew much of wandering by the way), minstrels, itinerant hermits, joined that large class of vagabonds whose homelessness and instability was seen not as a way of escaping the worldliness of the world but as a way of escaping the increasingly comprehensive networks of law and order.

Langland is also conscious, of course, of the friars, whose wandering abroad was a constant theme of complaint among the older established religious orders, and we are reminded, not for the only time, of the importance of the friars in the background of this description of the lunatic lollers. It was the friars who had themselves first appropriated this language of spiritual paradox, calling themselves, like these later 'lollares' (see lines 126, 136), God's minstrels, *joculatores domini*, or God's fools, *mundi moriones*, to emphasise the divine foolishness and carelessness of the world that made them voluntarily poor and beggars.[11] As often, Langland, whose criticism of the friars is criticism of the betrayal of the highest Christian ideal, seems to be trying to reinvent a new Franciscanism or at least to find it in new places. Langland is also conscious of himself as a wanderer, and of the way he initially described himself in the poem, going forth into the world, not as a pilgrim but as a wanderer (cf. C X 1). The sense of urgency we have in the lunatic lollers passage, the way in which the new subject is invested with such intensity and importance, has partly to do with Langland's own desire to recognise himself among this class of privileged lunatics, and it is striking that one of the characteristics attributed to them,

---

[9] See M. W. Bloomfield, *Piers Plowman as a Fourteenth-century Apocalypse* (New Brunswick, N.J., n.d. [1961]), pp. 24 – 5.

[10] Brian Stock, *The Implications of Literacy: Written Language and Models of Interpretation in the Eleventh and Twelfth Centuries* (Princeton, 1983), pp. 476 – 9.

[11] E. Talbot Donaldson, in his important discussion of this passage in *Piers Plowman: The C-Text and its Poet* (Yale Studies in English 113, New Haven, 1949), p. 146, considers that Langland was probably well aware of the Franciscan tradition, and that his phrase 'God's minstrels' is a conscious translation of *joculatores Domini*. Kathryn Kerby-Fulton, in a so far unpublished D.Phil. dissertation, 'The Voice of Honest Indignation: A Study of Reformist Apocalypticism in relation to *Piers Plowman*' (University of York, 1986), has a valuable discussion of the passage in which she suggests that the reference to 'Prophecy' (line 114) may indicate Joachite influence (p. 521).

that of having no care for the social conventions and etiquette of rank (lines 122 – 3), is so reminiscent of the dreamer's description of himself in B XV 1 – 10:

> Ac after my wakynge it was wonder longe
> Er I koude kyndely knowe what was Dowel.
> And so my wit weex and wanyed til I a fool weere;
> And some lakked my lif — allowed it fewe —
> And leten me for a lorel and looth to reverencen
> Lordes or ladies or any lif ellis —
> As persons in pelure with pendaunts of silver;
> To sergeaunts ne to swiche seide noght ones,
> 'God loke yow, lordes!' — ne loutede faire.
> That folk helden me a fool; and in that folie I raved.

Langland's whole account of the dreamer here as one who is thought to be a fool is removed in C, and elements reintegrated in the description of the lunatics in C IX, which may have something to do with Langland's re-representation of himself in the later version of the poem, especially in C V.

The description of the lunatic lollers is, as I say, full of this language of paradox: they are 'godes boys' (127) — 'boys' was still pretty universally a pejorative term; they are 'godes munstrals' (136), minstrels being thought of by Langland as a rather dubious class, again perhaps partly because he saw himself as in a way a member of it;[12] they are 'bourdyors' (127, 136) or jesters, a term which was used to describe an even more disreputable class of entertainers, and was so used in the earlier passage (C VII 108) in which Langland made his first attempt to associate beggars with God's minstrels. Even 'mesageres' (136) had a bad reputation, and were associated with minstrels in welcoming Liar after he had been expelled from the king's court (C II 237) — though there is a later passage in C XIII where messengers are contrasted favourably with merchants because of their lack of investment in things of the world, which is the way their footloose, precarious, dependent life comes to seem in Langland's ethics of poverty.

But Langland, of course, is not really using Paul's language of paradox in the same way as Paul. Paul was concerned to make an intellectually respectable case for what the world, and he himself in his earlier life, were bound to regard as foolishness: the rhetoric of paradox is designed to assert an intellectual superiority through the manner in which it speaks of a deliberate embrace of inferiority. The wit and intellectuality is evident, as it is too in Erasmus's *Praise of Folly*, which exploits essentially the same vein of wit. Langland, however, in a very characteristic way, represents the metaphor of folly in its literal sense: his fools are *real* fools and madmen, in whom the exercise of God's grace and power, since they have a special

---

[12] See Donaldson, *The C-Text and its Poet*, pp. 136 – 55, especially pp. 150 – 55.

access to God's protection and God's truth, is even more strikingly exemplified than in those who deliberately and as it were of their own will make themselves fools for Christ's sake. In that sense, Langland's lunatics do not really belong to the class to which they may seem most allied, the 'fools of God', the 'fous pour le Christ', or 'perfect fools', in whom the call fully to live the life of Christ results in a rejection of all that the world calls sane, sensible, decent, even virtuous.[13] Francis of Assisi is perhaps the model: he says, 'God called me and told me that he wanted me to be a new fool'. He joyed therefore in what made him the object of mockery and scorn and incomprehension, and in behaving in ways that caused people to think of him as insane, going about naked, singing strange songs, talking to the birds, scraping a tree branch over his arm as if it were the bow of a viol and singing to the imagined accompaniment. In the history of early asceticism there are many such stories, including the stories of those who deliberately mimicked the behaviour of clowns and jesters, dressed in the garb of fools and prostitutes, performed ridiculous dances, interrupted church services. An important desire is to assert kinship with the most wretched of God's creatures — beggars, lepers, outcasts and pariahs of all kinds — and to be ever wandering, living in abject poverty. It will be seen that there is a distinction between these fools of God, in whom folly is a strenuously artificial pretence, and Langland's fools, who are *real* fools.

In putting forward fools and madmen as those beggars who are most unambiguously worthy of charity and who most clearly demonstrate God's providential care of those who have no care of the world, Langland draws on a number of traditions, at the same time that he has to get round a number of problems. He calls his fools lunatics and has them growing more or less mad according to the phases of the moon, but they are clearly not mad through mental illness or disturbance, but rather congenitally feeble-minded. In medieval terms, the distinction is between mania and melancholy on the one hand and idiocy on the other.[14] The former were transitory states, the latter permanent, and there tended therefore to be much more attention given to the former. In those afflicted with mania or melancholy, madness was seen as a form of disease, sent by God, like all

[13] See John Saward, *Perfect Fools: Folly for Christ's Sake in Catholic and Orthodox Spirituality* (Oxford, 1980); also Roland Maisonneuve, 'Margery Kempe and the Eastern and Western Tradition of the "Perfect Fool" ', in *The Medieval Mystical Tradition in England*, Papers read at Dartington Hall, July, 1982, ed. Marion Glasscoe (Exeter, 1982), and the further references there cited.
[14] For discussion of ideas of madness in the Middle Ages, with specific reference to the representation of madness in literature, see Penelope B. R. Doob, *Nebuchadnezzar's Children: Conventions of Madness in Middle English Literature* (New Haven, 1974); Judith S. Neaman, *Suggestion of the Devil: Insanity in the Middle Ages and the Twentieth Century* (Garden City, N.Y., 1975). Neaman discusses the *Piers Plowman* passage briefly, pp. 131 – 3 (she seems to misunderstand *lepares* as 'lepers').

diseases, as a form of punishment or purgation, or both. The classic model was Nebuchadnezzar, who is reduced to the state of a beast without reason because of his pride and who learns humility; the model is frequently present in the secular world of medieval romance, first and best exemplified in Yvain in the romance by Chrétien of that name. Charles VI of France and Thomas Hoccleve are real-life examples of the manic and depressive forms, respectively, of mental illness in the later Middle Ages. These clearly have nothing to do with Langland's lunatic lollers.

Fools, though, are a larger and more amorphous class, and there was no general agreement on the place assigned to them in God's providence nor on the place to be assigned to them by society.[15] Their babbling was not always inspired idiocy — it was, after all, a fool (*insipiens*) who said in his heart, there is no God (Psalm 52) — and they were excluded from all the sacraments except baptism (though there is evidence that in some churches they were allowed to attend mass as long as they were kept separate from the rest of the communicants). To some extent, therefore, there was moral and spiritual as well as mental deprivation. The Middle Ages were also very well aware of and doubtful about the professionalisation of folly. Courts and household fools were commonly kept for amusement, and the descriptions of their behaviour do suggest in certain instances that they were genuinely deranged. The amusement that such court fools gave should not be idealised: no doubt their weakness of mind made them so obviously inferior and dependent that what they said or did could not be taken offence at, and therefore constituted a kind of legitimised subversion; but we should recall also Lear's 'Take heed, sirrah, the whip' (*King Lear*, I. iv. 116), and recognise the complacency and limitations of that allowed licence and its basis in what Hobbes describes as the cause of laughter — 'sudden glory at the sight of an inferior'.[16] Nor is the distinction between natural and artificial fools easy to make: someone with a 'comic' physical disability or deformity could easily 'play the fool', but someone mentally retarded could also learn to exploit that infirmity and become renowned for spectacular acts of lunacy, such as jumping out of high windows.

Langland's lunatic lollers clearly have nothing to do with this world of mutual exploitation. He draws more on an older tradition of the idiot as one whose lack of wit places him under God's special protection and also makes him the instrument of powers beyond himself, with access to hidden

---

[15] For discussion of fools and folly in the Middle Ages, see Barbara Swain, *Fools and Folly during the Middle Ages and the Renaissance* (New York, 1932); Enid Welsford, *The Fool: His Social and Literary History* (London, 1935).

[16] Hobbes is quoted thus in Welsford, *The Fool*, p. 50: this exact phrase does not appear in Hobbes, but it is a not inaccurate summary of the paragraph in which he speaks of the subject, in *Leviathan*, Part I, Chapter 6, in *English Works*, ed. Sir William Molesworth (London, 1839), Vol. III.

knowledge and mysterious prophecy (as in line 114). Popular prophetic writing often takes the form of inspired babbling, 'pleyinge, as it were' (114), as if to lay claim to this kind of origin.[17] Enid Welsford gives many examples of fools as poets and prophets and clairvoyants in Hebrew, classical, Islamic and other traditions. One of the most interesting stories is that of the Irish King Suibhne, who was afflicted with lunacy at the battle of Magh Rath in A.D.637:

> In this state he began to feel as if feathers were growing on him, and went flying about from place to place uttering lamentations in verse. At last he reached ever delightful 'Glen Bolcain', a place where all Irish lunatics used to assemble after the completion of a year of lunacy . . .[a place which has] 'a wood, very beautiful, very pleasant, and clean-banked wells and cool springs, and sandy clear water streams, and green-topped watercress . . . The madmen moreover used to smite each other for the pick of the watercress of that glen and for the choice of its couches'.[18]

There Suibhne meets the leading lunatic of the time, a certain Ealladhan, who calls himself Fer Caille, Man of the Wood, with whom he finds himself to have much in common, including prophetic power and knowledge of hidden mysteries.

It will be seen, though, that there are differences here too: Suibhne and Fer Caille are not lunatics like Langland's but wise men in whom the activity of reason has been temporarily or even permanently suspended so that they may be witnesses, in states of ecstasy or prophetic trance, to divine truth. They are like the holy wild men of medieval traditions, the desert saints, or Merlin driven mad into the wilderness at the corruption and hypocrisy of the world, in Geoffrey of Monmouth's *Life of Merlin*, and there pouring forth prophecies; they are, in a way, like all prophets and mystics. 'When the mind reaches God in contemplation, the rational sense fails', says Caesarius of Heisterbach in his *Dialogue on Miracles*, and Jacques de Vitry, in *The Alphabet of Tales*, in a passage that would have pleased Margery Kempe, describes 'devout women, that were so hugely ravished with thought of holy living, that of all the day there was no wit in them unto no outward thing'.[19]

---

[17] Donaldson (*The C-Text and its Poet*, p. 146) thinks it may have been 'prophecies' of the kind that Langland speaks about that may actually have got into popular alliterative verse. For some extraordinary specimens of similar verse from a later period, especially interesting in relation to the discussion below of 'Poor Tom' in *King Lear*, see *Loving Mad Tom: Bedlamite Verses of the XVI and XVII Centuries*, ed. Jack Lindsay (London, 1927).
[18] Welsford, *The Fool*, p. 98. There may be some allusion to this Irish hero in T. S. Eliot's choice of the name 'Sweeney' for his representation of primitive man, unaware of civilisation and therefore unencumbered by it.
[19] For these illustrations and quotations, see Doob, *Nebuchadnezzar's Children*, p. 32.

Another parallel will suggest itself to readers of Tolstoy's *War and Peace* (Book 5, Chapter 11), who will remember how Princess Mary surreptitiously entertained in her father's kitchen a group of wandering pilgrims called 'God's folk', who went begging from shrine to shrine all over Europe, many of them half-witted or deformed, or both. The Princess was half-ashamed, but regarded them with awe as well as pity, as in some way the possessors of a mysterious holiness. Prince Andrew was openly contemptuous, and brought his friend Pierre to join with him in mockery. Pierre was not so amused. The two of God's folk we see, it is true, the old woman and the young boy, are superstitious simple folk rather than lunatics, but we do hear of another member of the group, Crazy Cyril of Kiev, who goes barefoot summer and winter and has a great reputation for holiness.

But literature offers no better parallel for Langland's lunatic lollers than Shakespeare's *King Lear*. There is of course the Fool himself, though he seems more the type of cultivated fool, whose assumption of folly is here shrewdly directed to the education rather than the amusement of his master. But I am thinking more of Edgar, and of his escape from danger disguised as Poor Tom, a Bedlam beggar.

> My face I'll grime with filth,
> Blanket my loins, elf all my hair in knots,
> And with presented nakedness outface
> The winds and persecutions of the sky.
> The country gives me proof and precedent
> Of Bedlam beggars who, with roaring voices,
> Strike in their numb'd and mortified bare arms
> Pins, wooden pricks, nails, sprigs of rosemary,
> And with this horrible object, from low farms,
> Poor pelting villages, sheep-cotes, and mills,
> Sometime with lunatic bans, sometime with prayers,
> Enforce their charity.   (II. iii. 9 – 20)

Edgar clearly shares a conventional view that these Bedlam beggars, or 'Abraham men', as they were also called, were professional beggars, who used various tricks to enforce, as he calls it, charity. It was commonly believed that such beggars feigned madness and claimed that they had been kept in Bedlam a long time. Bedlam, or Bethlehem, was the hospital of St Mary of Bethlehem, in London: the house of St Mary was founded as a priory in 1247, became a hospital in 1330, and seems to have been specialising in lunatics by 1402, when six of its nine inmates are said to have been *mente capti*.[20] In 1547, after the dissolution of the monasteries, it

---

[20] See R. M. Clay, *The Medieval Hospitals of England* (London, 1909), p. 104; *OED*, s.v. 'Bedlam'; Neaman, *Suggestion of the Devil*, p. 137; Andrew McCall, *The Medieval Underworld* (London, 1979), pp. 135 – 6.

became a royal foundation for the reception of lunatics. The institutionalisation of lunacy is of course one of the themes of the important book by Michel Foucault, *Madness and Civilisation*, where it is argued that the new hospitals for the insane, though they seem to be a sign of corporate concern, were custodial rather than therapeutic; that they acted to remove a blight from the eyes of society (as lepers had been removed in previous centuries) and in so doing institutionalised a loss of rights as well as responsibilities, a deliberate erasing of self and identity.[21] The appalling nature of these Bedlam hospitals, and the appalling nature of the people who made visits to them as places of fashionable resort, is clear enough, though it would not do to take refuge in too rosy a picture of the Middle Ages, where the lunatic, though not put away, was most often beaten and abused, or harried from dwelling to dwelling, or put to the most servile drudgery.

However, it is as beggars that the Abraham men, or Bedlam beggars, were best known, inmates or supposed inmates of the hospital who had been discharged even though only half-cured, and who were licensed to beg, wearing as a badge a tin plate on their left hand or arm. And it is as beggars, and for the claim that they make on human charity, that they are introduced in *Lear*, first of all in Lear's own apostrophe, made before Poor Tom enters:

> Poor naked wretches, whereso'er you are,
> That bide the pelting of this pitiless storm,
> How shall your houseless heads and unfed sides,
> Your loop'd and window'd raggedness, defend you
> From seasons such as these? O, I have ta'en
> Too little care of this. Take physic, Pomp;
> Expose thyself to feel what wretches feel,
> That thou mayst shake the superflux to them,
> And show the heavens more just.   (III.iv. 28 – 36)

To 'shake the superflux' is of course a nice reversal of the phrase, 'extract the surplus', and Gloucester echoes Lear's impulse to charitable redistribution of wealth when he gives money later to Poor Tom:

> So distribution should undo excess,
> And each man have enough.   (IV.i. 70 – 71)

This however is only one function of Poor Tom. His other is to bring Lear to a recognition of what man is, stripped of all his pomp and ceremony. He recognises in him

> the thing itself: unaccommodated man is no more but such a poor, bare, forked animal as thou art   (III.iv. 109 – 11)

---

[21] Foucault, *Madness and Civilization: A History of Insanity in the Age of Reason* (New York, 1965), translated by Richard Howard from the French work originally published under the title *Folie et déraison: Histoire de la folie à l'âge Classique* (Paris, 1961).

The lunatic, in whom the world and all its values are repudiated, becomes the means to spiritual regeneration — and the fact that the lunatic is an impostor does not of course make this process invalid but only makes of it a more powerful demonstration of the mysterious ways in which man may come to grace. And what it brings Lear to, eventually, is a recognition of the other fool in the play, namely Cordelia. 'For it hath ever best liked me to speak straight what so ever lay on my tongue's end', says Folly, in Erasmus's *Praise of Folly* (Chapter 4). Cordelia too spoke straight, like a fool, but, through her folly, redeemed the world.

The role of the lunatic lollers in *Piers Plowman* is remarkably similar. Represented first as beggars, and as an answer to the question, Who is worthy to have? they become the means to an understanding of the true nature of the spiritual life in its rejection of all worldly concerns, its carelessness of the means of life, its divine recklessness. Long before the pardon-scene has come to an end, and rendering now superfluous that later, more explicit passage in B (VII 118 – 30) where Piers comes to his painful recognition that the way to truth is not through care of the world, the lunatic lollers have shown the way.

INTERPRETATIONS OF JUDAS IN MIDDLE ENGLISH LITERATURE

RICHARD AXTON

Apocryphal stories of Judas are told in most of the European languages; they show how curiously medieval people speculated about the life and motives of 'him who did betray the best'.[1] These narrative speculations seem to have been prompted by gaps or puzzles in the Gospel accounts of the Betrayal, and they continue the process of rationalization of the 'history' which the evangelists themselves wrestled with. The relationship between the four gospels has been stimulatingly discussed as an example of interpretation by the invention of narrative. Frank Kermode entertains the conjecture that 'there was originally no Judas at all', drawing attention to Paul Winter's derivation of the name Iscariot from an Aramaic word for betrayal.[2] Since Betrayal requires an Agent, Judas was invented and then given motives: 'narrative begot character, and character begot new narrative'.[3] The application of such a formalist methodology brings the ambivalence of Judas' function into a very clear light: he is a necessary agent, both Helper and Opponent of his Master. Once this is granted, the moral and theological implications are troubling and, as I hope to show, this was a perplexity experienced by medieval people, both learned and lewed.

Before considering some of the medieval evidence it may be useful to review the 'development' of Judas' role and motivation in the gospels. Although the priority of Mark is now quite generally upheld, it will be convenient to begin with St Matthew, whose account is in some ways

[1] The pioneer study is by Paul F. Baum, 'The Medieval Legends of Judas Iscariot', *PMLA* 31 (1916) 481 – 631. The present essay is part of a forthcoming book, *Lives of Judas in the Middle Ages*. I am grateful for suggestions made by Margaret Bridges and by Renate Fichte when the paper was read in Perugia.

[2] Frank Kermode, *The Genesis of Secrecy* (Cambridge, Mass. and London, 1979), p. 94, cites Paul Winter, *On the Trial of Jesus*, 2nd ed., *Studia Judaica*, Band I (Berlin and New York, 1974), p. 196. Historical criticism favours the view that Judas was a political zealot (Iscariot may be a corruption of Lat. *sicarius*: assassin) who, according to a line of thought going back to Thomas de Quincey in 1857, was disappointed in Christ's otherworldliness. This tradition is not wholly unknown in the Middle Ages. A 14C English book of hours shows Judas as an impetuous young man with flowing hair and 'the face of a freedom fighter' (See the reproduction in *Rendells Sale Catalogue* 146, Newton, Mass. 1979, No. 79; I am grateful for this reference to Professor Margaret Bent).

[3] Kermode, p. 91.

'archetypal' and contains an implausibility avoided by the other three.[4] Jesus informs the twelve that one of them is a traitor and publicly identifies the culprit, yet no one objects or tries to prevent the betrayal. The words which Matthew ascribes to Jesus emphasise Judas' necessary role in the drama of God's purpose as prophesied in the Old Testament:

> The son of man goeth as it is written of him; but woe unto that man by whom the son of man is betrayed. It had been good for that man if he had not been born. (Matt 26:24)

It is consistent with St Matthew's tragic view of events that he alone records (27:3 – 10) that Judas repented of his bargain when he saw Jesus condemned, and that he hanged himself. In Acts (1:18) this is elaborated: Judas bought a field with the 'rewards of his wickedness, and falling headlong he burst open in the middle and all his bowels burst out'.

The gospels of Mark and Luke avoid the public identification of Judas. Luke adds, before recounting the Last Supper, that 'Satan entered into Judas Iscariot' (22:3). St John underlines the theme of diabolism and introduces the motive of theft. Before the washing of feet, John says, the devil 'put into the heart of Judas Iscariot to betray Jesus' (13:2). Again, at the moment Judas received the sop from Jesus — a gesture which recalls and fulfills prophecy in the Psalms[5] — 'Satan entered into him' (13:27). Jesus' words, 'That thou doest, do quickly' are spoken in secret and prompt some of the disciples to think, 'because Judas had the bag, that Jesus had said unto him, ''Buy those things that we have need of against the feast'' ' (13:29). St John does not explain how Judas came to this position of trust; this is curious since, according to him, a year before the crucifixion, Jesus knew of Judas' diabolic nature ('Have not I chosen you twelve, and one of you is a devil?' He spake of Judas Iscariot (6:70 – 71)). So it is St John, then, who is responsible for reducing Judas' motive to avarice and for making him a habitual thief ('he was a thief and had the bag, and bare what was put therein' (12:6)).

The gospels, then, provide three explanations: avarice, diabolic possession, and the fulfilment of prophecy or divine necessity. You might expect medieval people to be content with the first two and, indeed, it is true that preachers used Judas as a type of avarice, and that playwrights showed Judas' bargain with the Jews as the prompting of the devil. However, the Church Fathers stressed the redemptive purpose of the crucifixion and the triumphant outcome of God's plan of redemption. St Augustine's dark

---

[4] See Enoch Powell's letter to *The Times*, 27 July 1985, in reply to J. Gosling, 29 June. Kermode (p. 81) assumes the priority of Mark, while asking the reader to imagine 'what it was that the evangelists set out to interpret'.

[5] Ps 40:9 (Vulgate), in AV: 'Yea, mine own familiar friend, in whom I trusted, which did eat my bread, hath lifted up his heel against me'.

notion of 'necessary evil' recognises the force of Christ's command to Judas and of His reference to fulfilment of the prophecies in Psalms.[6] In support of this interpretation he cites Psalm 108, in which he sees David's slanderous enemies 'under the person of Judas'. The vehemence of the Psalmist's curse is worth quoting, especially since its terms hold the narrative seeds of the apocryphal medieval stories of Judas:

Set thou a wicked man over him: and let Satan stand at his right hand.
When he shall be judged, let him be condemned: and let his prayer become sin.
Let his days be few; and let another take his office.
Let his children be fatherless, and his wife a widow.
Let his children be continually vagabonds, and beg: let them seek their bread also out of their desolate places. (Ps 108:5 – 10)

In spite of the way in which patristic allegory discovers justification for Judas' role in the Psalm, St Augustine maintains that Judas excercised free will. The argument for free will, according to which the divine prophecy and Christ's prediction did not *compel* Judas' act of wickedness, seems, however, to have been hard for ordinary people to understand, perhaps because popular belief always inclined to fatalism and expected religion to have predictive and constraining powers.

A typical common man's view of the matter is expressed in a fifteenth-century English dialogue of instruction, *Lucidus and Dubius*. The doubting layman, Dubius, asks:

God wold that his sonne Jesus
For man deed be sholde:
That, Y wolde wyte, what dede Iudas amys
That hym betray wolde?
For sith God wolde þat he sholde be deed,
And Iudas dede the same,
And Iudas was not to blame,
It semyth thei wroʒt by oo reed,
For there may no man spylle
That fulfyllyth Goddis wylle.[7]

All is made plain by Lucidus, a doctor of theology, who distinguishes the motives: God acted from charity and 'love on all wyse', whereas 'Iudas hym

[6] Augustine (*Tractate* LIX, on St John 13:16 – 20) speaks coyly of Judas being chosen for some purpose for which he was necessary, but 'not blessedness'. In *Sermon* I on the New Testament, ch.11, he speaks of God's use of heretics and wicked men. In his commentary on St John 17:9 – 13 (*Tractate* CVII) he notes that Judas was foreordained to perdition and cites Psalm 108.
[7] Winchester College MS 33, f.34b. I am grateful to Dr Richard Beadle for transcription of this text. See also *A Manual of the Writings in Middle English, 1050 – 1500*, ed. J. Burke Severs, Albert E. Hartung et al., 7 vols. (New Haven, 1967 – 87), III 743.

solde sylver to have / Only for fals covetyse'. This bald explanation relies on an orthodox polarity of *caritas* and *cupiditas*. Dubius' question, naive and loaded as it is, nevertheless signals a strong curiosity about the place of destiny in the theology of salvation, and it suggests that the bizarre legends about Judas' life which flourished in the Middle Ages deserve to be taken seriously.

Judas as Oedipus

The story that Judas was a foundling who grew up to kill his own father and marry his own mother appears in Latin in the twelfth century. P.F.Baum in 1916 showed how the story was recast in the *Golden Legend* and from there spread into the vernaculars: by 1300 there are versions in English, French, Welsh, Catalan, Czech; by 1400, in German, Dutch, Provençal, Italian, Swedish, Danish. It survives as a ballad in nineteenth-century Serbia.[8]

In the early Latin prose version Judas' father sees in a vision that his unborn child will murder him. When the child is born, rather than kill him, the parents expose him in a wilderness after piercing his feet. The baby Judas is found by shepherds and raised by a woman in the land of Iscariot. He grows up strong to become a thief and a servant of Herod's. One day Herod fancies some special apples for a feast and Judas goes to rob the orchard, not knowing that it is his father's. They meet and son kills father. When the widow pleads for justice, Herod protects Judas, forcing her to marry him in order to retain her property. One night in bed she notices the scars and recognises her son Judas. He leaves his mother and seeks forgiveness of his sins from Jesus, who makes him a favourite and his purse-bearer. But Judas steals from the purse and finally sells his master. He despairs of forgiveness and hangs himself.

This version has a simple dignity and pathos, but what meaning did the author see in the story? His cryptic comment, 'Nothing is hidden which shall not be revealed', recognises the idea of an ineluctible fate. The second idea expressed is concerned with moral justice: 'Whoever persists in evil shall suffer for it; whoever perseveres in goodness shall be saved'. Thus the full story of Judas' life shows that he is inherently wicked, but also that he is the victim of fate, in that he is unaware of the full monstrousness of his crimes — parricide and incest. These crimes are forgiven him. We can note, then, two cycles of sin in Judas' life: the first concludes with repentance and forgiveness, the second, with despair of forgiveness and suicide. There seems nothing unorthodox about the implications.[9]

---

[8] See Baum, note 1 above.
[9] In his commentary on Ps 108:6, Augustine holds that it was possible for Judas to have prayed for forgiveness, while also supposing him to be in Hades for an unpardonable crime.

The similarity of the story to that of Oedipus is obvious (particularly suggestive are the piercing of the child's tibias and his being found by shepherds), and it suggests a learned source, perhaps in Book 2 of Origen's *Contra Celsum*, where the Greek and Christian stories are discussed as parallel examples of prophecy which does not preempt freewell.[10] It is a story, too, which, though it is apocryphal, neatly maps the Psalmist's 'wicked man', at whose right hand Satan stands, and whose children are 'fatherless'.

Legenda Aurea

The legendary life of Judas is not recounted or alluded to by any reputable ecclesiastical authority except Jacobus de Voragine, who included it in his *Legenda Aurea* (c.1270) with the prefactory comment that it is 'apocryphal and little worthy of credence'.[11] Jacobus introduces the story under the life of St Mathias, the apostle who replaced Judas (the Psalmist's 'other' who 'took his office') and this is the company it keeps in the Middle English accounts based on *Golden Legend*: Mirk's *Festial* and the *Scottish Legendary*. Almost exactly the same story appears independently in the Middle English legendaries which couple Judas with the apocryphal life and death of Pilate, notably the *South English Legendary* and the metrical *Titus and Vespasian*.

[10] Origen's Gnostic opponent Celsus has argued that if Jesus had really been a god he could not have allowed himself to be betrayed by a wicked disciple; and that if he was a god and foretold Judas' betrayal and Peter's denial of him, then he was guilty of corrupting his own men. Origen replies that Christ knew Judas' cupidity and Peter's lack of firm loyalty, and that he predicted correctly the acts of betrayal, but he insists that these events did not take place *because* they were predicted by Christ. To make the point, he compares the prophecy of Judas' betrayal attributed to the Saviour in Psalm 108 with the oracle made of Laius, and quotes:

'Beget no children against the will of the gods,
For if you do produce a child, your offspring shall slay you,
And your whole house shall be steeped in bloodshed'.

As for Judas' suicide, Origen does not inveigh against despair: rather, he is impressed by the vestige of moral thinking in Judas' soul, implanted by Christ's teaching and evident in his recognition. 'I have betrayed innocent blood'. Origen's Greek view here contrasts strikingly with the later emphasis of the Latin fathers of Judas' sin of despair. *Contra Celsum*, trans. Henry Chadwick (Cambridge, 1953), pp. 85ff.

The *Contra Celsum* was current in Latin MSS of the twelfth and thirteenth centuries, so that a medieval scholar, struck by the similarities, could have invented from them the early life of Judas.
[11] *The Golden Legend* trans. G. Ryan and H. Ripperger (New York, 1969), p. 172.

In the *Golden Legend* version the baby Judas is put to sea in a wicker basket. He washes up on the isle of Iscariot and is adopted by the childless queen, who gives out that she is pregnant. Later the queen conceives a son, whom Judas bullies and one day, after being told that he himself is a foundling, kills. Judas flees to Jerusalem, joins Pilate's court and becomes his steward. In this version it is Pilate who has a craving for apples, urges Judas to steal from the orchard in which he meets and kills his father, and forces the widow to marry her husband's murderer. In her sorrow the woman reveals to Judas the story of her lost son and slain husband; he confesses, and on her advice receives shrift from Jesus. Judas is now entrusted with the communal purse and from it he customarily steals ten per cent of the alms received. At this point the story links with the gospels. When Mary Magdalene broke her box of ointment upon Christ's feet and three hundred pence were seen to be wasted, Judas considered that he had personally lost thirty pence. So, to regain his tithe, he sold Christ to the Jews. When finally he hanged himself, his soul could not pass from his body through the mouth which had kissed Christ; his bowels burst, releasing his soul to the devil.

Clearly many of the motifs here spring from biblical stories; the exposure of the child by water, his royal upbringing and killing of his step-brother seem to be assimilated from the life of Moses (with a glance at Cain), just as the apple-picking sequence appears as an inverted replay of the garden of Eden. More central and significant is the ingenious explanation of the thirty pence as a tithe, which is nevertheless stolen. The gospels of Matthew (26:14) and Mark (14:10) had suggestively juxtaposed the disciples' outcry at the wasted ointment with Judas' visit to the high priests. Again, as we have seen, it is St John (12:3 – 6) who elaborated Judas' unworthy motive, explaining that his objection to the loss of 'three hundred pence' was 'not that he cared from the poor, but because he was a thief and had the bag and bare what was put therein'. The relationship between three hundred pence and thirty pence had been lurking in the gospels, waiting to be discovered by medieval minds which loved pattern and which were also recurrently preoccupied with the problem of usury. In terms of narrative structure, as we shall see, the explanation of the origin of the thirty pieces of silver forced the crucial link between Judas' old life and his role in the gospels.

English Legendaries

The *Golden Legend* version of Judas' story seems to have attracted two lines of interpretation in the derivative English texts: the possibly Manichean idea of inherent evil, and the idea of destiny. The notion that Judas was inherently wicked is the theme of the powerful account of his life given in the *South English Legendary* c.1300.[12] 'Iudas was a luþer brid', it begins: Judas was a wicked fellow. As a child he was handsome, but 'Hyt hys noȝt al god þat is vayr'. The poet has a liking for proverbs and finds that Judas' behaviour proved the wisdom that 'Ever it is croked þat wil be wrong'. When Judas joins forces with Pilate, 'þe o schrewe wyþ þe oþer', the poet comments that 'ech þyng loueþ hys ilyk' (l.66). Judas' wickedness comes out early when he strikes other children and 'breke ȝare heued'. This spare, forceful language is particularly effective in conveying the recurrent violence of Judas' behaviour. Judas kills his father brutally with a stone:

> So þat he smot him mid a ston · bihinde in þe pate
> Þat al þe scolle todaȝte · þe brayn veol out þer ate   (83 – 4)

The question of Judas' repentance is of particular interest to the author of the *Legendary*, who is generally thought to have been a Dominican friar: the administration of shrift and the begging of alms were of special importance to that order. In telling how Judas became 'bourser', the poet commends the generosity of those 'þat were of gode þoȝt / To sosteny his apostles' and condemns Judas because 'þe teoþinge he wolde stele'. So far as the poet is concerned the story serves only to show how inherently bad Judas was: 'A schrewe he was al hys lyf' (l.120). Why then did Jesus trust him? He answers with a paradox:

> Wel wuste oure Louerd what he was · & alle hys luþer dede,
> Ac naþelas he most voluulle · þat þe prophetes of him sede. (122 – 3)

But this is also enigmatic, since 'he' of line 123 could refer to Our Lord himself, as well as — more obviously — to Judas. The sayings of the prophets (Psalm 108, and Jesus' own words in Matt 26:24) will be fulfilled by the cooperation of the two men. The poet quickly turns from such philosophical matters to assert that such a man as Judas deserved to hang, though suicide is parenthetically condemned:

> He was a strong þeof & manquellare · & also endede hys lyf
> & suche men scolleþ anhonged be · & þo noman hyt nolde do
> Hym sulf he heong vppon a treo.   (138 – 40)

The exemplum ends with a prayer that the audience may be shielded from the wicked place they know Judas has gone to.

The earliest of the *South English Legendary* manuscripts to contain this story place it at the very end of the secular calendar, where it is followed immediately by the Life of Pilatus.[13] Judas and Pilate are presented as birds of a feather: 'Pilatus was a luþer man' echoes 'Iudas was a luþer brid'.

---

[12] *The South English Legendary*, ed. Charlotte D'Evelyn and Anna J. Mill, 3 vols. (EETS, London, 1956 – 59), II 691ff.

[13] Harley 2277 and Corpus C.C. 145, both c.1300. See *Manual* II 414.

When Judas becomes Pilate's steward, the liaison is seen as proverbially inevitable:

> Vor twei schrewen wolleþ beo freond · þei noman elles nere.   (100)

Like Judas, Pilate 'gaderede tresur'; unlike him, Pilate 'spak vayre & was mylde & was euere stille' preferring to work through 'quoyntises' than violence. There are also striking similarities between the lives of these two villains: as a child Pilate kills his step-brother, a motif which is repeated; through his cunning he becomes useful to Herod who makes him 'maister of Ierusalem'. Like Judas he is a suicide; he kills himself in gaol by begging an apple and a knife to peel it with. His body, 'ded as a ston' causes natural disturbances but eventually comes to a rock which 'toclef amydde atwo' to swallow it. The similarities between these two lives, in motifs and in verbal formulae, suggest an archetype of wickedness (though Pilate's case is less interesting in that, although he is the son of an adulterous king, his own life is uncomplicated by sexual intrigue), and establish Judas and Pilate as a pair of villains.

A more sophisticated interpretation of Judas' double villainy is given by the English poet of the *Titus and Vespasian*, usually dated around 1370, written in octosyllabic couplets, and treating the lives of both Judas and Pilate as part of the story of the destruction of Jerusalem.[14] The London poet is superficially interested in the notion of destiny:

> Soo gan Judas wickede to be
> Bothe þrugh blode and destyne.   (4581 – 82)

When Judas enters the orchard the poet digresses to remind us that although his parents thought the sea had done away with Judas,

> But his desteyne soo no wolde,
> Hit most ben right as it sholde.
> Þogh men wene to stoppen Goddes cast,
> Hit wil forth goon at þe last.   (4693 – 96)

The implications of God preserving Judas for a special destiny by having him slay his own father are not explored, but a similar note is struck at the end, when the poet says that Christ would have forgiven Judas his betrayal of Him,

> But he most nedes be lorn
> As it was loked him biforn.   (4837 – 38)

---

[14] *Titus and Vespasian*, ed. J. A. Herbert (Roxburgh Club, London, 1905), p. 202, lines 4487 – 4885.

The alternative manuscript reading of 'ordeyned' for 'loked' shows that scribes in Chaucer's time were alert to the doctrinal implications of the story. Indeed, it may be that the poem has been dated too early and that the poet's strain of fatalism is itself a literary debt to Chaucer. However that may be, *Titus and Vespasian* is unusual in making explicit the thread of fatalism which connects the apocryphal and biblical stories of Judas; in some unarticulated way Judas is seen as victim of 'Goddes cast'.

It would be misleading to suggest that any of the texts so far discussed expresses any *sympathy* for Judas, either overt or covert. His destiny is clearly extraordinary, but the story we have been following makes him guilty, objectively at any rate, of the most abhorrent crimes known in medieval society; it is a tale of homicide, parricide, incest, betrayal, and suicide. Preachers of homilies are not likely to blur the edges of a clear-cut moral and they are usually unwilling to draw any but the most trivial and complacent inference from the double cycle of sin and misfortune.

One point of the story presents particular interest and difficulties to the medieval religious orders: this is the link which explains how Judas came to be purse bearer. To the mendicant orders in the thirteenth century it was a source of some embarrassment that Christ had a purse at all. The Franciscan St Bonaventure explained in his *Apologia Pauperum* that the purse was not an incitement to cupidity but a consolation to the poor: Jesus set an example to the Church to dispose of its wealth; it was thus a distinction between covetousness and charity that Jesus had in mind when he gave the money bag to Judas knowing that he would succumb to temptation and betray him. The purse, like Judas himself, was a necessary evil, a condescension to the evil of the world.[15]

The Drama

The same story sounds startlingly different if we hear it from Judas' own lips — as happens in the medieval drama. Coming from Judas himself, his biography can appear as a tale of misfortune rather than wickedness, a plea for self-justification in the forum of dramatic debate. Structurally the playwrights explored two possibilities: either they introduced the story at the crucial point of Judas' decision to betray Christ, or they delayed it until before Judas' despair, so as to heighten the horror and pathos of his self-destruction. There is only one Middle English play which makes use of the apocryphal life of Judas, the Towneley MS *Suspencio Judae*; this occurs as

---

[15] Bonaventure's *Apologia Pauperum* ch. 10 is discussed by M. D. Lambert, *Franciscan Poverty: the Doctrine of the Absolute Poverty of Christ and the Apostles in the Franciscan Order, 1210 – 1323*, (London, 1951), pp. 135 – 38. The use of *loculos* (Judas' little purses) was specifically abjured by the Friars Minor.

an addition to the cycle of plays, added in the sixteenth century; moreover, it is unfortunately incomplete.[16] The playwright takes the second of the structural options, giving to Judas before he hangs himself a ninety-six line monologue, in which he laments that 'waryd and cursyd I have been aye' and tells of his wretched childhood.

In the French *mystères* Judas' legend does not appear before the fifteenth century. Arnoul Greban includes it at the point where Judas asks to become a disciple; Jean Michel dramatises much of the story, from the fratricide onwards, in six separate interlaced scenes.[17] However, by far the earliest, least known, and most interesting of the dramatic treatments is that of the Provençal *Passion* in the Didot MS.[18] There are so many idiosyncratic features in this version of the story that P. F. Baum suggested that it represents a very archaic form.[19] What Baum did not remark is that these elements form an astonishingly sympathetic interpretation of Judas' motivation, offering a new explanation of the ten per cent and mitigating Judas' guilt by extending the juxtaposition of him with the disciple Peter.

The Provençal *Passion* tells the legend of Judas in the first of three monologues (the other two are the parallel scenes contrasting Judas' remorse and Peter's). A vernacular stage direction says, 'When Judas sees the ointment poured in Jesu Christ he gets on his feet and speaks these words

[16] *The Towneley Cycle: a Facsimile of Huntington MS HM 1*, ed. A. C. Cawley and Martin Stevens (Leeds, 1976), f.131v – 132r. The *Suspencio Iude* (play 32) should come after *Coliphizacio* (21) (see p. xi).

[17] Baum, pp. 542 – 53.

[18] The Didot MS is a collection of Provençal popular religious poetry and *chansons de geste*. It was written by a number of amateur scribes in around 1345. The language of the play is a *mélange* of dialect forms, suggesting earlier *remaniements* of the play and locating it within about 100 km of Toulouse, an area within which many heresies flourished in the thirteenth and fourteenth centuries. Most of these Cathar beliefs stem from the same assumption that the world is evil and Christ is a god of spirit. Among the most striking heresies is the recurrent assertion that suicide is legitimate and honourable in that it hastens deliverance from fleshy bondage (most historical cases appear rather to have been to avoid prosecution for heresy, however); and the argument that incest is preferable to marriage, since in incest the true wickedness of the flesh is more readily perceived. Both arguments are suggestive in relation to the sympathetic treatment afforded Judas in the Provençal *Passion*. More curious still is the view, publicly confessed by a heretic called Lepzet (probably from South Germany in around 1300) that if a man wished to lie with his mother he must pay her eighteen pence: sixpence for having conceived, sixpence for bearing him, sixpence for nursing him. Sisters, however, cost only sixpence. No doubt incest was commoner in the Middle Ages than now. With Lepzet and his sect, however, we seem to be at the lunatic fringe. I hesitate to claim that the Didot *Passion* is a Catharist work and a good deal more work needs to be done to establish in what sense this might be true. In most respects the play's statements are perfectly orthodox, though the omission of Christ's words instituting the eucharist is curious. A certain element of Manicheism seems implicit in many medieval Passion plays, simply as a result of having to embody the forces of evil which crucified Christ.

[19] Baum, pp. 552 – 59.

before all'[20] clearly signalling that the speech is a direct appeal to the audience. The story itself is simpler and more coherent than any version we have met so far. There is no premonitory dream, no fratricide, no picking of forbidden paternal apples. Judas is made an exact contemporary of Jesus. When Herod ordered the slaughter of innocents, Judas' parents put him to sea in a little boat. Thus his escape and that of the Christ child are complementary; they are preserved for one another. Judas' mother brands his back with a hot iron and later recognises him by the scar. Judas is raised by a king. His father comes to the land and, in an inexplicable act of folly and wickedness, Judas kills him. He then flees to Jerusalem, where a woman falls in love with him and he with her. They marry and have two children. When Judas is recognised by the scar, both man and wife, mother and son, go to Jesus for forgiveness. This Provençal emphasis on a love-match is unique and the account of recognition and parting is told with dignity and compassion.

In all the versions discussed so far it is the linking of the early life and the biblical story which is the weak — but crucial — link. The Provençal playwright solves this problem astonishingly. Judas tells how when Christ made him bursar (*majorals*), he told him to think no more of his mother 'than of a sheep'. Judas relates that he willingly agreed to part from her but said, 'Lord, I am anxious for my two children. Who will feed them and bring them up?' Christ replied briefly, 'They shall grow up with their mother, and I shall give them what they shall eat. Of all that God shall give us, the tenth part shall be for them. From such gifts, I swear to God, your sons shall live'.[21] In all other versions, Judas' ten per cent is a mark of his profession as thief and usurer; here it is the crucial link with a tragic past, the price agreed by Christ as an act of charity.[22] Thus when Judas turns from the audience towards the table of the Last Supper, and asks Christ why he allows the waste of such precious ointment, when the money from its sale could have fed the poor, the audience must be as startled as Judas is by Christ's fierce response: 'Cursed Judas — you have little care for the poor; you are a false usurer'.[23] The effect of transposing St John's commentary into Jesus' mouth is disconcerting. Judas now denounces his master, 'You

---

[20] *La Passion Provençal du MS Didot*, ed. William P. Shepard (SATF, Paris, 1928), after l.480.

[21] *ibid.*, lines 560 – 71.

[22] Among scholastic commentators I have found only Peter Comestor who suggests that Judas had a wife and family to keep:
'Judas vero propter lucrum, quia fur erat, et loculos Domini habens, quae mittebantur portabat, id est non solum ferebat, sed asportabat. Habebat enim uxorem et filios, sicut scriptum est de eo: "Fiant filii eius orphani, et uxor eius vidua, etc. (Psalm cviii)". Uxori ergo et filiis dabat quae furabatur'. (*Historia Scholastica, in Evangelia* cap. cxvi, *PL* 198, col.1597 – 98).

[23] *Passion Provençal*, ll.611 – 14.

are a fine traitor — good for nothing but to eat bread!'[24] — a startling indictment of the eucharist. He leaves the table and goes to Caiaphas' scaffold (*catafalc*), where he asks the Jews to arrest Jesus for debt.

The mitigation of Judas' guilt is emphasised later by having Peter address his self-accusations directly to the audience, too. Peter recalls how Jesus favoured him and gave him gifts. 'How can I live?', he asks, 'without wealth of my own I shall die of hunger. Why not hang myself?' Unfortunately the manuscript is torn away at this point, but one can read enough to make out the recurrence of ideas of honour, loss of wealth, betrayal, and self-hanging.[25] Peter is prudent, however, and decides to ask pardon. At once a Jew announces that Christ is to be hanged. Then Judas enters and asks the Jews to free his master. He accuses himself of disloyalty, judges that he is beyond the help of Christ's power and hangs himself. Judas' dignified suicide is only one of several features in this play from the region of Toulouse which suggest the heretical interpretations of the Cathars. [26] Freed from the constraints of textual authority, popular medieval imaginations seem determined to transform the villain into suffering hero.

The Judas ballad

Of all medieval interpretations of Judas the most intriguing is an English song in Trinity College MS B.14.39 (formerly MS 323). The manuscript is thought to be a Dominican or Franciscan commonplace book produced in the Worcester – Hereford area, c.1255 – 1260, and containing 140 poems and sayings, mostly in English, but also in Latin and French.[27] Many of the English poems read like friarly incitements to devotion; worldly wealth is

[24] *ibid.* ll.633 – 34.
[25] *ibid.* ll.1138 – 59.
[26] In accounting for his life and actions, the Provençal Judas describes himself as *desastruc*. The word *desastruc* is glossed in the earliest Provençal version of Donatus' grammar as *infortunatus*, with two alternative etymologies: *des nasques* = ill-born, and, relating it to *desastre*, star-fated. Two kinds of men are said to be *desastruc*: 'those who have no grace of God nor any honour in the world' and 'those who do evil when they seek to do good'. *Desastruc* seems, then, implies that a man is both unlucky and that he brings bad luck on others. The Provençal poet Matfre Ermengaud, who wrote against the Waldensian heretics, says in his *Breviary of Love* that Jesus told his disciples to wash because they were not pure, explaining that 'He said this on account of the *desastrug* Judas who had to betray him (*devia trazir*)'. The word is uncommon in *langue d'oc* and it seems that Judas defines the word rather than the word him; he is the classic case of a man *desastruc*.
[27] Karl Reichl, *Religiöse Dichtung im Englischen Hochmittelalter: Untersuchung und Edition der Handschrift B.14.39 des Trinity College in Cambridge* (Münchener Universitäts-Schriften, 1974). D. Jeffrey thinks the manuscript of Franciscan provenance (*The Early English Lyric and Franciscan Spirituality*, Lincoln, Nebraska, 1975, p. 207). See also *Manual*, VI 1759.

denounced and shrift is urged. The Judas song, recognised by Child as the 'first English ballad'[28] begins, 'Hit wes upon a sereþorsday'. Maundy Thursday was a day specially for 'schering' or purification by shriving, and also a day when monastic observances commemorated Judas' treachery.[29]

Composed in long-line couplets, the poem makes up four brief, dramatic scenes mostly in dialogue, with abrupt transitions between them. However, the song-like repetition of lines 8, 25 and 30, which have become familiar in modern editions of the poem, are probably not warranted by the manuscript, and the figures .ii. which appears in the right hand margin beside these lines more likely indicate, as Skeat suggested, that the singer should repeat the second stave of the tune so as to adapt it to triplet form, as indeed he must mould the lines of varying syllabic length to the shape of his melody.[30] If this more conservative view is right, then the poem has three triplets and its economy is made even more extraordinary by the fact that the total number of lines is seen to be thirty-three; and this, for a poem which tells of the betrayal of Christ, might be thought significant. This is how I present the text:

'Judas' [Trinity College, Cambridge MS B.14.39 f.34r]

Hit wes upon a sereþorsday   þat vred louerd aros,
Ful milde were þe wordes   he spec to Judas:

'Judas, þou most to Jurselem   oure mete for to bugge;
þritti platen of seluer   þou bere up o þi rugge.   4

þou comest fer in þe brode stret,   fer i þe brode strete,
Summe of þine cunesmen   þer þou meist imete.'

Imette wid is soster,   þe swikele wimon:
'Judas, þou were wrþe   me stende þe wid ston,   .ii.   8
For þe false prophete   þat tou bileuest upon.'

---

[28] F. J. Child, *The English and Scottish Popular Ballads*, 5 vols. (Boston, 1882 – 98, repr. New York, 1965), No. 23, I 243 – 4.

Reichl (pp. 116 – 18) has drawn attention to a twentieth-century ballad version from Tennessee in *The Ballad Book of John Jacob Niles* (Boston, 1961), No. 16.

[29] In the Maundy Thursday Rites of Durham, the monks drank from a 'goodly great mazer called Judas cup, which was also edged largely and finely about with silver and double gilt with gold . . . which was never occupied but on Maundy Thursday at night in the fraterhouse'. See John McKinnell, 'Drama and Ceremony in the Last Years of Durham Priory', *Medieval English Theatre* 10 (1988), 100 – 1.

[30] T. Mitsui, 'Notes on the Stanzaic Division and the Metre of *Judas*', *Studies in English Literature* (ELS, Japan) 44 (1979), p. 209.

'Be stille, leue soster,   þin herte þe tobreke!
Wiste min louerd Crist,   ful wel he wolde be wreke.'

'Judas, go þou on þe roc   heie upon þe ston,   12
Lei þin heued i my barm,   slep þou þe anon.'

Sone so Judas   of slepe was awake,
þritti platen of seluer   from hym weren itake.

He drou hymselue bi þe top,   þat al it lauede ablode.   16
þe iewes out of Jurselem,   a wenden he were wode.

Fforet hym com þe riche ieu   þat heiste Pilatus:
'Wolte sulle þi louerd   þat heite Jesus?'

'I nul sulle my louerd   for nones cunnes eiste,   20
Bote hit be for þe þritti platen   þat he me bitaiste.'

'Wolte sulle þi lord Crist   for enes cunnes golde?'
'Nay, bote hit be for þe platen   þat he habben wolde.'

In him com ur lord gon   as is postles seten at mete: 24
'Wou sitte ye, postles,   ant wi nule ye ete?   .ii.
Ic am iboust ant isold   today for oure mete.'

Vp stod him Judas: 'Lord, am I þat?
I nas neuer o þe stude   þer me þe euel spec.'   28

Vp him stod Peter   ant spec wid al is miste:
'þau Pilatus him come   wid ten hundred cnistes,   .ii.
Yet ic wolde, louerd,   for þi loue fiste!'

'Stille þou be, Peter,   wel i þe icnowe.   32
þou wolt fursake me þrien   ar þe coc him crowe.'

There are four episodes. Jesus sends Judas to buy meat for the passover, giving him thirty pieces of silver. Judas encounters a treacherous woman who is his 'sister' and sleeps in her lap. He wakes to find the silver gone; then Pilate appears and bargains with him. Finally, back in the room, Judas denies that he has been a conspirator and Peter boasts of his loyalty.

The listener must be struck at once by the text's extraordinary density — it suggests much in few words, leaving him to make connections and solve puzzles. It is an argument for the completeness of 'Judas' that this riddling quality is characteristic of other poems in the manuscript. A proverb on avarice —

>   þeues frent ant louerides purs,
>   Cunnes cheste ant Cristis curs.   (Reichl No.43)

('Friend of thieves, purse of lords, quarrelling of kindred, curse of Christ') — has a similar compactness. That the author of the couplet had Judas in mind is evident from his rendering of the Latin prose 'malediccio omnium' as 'Cristis curs'.[31]

The economy of the action in 'Judas' is entirely controlled by Christ's bitter and tragic words, 'I am bought and sold today for your meat'. Jesus gives into Judas' hands — or, more exactly, he loads onto Judas' back — the very price of redemption, the thirty pieces of silver by which His own body and blood are bought for all mankind. The command, 'þou bere up a þi rug' suggests that Jesus lays on Judas a burden equivalent to his own ('He bringet þe rode up on his rug' — Reichl No.52, 1.102). Indeed, the entire poem seems dominated by the burden of the silver; they are not pennies as in other accounts of the betrayal, but 'platen' — plates or pieces of silver coin.[32] They seem to have an independent life of their own, linked perhaps to Joseph's silver in the story of Genesis, or to the strange legend told by Godfrey of Viterbo in his *Pantheon* of the descent of the thirty pieces from their coining by Abraham's father.[33]

Judas labours with the silver 'platen' on his back up onto a high rock, where he rests. Finding them — and the woman — gone during his sleep, he rages inconsolably and tears at his hair till it runs with blood. Obsessed with his loss of the pieces entrusted to him, he refuses Pilate's offers of gold or 'any other kind of wealth'. To modern thinking, Judas behaves like a child or an idiot in his obsession, yet I think that the mentality can be understood in medieval terms. Ronald Finucane's book on popular beliefs in medieval England refers to the English practice in the twelfth and thirteenth centuries of bending silver pennies in confirmation of a vow to a saint:

> One must offer *this* coin only or present *that* candle and no other; a preference for the literal and concrete over the figural and abstract. The saint must be given *precisely* the candle or coin indicated when the vow was made.[34]

In this light Judas is no common thief, and there is something moving in his heroic refusal of the wealth offered by the rich Jew Pilatus, his insistence on

[31] A Franciscan sermon for Schere Thursday (Oxford, Merton College MS 248) speaks in riddle that is also suggestive: 'Trewe loue is a robbour & doþ noman unriʒt'. (Quoted by Homer G. Pfander, *The Popular Sermon of the Medieval Friar in England* (New York, 1937), pp. 50–1.
[32] Reichl No. 70 has 'þritti poneues'. *The Northern Passion* (ed. F. A. Foster, EETS 145, London, 1913) speaks of 'Thretty plates of penyes rounde' (1.1956). In the thirteenth-century *Genesis and Exodus* (ed. R. Morris, EETS 7, rev. ed., London, 1873), 'Ioseph solde ðe bredere then / For xxx plates to ðe chapman' (200–1).
[33] E. Du Méril, *Poésies populaires Latines du Moyen Age* (Paris, 1847), p. 321. Kermode develops the idea that parts of the gospel narratives were composed as *midrashim* on older 'testimonies' and notes St Matthew's finding of thirty pieces of silver in Zechariah (11:12): 'They weighed for my price thirty pieces of silver' (*The Genesis of Secrecy*, p. 86).
[34] Ronald Finucane, *Miracles and Popular Beliefs in Medieval England* (London, 1977), p. 74.

recovering what has been entrusted ('bitaiste') to him by his master.[35] His formulaic resistance to temptation links him, oddly, with the martyr St Margaret in the Trinity MS poem.[36]

Perhaps the most intriguing feature of the story — one parallelled only, it seems, in the apocryphal Coptic Gospels[37] — is the temptress, the 'swikele wimon', who is mysteriously in league with Pilate. She is Judas' 'soster', one of the 'cunesmen' (kinsmen) of whom Christ speaks. Judas addresses her as 'leue soster', yet she seems also to be his lover (a term licensed by the *Song of Songs* and used familiarly, to express endearment).[38] Her scornful denunciation of 'þe false prophete þat tou bileuest upon' shows resentment at Judas' betrayal of his own kin and must allude to his having given her up for Christ. This, of course, is exactly what happens in the apocryphal life of Judas. The incestuous love has been redirectly from mother to sister.

The diabolic temptation 'high upon the stone' — at once a secret tryst and an exposed place — is immediately qualified by the seductive voice coaxing Judas asleep. Tormented by insecurity, denounced for his new allegiance, reproached for betraying his former life, Judas takes refuge in sex and sleep. Since the Middle English 'barm' of line 13 can mean equally 'breast' and 'lap', the image of Judas cradled asleep after the quarrel and love-making is insistently motherly. Yet, although her vehement denunciations of Christ allow Judas to appear in a sympathetic light in defence of his master, Judas' words are equivocal. His urging her to silence and secrecy may indicate merely his desire not to be found out reverting to his old ways. Although there is evident irony in his conditional, 'Wiste min louerd Crist', since the listener knows that Christ *does* know, the nature of divine foreknowledge is an aspect of the poem that comes to disturb us more and more.

In the woman's threatening of Judas with stoning (which, as we saw in the *Southern English Legendary*, was the way Judas is said to have killed his own father), there is a suggestion of the death suffered by St Stephen. This boy hero of the second oldest English ballad (fifteenth-century) is led out of

---

[35] The crucial word *bitaiste* occurs a few pages later in the Trinity MS, in the dialogue of Body and Soul at Doomsday (Reichl No. 52), where the poet distinguishes between avarice and a true attitude to wealth, which is thankful to God for His gifts. Soul urges Body to sing masses in thanks for 'þat he þe bitaiste', and blames it for having always been busy about increasing its personal wealth ('to echen þin haiste'). The distinction heightens the paradox of Judas' behaviour in lines 21 – 2.

[36] St Margaret resists both 'gold ant fee' and the pagans' denunciation of 'the prophete': 'I nule leten is loue for oþer neuer on' (l. 89) 'Awaried worþe þine godes þat tou leuest inne' (225).

[37] Carleton Brown, ed., *English Lyrics of the Thirteenth Century* (Oxford, 1932), p. 183.

[38] 'I have a ȝong suster' (Brown-Robbins, *Index* 1303) Cf. *PP* B.5.650-1: 'By Crist! quod a commune womman, þi compaignie wol I folwe./ Thow shalt saye I am þi suster!'.

town by Herod's men, who 'stonyt hym wyth ston'.[39] The listener's imagined apprehension of suffering becomes a reality in the scene where Judas tears at his hair until his head runs with blood. This conventionalised icon of impotent rage and madness (the Jews 'awenden he were wod') may recall Samson, betrayed as he slept in Delilah's lap and she cut off his hair.[40] The image is even more startling if, recalling that Judas' hair was held to be angry red,[41] we see it as a violent form of self-purification appropriate to Schere Thursday (as clergy shaved their heads and beards in token of penitence).

This haunting portrait of demonic possession, isolation, and suffering, occupies the exact centre of the poem (17/33) and is made more intense by being imagined viewed by an audience — the crowd of Jews outside the walls of Jerusalem. Our sense of their mocking the man whose 'top . . . lauede ablode' disturbs us as a response dislocated from its normal association with Christ, suggesting Judas as a parody — if a compassionate one — of God's Passion.[42]

In the 'swikele wimon' who tempts Judas can also be seen a curious recasting of the serving woman of St Matthew (26:69) who accuses Peter of being one of Jesus' followers. Judas' attempt to shame her, weak though it is, compares favourably with Peter's denials in the gospel source. That the poet of 'Judas' meant the contrast cannot be doubted, in view of the ballad's climax and conclusion, where Peter boasts of his strength and loyalty to be answered quietly by Jesus' prediction of his betrayal.

It is not possible to sustain a completely sympathetic interpretation of Judas as victim of female deceit. His denial of complicity, 'I nas neuer of þe stude þer me þe euel spec' (I was never in the place where men spoke evil of you), sounds like the disingenuousness of a man who cannot say yea or nay.

---

[39] British Library, Sloane MS 2593. R. L. Greene, *Early English Carols*, 2nd ed., (Oxford, 1975), No.57. The boy Stephen's refusal of Herod's 'gold and fee' and his oath by the capon which crows from the cooking pot (a motif in Judas' story in the *Cursor Mundi* ll.15961 ff.) link his story with Judas.

[40] As in the splendid bas relief on the fontana maggiore in Perugia. Cf. Judges 16:19.

[41]   Þe rede mon he is a quet
      for he wole þe þin iwil red,
      he is cocker þef & horeling
      scolde of wreche-dome he is king.'
(*Proverbs of Alfred*, ed. Helen Pennock South (1931, repr. New York, 1970), lines 661 – 64).

    Judas' hair seems an important feature of his iconography, see note 2 above. In SEL, in the struggle of Judas and his father, 'hii nome eyþer *bi þe top*' (1.81) while Pilate's childhood wickedness is shown by fighting with his half-brother, 'hii *toppede* ofte' (1.15).

[42] Borgés, in his 'Three Versions of Judas' entertains the idea of Judas as sacrificial counterpart to Christ, the only disciple who perceived his secret divinity and terrible purpose. *Fictions*, ed. and trans. Anthony Kerrigan (London, 1965, repr. 1974), pp. 138 – 43.

Yet, just as we might conclude that Judas has lost all moral sense and is brazening out the notoriously difficult public scene, the poet pushes Peter into the foreground. The extravagance of his boast contrasts beautifully with the quietness of Christ's prophecy. Peter the rock will not be undone by anything so spectacular as a hundred of Pilate's knights, but by the mere words of another woman. Once again, the cryptic silence of the ballad leads the listener to fill out the action from his familiarity with the larger story. There is no need to suppose that the song is only fragmentary: thirty-three lines are enough.

The ballad ends, as it began, with prophecy. Christ's 'milde' words to Judas have been proved true in Judas' actions and will prove true in Peter's. This is no 'false prophete'. Christ's words to Judas become fact almost at once, in the space between lines 6 and 7, between the conditionally possible 'þou meist imete' and the past indicative 'Imette'.[43] The linguistic shift is repeated between lines 13 and 14, where Judas' fatal sleep occupies the space between the sister's imperative 'slep þou þe' and the narrator's 'Sone so Judas of slepe was awake'. As a result Judas seems robbed of active power, to be merely the object of commands thrust upon him by others — Christ, the woman, Pilate. It is notable that his most decisive action is violence against himself — a proleptic image of suicide. Christ's words to Judas began as compulsion ('þou most') and imperative ('þou bere'), but then modulate ('þou comest' may be understood as a future or a conditional: 'When you come') into the possible: 'þou *meist* imete' contrasts meaningfully with 'þou *most*'. The juggling of verb forms cleverly leaves Judas technically a free agent and Christ's enigmatic words can be interpreted as a warning against a danger which both He and Judas know may assail him once he goes into Jerusalem. Since Judas has to buy goods, the most natural interpretation of 'þe brode strete' would seem to be the High Street where the traders are (The Broad, as in Oxford), but what does Christ mean by saying — and repeating — that Judas will come '*fer i* þe brode strete'? To be 'far along' a broad highway would seem to be well on the road to perdition.[44] Like the high rock the broad street is part of a moral landscape, where there are only two roads and they lead to salvation and damnation. The ordeal which our Lord commands for Judas is thus much more terrible than in the gospels or in any other medieval account I know, because it is done in full knowledge of Judas' former weakness and of the scorned woman waiting for vengeance in the streets of Jerusalem.

---

[43] In ME *may* can be either model auxiliary, expressing the subjunctive of potentiality ('It is possible that you will meet') or an auxiliary in the future tense ('You will meet'). See Tauno F. Mustanoja, *A Middle English Syntax*, Part I (Mémoires de la Société Néophilologique de Helsinki XXIII, Helsinki, 1960), pp. 455, 494 – 5.

[44] See *MED brod* 7c and the 'lata porta et spatiosa via' of Matt 7:13.

Conclusion

What, in conclusion, can be taken from the legends of Judas? What do they mean? Their importance seems to me to lie primarily in the fact that they are, as Jacobus would say, 'not authentic', not accepted as orthodox, and consequently they show medieval minds at work at the edges of difficult issues which the Church Fathers had failed to explain to the satisfaction of ordinary people. On the evidence of St John's gospel medieval people had little reason to quarrel with the received divine judgment of Judas as a 'son of perdition'. Dante places him at the lowest point of hell, his head and torso hidden inside the middle of Satan's three mouths, his legs kicking helplessly in the icy mist. Without such an image of perdition, perhaps, the idea of salvation would become meaningless. In contrast to Dante's vision (*Inferno* 33,55 – 62), how much doctrinal equivocation — yet also subtlety and curiosity — are displayed by the popular accounts of Judas' life. The dismal cycle of abandonment, parricide, incest, repentance, recognises that the man who had to betray Christ and then hang himself must have a special destiny, finely balanced between misfortune and wickedness. That the events of the first cycle are, in a sense, neutral is borne out by the fact that this Oedipal plot forms the basis of the medieval saint's legend of Saint Gregory. The point seems to be, rather, that Gregory and Judas are both men destined for extraordinary undertakings. Repentance of his early sins gives Judas a fresh start and brings him into the Christian story; yet the medieval authors do not usually point to the *contrast* between the two cycles of sin; rather, they seem fascinated by the way in which his deeds fulfil a divine prophecy, and by the small space which that seems to allow for the operation of freewill.

In linking the two cycles of Judas' life the function of the thirty pieces of silver is crucial. Judas' role as bearer of the common purse seems to have held a special importance for the preaching friars, who were largely responsible for popularising the apocryphal life. Though it would have been easy to present Judas merely as a type of avarice, his motives were made more complex than that. The 'swikele wimon' looks at first sight like a piece of friars' misogyny, but if my interpretation is correct, her appearance in the poem is deep-rooted in a tragic past; she might be seen as Judas' fate, cooperating in the economy of salvation to make Judas' bargain a double destiny that is both psychologically and theologically disturbing. Finally, and even more speculatively, it may not be irrelevant to observe that the equivocal sympathy afforded Judas in the stories spread by preaching friars is gained at the expense of St Peter, the rock of the established Church.

THEOLOGICAL DOCTRINE AND POPULAR RELIGION IN THE MYSTERY PLAYS

HANS-JÜRGEN DILLER

'Popular religion' is an ambiguous term. It may mean beliefs held by the people and suspected by the Church. This set of beliefs has received considerable attention from social historians in the recent past. It may suffice in this context to mention Natalie Zemon Davis and the Soviet cultural historian Aron Gurevitch.[1] As far as I am aware, popular religion in this sense of the term does not play an important part in the English mystery plays — apart, of course, from the Mak episode in the *Secunda Pastorum*. Mak does use magic to ensure the soundness of the Shepherds' sleep, and he and his wife resort to superstition when they claim that the 'child' in the cradle has been transfigured by an elf. But when they do this their situation is so clearly desperate that nobody will take their claim seriously. The Wakefield Master obviously wanted to make superstition look ridiculous. While this may imply that he felt the need to combat it in his audience, it certainly does not betray any secret sympathies, as certain ritually-inclined critics seem to believe.[2] Other instances of popular customs which may go back to pagan times, such as the wrestling in the Chester Shepherds Play, are equally clearly part of the counter-world which is overcome by the advent of Christ.

Important as this kind of popular religion certainly was during the Middle Ages, it has left only the scantiest of traces in the mystery plays. What we have to deal with is popular religion in the sense not of religion of the people, but religion for the people, i.e. religion as taught the lay population by the Church. This sort of religion, which borders on popular piety, has to

---

[1] Natalie Zemon Davis, 'Some Tasks and Themes in the Study of Popular Religion', in *The Pursuit of Holiness in Late Medieval and Renaissance Religion. Papers from the University of Michigan Conference*, ed. Charles Trinkaus and Heiko A. Oberman (Leiden, 1974) [Studies in Medieval and Reformation Thought, 10], pp. 307 – 36; Aaron J. Gurjewitsch, *Mittelalterliche Volkskultur* (Dresden, 1986). The German translation of Gurevitch contains a postscript which updates the Russian original (Aron Ja. Gurevitch, *Problemy srednevekovoj narodnoj kul'tury*, Moscow, 1981).

[2] John Speirs, 'The Towneley "Shepherds' Plays" ', in *The Age of Chaucer* (rev. edn. Harmondsworth, 1959) [The Pelican Guide to English Literature, Vol. I], p. 169, sees in the 'Mak farce as a whole [. . .] an expression of the jollity of the folk as the rebirth significance of the midwinter festival overcomes the death significance'.

be seen in relation to what I have called 'theological doctrine', not in opposition to it.

The mainstream of English-speaking scholarship seems to use 'popular religion' in the second sense. It stands for religion as it was received by the lay population thanks to the popularizing efforts of the Church, especially after Lateran IV (1215). After this council the teaching of the elements of the Christian faith no doubt became increasingly important.[3] In 1977, at the First International Symposium on Medieval Drama, A. C. Cawley read a controversial paper on 'Medieval Drama and Didacticism'[4] which was followed by an equally controversial discussion.[5] Cawley believed that the plays were under the massive influence of the manuals of religious instruction which stemmed from the Council of Lambeth (1281), especially of the *Lay Folks' Catechism*.[6] He supported his thesis with the argument that '[i]nstruction in many of these doctrines [as promulgated in the *LFC*] is given in the vernacular Corpus Christi plays'.[7] In the discussion a good many points were raised, but a good many others were not. Although it may seem impertinent to go back to a discussion of 14 years ago, I shall add a few objections of my own, because they will help me define the 'popular religion' we are dealing with in the mystery plays:

(1) The *Lay Folks' Catechism* and its Latin original are presented as exhaustive catalogues of what the Christian penitents have to know at their annual confession. This knowledge is necessary for their souls' eternal bliss, lack of it puts the believer's soul in serious danger (*LFC*, 33, 37).[8] The elements of the faith contained in the *LFC* are thus a matter of utmost importance. Every parish priest is in duty bound to teach them. Negligence in this matter would be a very serious offence indeed.

(2) If I, as a Lutheran, may compare the teaching of the *LFC* with that of Luther's 'Smaller Catechism', which in my youth was still the staple of religious teaching, I must admit that I find the teaching of the *LFC* enormously detailed and a considerable burden on the powers of abstract thinking. That God is one god in three persons and that the Holy Ghost proceeds from the Father and the Son — these doctrines, for instance, are not part of Luther's Smaller Catechism.

---

[3] Leonard E. Boyle, 'The Fourth Lateran Council and Manuals of Popular Theology', in *The Popular Literature of Medieval England*, ed. Thomas J. Heffernan (Knoxville, TN, 1985) [Tennessee Studies in Literature, 28], 30 – 43.

[4] *Proceedings of the Colloquium Held at the University of Leeds, 10 – 13 September 1974, on the Drama of Medieval Europe* (Leeds, 1975), pp. 3 – 12.

[5] *ib.*, pp. 13 – 21.

[6] T. F. Simmons and H. E. Nolloth, eds., *The Lay Folks' Catechism*. EETS OS 118 (London, 1901). [henceforth '*LFC*']

[7] Cawley, *art. cit.*, p. 6.

[8] Unless indicated otherwise, line references are to the 'T' version of the *LFC* (from Archbishop Thoresby's own register).

(3) It is therefore not surprising that, as far as the doctrines of the *LFC* are treated in the plays at all, that treatment is far shorter and less systematic. The plays are sometimes even disappointingly neglectful of doctrinal content. For instance, the double procession of the Holy Ghost is never even mentioned in the Pentecost plays. It does figure prominently, though, in the N.Town Incarnation scene.[9] The institution of the Eucharist is even absent from the Towneley cycle (which may be owing to the fact that the play in question, the *Conspiracio et Capcio*, is a rather confusingly composite text).[10] The tenet that belief in the doctrines of transsubstantiation and concomitance is essential for salvation is expounded only in the N.Town cycle:[11]

> bretheryn be þe [vertu] of þese wordys þat [re]hercyd be
> Þis þat shewyth as bred to ȝour Apparens
> Is mad þe very flesche and blod of me
> To þe wech þei þat wolde be savyd must ȝeve credens.'
> (N.Town 'Passion Play I', 702 – 5)[12]

Considering that this doctrine emphasizes like no other the power of the clergy (who for this very reason are said to have more power than the angels),[13] it receives surprisingly little attention in the plays. The *LFC* also

---

[9] The name 'N.Town' is now generally accepted for the misnomer 'Ludus Coventriæ'. For justification of the name cf. Peter Meredith's new edition *The Mary Play from the N.Town Manuscript* (London, 1987), p. vii.

[10] Cf. Mendal G. Frampton, 'Towneley XX: The *Conspiracio (et Capcio)'*, *PMLA* 58 (1943) 920 – 37. In York the Last Supper presumably was on a leaf between ff. 132 and 133, now lost. Cf. Beadle, ed., pp. 230f.

[11] The doctrine of concomitance, which goes back to Alexander of Hales' *Summa universae theologiae* (1st half 13th century), claims that the bread of the communion is changed into both the flesh and blood of Christ. It thus justifies the withholding of the chalice from the lay congregation. This doctrine is possibly hinted at in the Chester Pentecost play, Ch XXI 345f.:
> that Godes bodye granted us was
> to use in forme of bread.

[12] Unless otherwise indicated, quotations are from the following editions: *The Chester Mystery Cycle*, eds. R. M. Lumiansky and David Mills, EETS SS 3 (London, 1974); *Ludus Coventriæ, or: The Plaie Called Corpus Christi*, ed. K.S. Block, EETS ES 120 (London, 1922); *The Towneley Plays*, ed. G. England, EETS ES 71 (London, 1897); *The York Plays*, ed. Richard Beadle, York Medieval Texts, second series (London, 1982).

[13] Cf. *Mirk's Festial*, ed. Theodor Erbe, EETS ES 96 (London, 1905), p. 169: 'for he [þe prest] haþ of Godis ȝeft here in erth þat he ȝaf neuer to no angele in Heuen: þat is, forto make Godis body'. Cf. also *Everyman*, 735 – 9:
> God hath to them more power gyuen
> Than to ony aungell that is in heuen.
> With v. wordes he may consecrate,
> Goddes body in flesshe and blode to make,
> And handeleth his Maker betwene his handes.
> (*Everyman*, ed. A. C. Cawley, [Manchester, 1961].)

insists that whoever takes the sacrament of the altar unworthily works his own damnation (*LFC*, 327), a point which must have been of paramount importance for the pastoral care. Yet again, it is mentioned only in N.Town: When Judas approaches Jesus to take communion, Jesus says to him:

> Myn body to þe I wole not denye
> Sythyn þou wylt presume þer-upon
> Yt xal be þi dampnacyon verylye
> I ȝeve þe warnyng now be-forn.   (*ib.*, 774 – 7)

It is true that the other cycles also insist on Judas' damnation, but they attribute it to his suicide. The Towneley cycle in its fragmentary *Suspencio Iude* (T XXXII) retells the story of the *Legenda aurea*, according to which Judas was damned already in his mother's womb. Thus, one of the most important tenets of Christian doctrine is not only omitted, but is even obscured and sacrificed to the appeal of a legend. None of the Harrowing of Hell plays mentions any of the various theories of Redemption which figure so prominently in the criticism of the cycles;[14] confession is never even mentioned as far as I am aware. The list could probably be extended.

(4) Yet a fourth point which argues against the didactic aim of the mystery cycles deserves to be made: At the end of his paper Cawley points out that in the mystery cycles, the sinners, 'falsely and self-defensively, accuse the godly men and women of committing those very sins which they themselves are often guilty of'.[15] As examples, Cawley mentions the Torturers in Towneley who accuse Jesus of witchcraft, of allowing himself to be called God's son and of defiling the Sabbath. If they were true, these charges would make Jesus guilty of violating the first three commandments. This argument seems to me self-defeating. For if we accept that the audience of the Towneley Plays were capable of so categorizing these charges and thus appreciating their falseness, then it follows that they were in no need of having the commandments taught them. The commandments in question are *recalled* rather than *taught*.

From the arguments adduced it has become clear, I hope, that 'didacticism' is insufficient to define the function of the mystery plays. We can hardly say with Stanley J. Kahrl that '[t]he plays came into being in the first place to educate the general populace in the articles of the faith'.[16] The notion of 'didacticism' has to be qualified to be useful. As far as there is overt didacticism, as in the Chester Expositor, it mostly concerns points which do not figure in the manuals of religious instruction and which we

---

[14] *E.g.*, Timothy Fry, 'The Unity of the *Ludus Coventriæ*', SP, 48 (1951), 527 – 70; Claude Gauvin, *Un cycle du théâtre religieux anglais du moyen âge. Le jeu de la ville de "N"*, (Paris, 1973), esp. pp. 214ff.

[15] *Art. cit.*, p. 12.

[16] 'Secular Life and Popular Piety in Medieval English Drama', in Heffernan, ed., p.103.

may assume to have been peripheral to the teaching of the Church. The only cycle that is interested in matters that are central to the doctrinal teaching of the Church throughout seems to me to be the N.Town cycle.

Obviously, there are some tenets of the Christian faith which the mystery plays emphasize, and some which they neglect. Can we find a criterion which satisfactorily distinguishes between these two kinds of tenets? It is perhaps tempting to think that the contrast between myth and dogma might provide such a criterion, but such a distinction would run us into numerous difficulties, not the least important one being that 'myth' in modern criticism is a highly loaded term. Moreover, modern, de-mythologizing theology would claim that Christian dogma is just as 'mythological' as the stories told in the Old and New Testaments.[17] In this sense all of pre-Bultmann Christianity is mythological. Another possible distinction would be that between story and dogma; but this, too, has its drawbacks: in the Christian religion story and dogma are inextricably interwoven, witness the dogmas concerning the immaculate conception, the virgin birth, and many others.

The criterion which I propose is very simple but suprisingly workable, though at times also embarrassingly crude. I call it *tangibility*. It is largely identical with what Meg Twycross, borrowing from Nicholas Love's *Mirrour*, has called the 'bodily' (as opposed to the 'ghostly') side of the Christian faith.[18] I prefer my term because it seems to me more 'operational'. But more important than this terminological quibble is the fact that the mystery plays not only *prefer* the tangible or bodily aspects over the intangible or ghostly ones. They even *sacrifice* the latter for the benefit of the former. Doctrinal exposition is often passed over in silence, even when an event is likely to create an impression that is contrary to the teachings of the Church. Examples for this tendency were given earlier. Since the Middle Ages were fully aware of the fact that pictures are much more effective than spoken words — and living pictures even more so than dead ones —[19] we are forced to conclude that the majority of the mystery cycles were not meant to teach the 'ghostly' or 'intangible' aspects of the Christian faith. We may even have to assume that the Church was prepared to risk a certain confusion in the minds of the lay believers — unless, that is, it was very assured of the quality of its preachers.

[17] *E.g.* Rudolf Bultmann, *Jesus Christus und die Mythologie* (Gütersloh, 1980⁵), p. 14 (American original: *Jesus Christ and Mythology*, New York, 1958).

[18] Meg Twycross, 'Books for the Unlearned', *Drama and Religion*, ed. James Redmond [Themes in Drama 5] (Cambridge, 1983), p. 80.

[19] Cf. Clifford Davidson, ed., *A Middle English Treatise on the Playing of Miracles* (Washington, DC, 1981), ll. 211–19 and comment p. 67. Especially important is Davidson's reference to Reginald Pecock's defence of miracle plays in his *Repressor of Over Much Blaming of the Clergy*.

The Church which accepted these risks must have realized that an emotional response to the 'tangible' aspects of the faith was at least as important to secure the allegiance of the believers as a knowledge of the doctrine. The emotional side of the Christian faith is left severely on one side in the manuals of popular religious instruction. 'Tangible' facts have this advantage over 'intangible' ones that they can engage the reader's or hearer's imagination ever anew. 'Ghostly' or 'intangible' assertions will be either accepted or rejected, or (a third possibility) accepted and then forgotten. Unless we are specialists for abstract thinking, they will not preoccupy us very much.

Christ shares with many mythical heroes a miraculous birth and miraculous powers. The dogma of the virgin birth, which is 'tangible' in the very crudest sense of the term, was of course given ample space on the medieval stage. But it is probably correct to say that it was staged not because it was sanctioned as dogma, but because it engaged the imagination of the populace. Having disagreed with Stanley Kahrl's dictum that the plays' purpose was to teach the articles of the faith (cf. fn. 16), we can all the more heartily agree with his next sentence: 'They are part of the world of the *Lay Folks Mass Book* [not the *Lay Folks' Catechism*!], the Northern Passion, South English Legendary, the world of the saints' lives and the "late medieval cult of Jesus" '.[20]

A paragraph or so ago I said that the mystery plays concentrate on the affective side of the Christian faith, that they want to engage their hearers' imagination and emotions. It is not so easy to be very specific about the kind of emotions they are meant to arouse. The drama does not have the same means as the narrative or the meditative poem to guide its readers' responses. There is no 'guide persona' (to use Meg Twycross' happy phrase) who might 'step gently in and point the reader's attention'.[21] And the expositors and doctors that we find in Chester and N.Town are not very helpful in this respect, because the responses they solicit are less to the imagined reality than to the dramatic performance. Very occasionally they do ask the audience to hear 'the matter' 'with reverence', the Chester Expositor also offers typological interpretations of the events just seen. But more commonly these 'Presenters' ask the spectators' indulgence for imperfect acting or inform us that the short time at the disposal of the actors prevents them from presenting the entire story. Thus our attention is directed to the representation rather than to the represented reality. An emotional response to the story is asked for very rarely indeed.

---

[20] *Loc. cit.*; for the 'late medieval cult of Jesus' cf. J. W. Robinson, 'The Late Medieval Cult of Jesus and the Mystery Plays', *PMLA* 80 (1965) 508 – 14.

[21] *Art. cit.*, p. 75.

If there are 'guide personae' in Meg Twycross' sense, they are not 'authorial' but 'personal' (to borrow a term from Stanzel's theory of narrative).[22] We find them in the *dramatis personae* who address the audience. And they do not ask us to identify with them imaginatively, but to discover real identities. Most of these identities are of a rather homely kind: between Noah and henpecked husbands, between Mrs Noah and shrewish wives, between the Shepherds and poor English labourers. Even the identity between Joseph and husbands who suspect they have been cuckolded is of this 'homely' type. But there are more serious identities as well: between us and the quest-mongers and false swearers whom Pilate addresses in the Towneley *Conspiracio [et Capcio]* (T XX, 24f.). Much more important and above all more universal is the identity between us and the torturers of Christ, which is made clear in Christ's speeches from the Cross. But whether the identities be humorous or deadly serious, they always presuppose a distance between spectator and *dramatis persona*.

If we want to reconstruct the attitudes which the contemporary audiences were expected to take we can only proceed inductively: study individual plays and see whether there is a consistent 'tone' emerging in any one group of plays. I propose to do this with the Towneley and N.Town cycles. For the Towneley cycle I shall largely draw on the evidence collected by E. Catherine Dunn, although I shall use it to a rather different purpose. Dunn believed she had discovered a 'prophetic principle' in Towneley which went beyond the general constructive principle which W.W. Greg had postulated in the Old Testament plays of all known cycles.[23] I believe that her evidence, so far as it is not culled from the *Processus Prophetarum* (T VII), points to a mood of longing rather than to prophetic certainty. This longing turns into gratitude when the longed-for event has at last taken place. The sense of gratitude is particularly strong in the Shepherds Plays. In the *Prima Pastorum* the Shepherds devote more than a stanza to the privilege they are about to enjoy:[24]

1 Pastor: Wold God that we myght this yong bab see!   440
2 Pastor: Many prophetys that syght desyryd veralee,
To haue seen that bright.
3 Pastor: And God so hee
Wold shew vs that wyght, we myght say, perdé,
We had sene

[22] Franz K. Stanzel, *A Theory of Narrative* (Cambridge, 1984), esp. chapter 7.
[23] E. Catherine Dunn, 'Lyrical Form and the Prophetic Principle in the Towneley Plays', *Mediaeval Studies* 23 (1961) 80 – 90; W. W. Greg, *Bibliographical and Textual Problems of the English Miracle Cycles* (London, 1914), p. 16.
[24] The quotations from the Towneley Shepherds and Noah plays are from A. C. Cawley, ed., *The Wakefield Pageants in the Towneley Cycle* (Manchester, 1958).

That many sant desyryd,   445
With prophetys inspyryd;
If thay hym requyryd,
Yit closyd ar thare eene.
  2 Pastor: God graunt vs that grace!
  3 Pastor: God so do.   449

Similarly in the *Secunda Pastorum*:

  1 Pastor: Patryarkes that has bene, and prophetes beforne,
  Thay desyryd to haue sene this chylde that is borne.
  Thay ar gone full clene; that haue thay lorne.
  We shall se hym, I weyn, or it be morne,   695
  To tokyn.
  When I se hym and fele,
  Then wote I full weyll
  It is true as steyll
  That prophetys haue spokyn: 700
  To so poore as we ar that he wold appere, [. . .]

The patriarchs mentioned in the first line of this stanza have indeed
expressed something like a desire for the coming of Christ. When Noah, at
the end of the *Processus Noe cum Filiis*, is asked by his wife whether all the
victims of the flood will ever escape from the pain [of hell], he replies:

  Wyn [=escape]? No, iwis, bot he that myght hase
  Wold myn of thare mys, and admytte thaym to grace.   (T III 550f.)

The charitable feeling conveyed in this exchange compares rather
favourably with the smugness which we sense at the end of the York Noah:
When the York Uxor is worried about the prospect of the world ending in
fire one day, she is reassured by her husband:

  Beis noȝt aferde þerfore,
  ȝe sall noght lyffe þan yore,
  Be many hundreth yhere.   (Y IX 306 – 8)

The Towneley Abraham, at the beginning of his pageant, prays:

  Mightfull lord! to the I pray,
  Let onys the oyle of mercy fall,
  Shall I neuer abide that day,
  Truly yit I hope I shall.   (T IV 5 – 8)

Later in the same prayer he thinks of 'oure elders all' who have followed
Adam into hell (T IV 33, 43ff.). The fact that in this age the world is still
waiting for the Saviour is thus brought home to the audience more strongly
than in the other cycles. The same *Ubi sunt* topos is uttered by old Simeon in
the Towneley *Purification of Mary*:

> Bot yit I meruell, both euyn and morne,
> Of old elders that were beforne,
> wheder thay be safe or lorne,
> where thay may be. (T XVII 9 – 12)

In the further course of his speech he reminisces about the prophets 'that now ar dede' (*ib.*, 55) and who had foretold the birth of the Christ. He prays for the grace of seeing Him before his death (*ib.*, 65 – 72).

To return to the Towneley *Abraham*: God promises, without being heard by the patriarch:

> I will help adam and his kynde,
> Might I lufe and lewte fynd; [. . .]. (T IV 49f.)

God remembers this promise at the beginning of the *Annunciacio*:

> To abraham I am in dett
> To safe hym and his gett [=offspring]. (T X 41f.)

The feeling of fulfilled longing voiced by the Shepherds is also expressed by John the Baptist. After having baptized Christ, he says:

> Thou blys me, lord, hence or thou gang,
> So that I may thi frenship fele;
> I haue desyryd this sight ful lang,
> ffor to dy now rek I no dele. (T XIX 205 – 8)

The baptism plays of the other cycles do not express this feeling. Nor do the other Noah and Abraham plays foreshadow the coming of Christ in the way that is peculiar to Towneley. There is a doubleness of perspective here which makes the Redemption appear more urgently and more persistently awaited than in any other cycle: the *dramatis personae* express primarily their uncertainty about the fate of their forebears and a vague hope of salvation. To the audience this hope is a certainty, even a living reality. The attitude which the Towneley Plays instilled in their audience must have been one of gratitude to God, heightened by a sense of compassion with the patriarchs and prophets. It is remarkable that this attitude should be so consistently maintained in such a heterogeneous cycle.

I stated earlier that the N.Town cycle seems to me the only one with a thoroughgoing interest in the 'intangible' aspects of the Christian faith. This has already become apparent in the few remarks about the Last Supper scene in 'Passion Play I'. But the most impressive attempt at staging an 'intangible' aspect of the Christian faith is the Incarnation. To demonstrate this, I first have to retell the action of that scene. As is well known, the N.Town Incarnation follows closely the model of the Pseudo-Bonaventuran *Meditationes de Vita Christi*. Like the *Meditationes* and unlike all other cycles, N.Town presents the Incarnation as the answer to a prayer, again like the *Meditationes* it includes a Debate of the Four Daughters of God, an allegorical tale which was extremely popular in the Middle Ages.[25] The prayer is uttered at the beginning of pageant 11 by that ambiguous figure Contemplacio, who before has served as prologue but now becomes a factor in the action. He summarizes prayers from Isaiah and Jeremiah, thus establishing a continuity with the Old Testament which goes beyond that suggested by the Prophets play. But of more immediate importance is the fact that Contemplacio already strikes the keynote of the conflict which is to dominate the ensuing dialogue between the Four Daughters of God: Man would deserve ('were wurthy', 1063; 4)[26] to suffer endless pain for his offence, but that would mean that God's 'great mercy' has to 'perish' (1064; 5). Contemplacio asks God to follow mercy:

> Lete mercy meke [make submissive] þin hyest magesté.   (1067; 8)

Contemplacio's prayer is supported by the Virtutes, who correspond to the Angels of the *Meditationes*. Like those, they implore God to fill again those seats in heaven which have been vacant since the fall of Lucifer and his associates. The Virtutes, however, go beyond the Angels of the *Meditationes* in pointing out that Man was seduced by the Devil and that he is repentant, whereas the Devil 'in his obstinacy doth dwelle' (1103; 44). When God the Father begins to speak, he does not react to these arguments. He replies with a quotation from Ps 11:6, first in Latin, then in English:

> Propter miseriam inopum
> Et gemitum pauperum
> Nunc exurgam.   (1108 – 10)

God in His speech reacts exclusively to the cries for mercy, not to the arguments offered in the preceding speeches. He thus avoids showing Himself 'constrained', as it were, by the laws of logic. The issue of principle, which dominates the following debate of the Daughters of God, is thus neatly separated from God's decision, which is shown to be prompted solely by considerations of pity. God has already made up his mind, He cannot be swayed by the following debate:

---

[25] Out of the vast literature on the subject only the most important titles can be cited here: Hope Traver, *The Four Daughters of God*. [Bryn Mawr Monographs, 6] (Philadelphia, 1907); *ead.*, 'The Four Daughters of God: A Mirror of Changing Doctrine', *PMLA* 40 (1925) 44 – 92; Kari Sajavaara, ed., *The Middle English Translations of Robert Grosseteste's* Chateau d'Amour [Mémoires de la Société Néophilologique de Helsinki, 32] (Helsinki, 1967), pp.62 – 90.

[26] The quotations are from Peter Meredith's new edition (cf. fn. 9), which is more readable than Block's. Since to most readers Block will be more familiar, line references are given to both editions, with Meredith before and Block after the semicolon.

Now xal I ryse þat am Almyghty
Tyme is come of reconsyliacion.   (1114f.; 51f.)

Of the Four Daughters, Truth and Righteousness argue against, Mercy
and Peace in favour of pardoning Man. In giving the first word to Truth the
debate follows the mainstream of the tradition. This is logical when God has
already indicated how he is going to proceed. In the *Meditationes*, by
contrast, God does not react to the Angels' prayer, and thus the debate can
begin with Mercy's plea. In the N. Town play the debate makes an important
theological point in describing the first three Daughters as 'infinite' (1127,
1162, 1174; 65, 83, 100). In this the play follows the *Charter of the Abbey
of the Holy Ghost*.[27] But the play adds two arguments from Anselm's *Cur
Deus Homo*, thereby sharpening the feeling that the conflict between the
virtues cannot be solved by human reason: Justice observes that the infinite
God must insist on infinite punishment (1155; 93), and that, since Man can
never give satisfaction for his offence, he can never be released (1165f.;
103f.). Truth reminds God that by pardoning Adam he would be
contradicting himself (1126; 64). The logical dilemma which has thus been
planted can of course be overcome by the reference that 'the peace of God
passeth all understanding', which we find both in the *Charter* and in the play
(Horstmann, p. 351; Fanning, p. 51; 1177; 115). This allows the Four
Daughters to agree among themselves and then plead unanimously before
God in favour of Man. The author of the *Charter* was content with such a
solution, but our playwright preferred to have the conflict brought before
the second person of the Trinity. He defines and at the same time solves the
dilemma:

> I thynke þe thoughtys of pes and nowth of wykkydnes.
> This I deme to ses ȝour contraversy:
> If Adam had not deyd, peryschyd had Ryghtwysnes,
> And also Trewth had be lost þerby;
> Trewth and Ryght wolde chastyse foly.
> ȝiff another deth come not, Mercy xulde perysch,
> Þan Pes were exyled fynyaly;
> So tweyn dethis must be, ȝow fowre to cherysch.
>
> But he þat xal deye, ȝe must knawe
> Þat in hym may ben non iniquyté,
> Þat helle may holde hym be no lawe,
> But þat he may pas at hese lyberté.
> Qwere swyche on his, prevyde and se,

---

[27] Editions: Carl Horstmann, ed., *Yorkshire Writers: Richard Rolle of Hampole* (London,
1895), I, 337ff.; Clara Elizabeth Fanning, ed., *The Charter of the Abbey of the Holy Ghost:
A critical edition from all the known manuscripts with introduction, notes and glossary.*
Unpubl. Ph. D. diss, Fordham U., 1975 (Mic 76–4117). Cf. the notes in Meredith, ed.,
pp. 108ff.

And hese deth, for mannys deth, xal be redempcyon.
All hefne and erth seke now ȝe;
Plesyth it ȝow þis conclusyon?   (1199 – 1212; 137 – 52)

The opening words of the speech make it clear that the Redemption itself is not at issue. God's decision has not changed since he last spoke some ninety lines ago. The rest of the speech is devoted to the *method* of redemption. The judgment suggests that the method chosen is intelligible after all, and the four virtues are not really in conflict. God, by being merciful, does not cease to be just. But the two qualities can be reconciled only under very carefully specified conditions. These are largely the conditions spelt out in Anselm's *Cur Deus Homo*: Man, being finite, cannot give satisfaction to an infinite being; satisfaction therefore has to be vicarious, the measure of the satisfaction must be in proportion to the offence (*CDH* I, cap. 20),[28] the one who gives the satisfaction must be both god and man (*CDH* II, 6), he must be without sin, so that hell has no power over him. At the same time, God is not forced to act as he does (*CDH* II, 5).

After the judgment the Four Daughters discover that neither in heaven nor on earth is there anyone to meet the requirements specified by the Son. Peace now pleads:

He þat ȝaff þis counsell, lete hym ȝeve þe comforte alon,
for þe conclusyon in hym of all þese lyse.   (1229f.; 167f.)

The Son does not accept immediately but asks for a 'counsel of þe Trinité' (1233; 171). The Father replies:

In ȝour wysdam, Son, man was mad thore,
And in wysdam was his temptacyon;
Þerfor, Sone, Sapyens, ȝe must ordeyn herefore
And se how of man may be salvacyon.   (1235 – 8; 173 – 6)

After this the Son points out that the Saviour must be both god and man and that he is willing to 'were þat wede' (1240; 178). The Holy Ghost then affirms that he proceeds from both the Father and the Son and that he will 'lead' the Son to his 'lover' (1245; 183).

The appeal to the Son is prepared for very subtly: Justice accuses Man of having wanted to be as wise as God (1159; 97), Peace suggests that 'oure Lorde' should judge 'in his hyȝ wysdam' (1185; 124). In Mercy's reply

---

[28] Anselm von Canterbury, *Cur Deus Homo*, ed. and trans. Franciscus Salesius Schmitt (Munich, 1970³). On Anselm's influence on N.Town cf. Timothy Fry, 'The Unity of the "Ludus Coventriae" ', SP 48 (1951) 527 – 70, esp. pp. 534 – 5. Fry believes that the 'Abuse-of-Power' theory is at the heart of the Redemption in the N.Town cycle, but this affects only God's title over Satan after Christ's death; it makes no difference for the reasoning behind the Incarnation.

Wisdom has become a person (1186; 134). This person is of course the Son, who is traditionally identified with God's wisdom, while the Father stands for power and the Holy Ghost for love.[29] The Son's identification with wisdom makes it suitable for him to become the saviour of mankind.

Here the dialogue is used most skilfully to make a number of doctrinal points. By reaching his decision before the Four Daughters begin their argument, God makes it clear that his decision is a free one. Although the Redemption 'must' be brought about in a certain way, God is thereby not forced. Having freely willed the end, he now explains the suitable means. In true Anselmian fashion, the 'necessity' under which he operates is one that does not constrain him (*CDH* II 5 and 17).

This is not the only scene in which the N.Town cycle shows remarkable originality in transforming the 'intangible' aspects of the Christian faith into 'tangible' stage events. N.Town is also alone in giving scenic expression to the fact that only Christ's soul, not his body, descended into Hell.[30] Other cycles (Y XXXVII 23f., T XXV 23f.) render this circumstance only verbally, if at all. N.Town inserts a brief scene of fifty lines, called 'The Descent into Hell' by the editor and numbered '33' in the manuscript, between Mary's final lament in the Crucifixion (No. 32) and the Burial of Christ's body (No. 34). Two actors are thus needed to represent Christ. The 'Descent' monologue is spoken by Christ's soul while Christ's body is still hanging on the Cross. The actual Harrowing (No. 35) begins only after the Soldiers guarding the Sepulchre have fallen asleep. The 'Descent' monologue with its beginning 'Now all mankende in herte be glad',[31] forms a fine contrast to Mary's lament:

Here in þis temple my lyff I lede
And serue my lorde god with hertyly drede.   (*ib.*, 963f.)

This emotional contrast is not as effective as it might be, since Mary seems to have advance knowledge of her son's Resurrection (968). Nevertheless, the scene is another sign of the N.Town playwrights' desire to make even the more abstract of Christian doctrines visible on the stage. The pervasiveness of this tendency is just as remarkable as that of a different tendency is in Towneley. Since the effort to 'dramatize dogma' has its parallels in *The Castle of Perseverance*, it is tempting to speculate that this

[29] Cf. Meredith, note on ll.1235–7.
[30] Cf. *LFC*, 137ff.:
   The ferthe article is, that when he was dede,
   And his body tane doune, and wonden, and doluen
   Yit, to whiles that his bodi lai in the graue,
   the saule with the godhede went untill hell, [. . .].
[31] 'Passion Play II', 971 (Block, p. 305).

has something to do with the migratory character of both plays. The fact remains that among the Creation to Doom cycles, N.Town is virtually alone in showing an effort to dramatize such dogma as was considered essential by the Church authorities, while Chester, which also shows a doctrinal interest, indulges more in peripheral matter.

POETRY, THEOLOGY AND DRAMA IN THE YORK CREATION AND FALL OF LUCIFER

RICHARD BEADLE

Medieval English playwrights tackled a variety of dramatically intractable and theologically delicate subjects, amongst which was the creation of the universe and the fall of the rebellious angels from heaven. A play on this subject forms the first episode in all four of the extant mystery cycles, which otherwise are concerned essentially with the spiritual history of the relationship between man and God, from the Fall to the Last Judgement. The decision to dramatise what happened prior to the creation of man was theologically dictated. Lucifer's rebellion left a vacant place amongst the orders of heavenly beings, which God proposed to fill by a secondary creation in his own image. Plays on the Creation and the Fall of Lucifer therefore provided, in terms of the cyclical structure, an explanation of how mankind came to be created. They also furnished an account of the origin of evil in the world, by giving the devil a motive for wishing to subvert God's new creation through envy of his heavenly destiny. However, several difficult issues would enter the mind of a fourteenth-century playwright embarking on a subject of this nature, for as far as we know there was no precedent for its treatment in earlier dramatic tradition. Amongst the difficulties were the impersonation of God the Creator (a different matter from presenting him in incarnate form later in the cycle), the nuances of theological interpretation attaching to the offence of Lucifer, the problems of staging an epic action moving from heaven to hell, with only limited practical resources; and the development of a dramatic language and style appropriate to supernatural beings, but also suitable for reception by a predominantly unlettered audience. This study focuses upon the most successful surviving version, the York Barkers' pageant of the *Creation and Fall of Lucifer*,[1] and seeks to investigate the remarkably close integration of its poetic, dramatic and theological qualities.

A brief note of some factual matters is necessary to place the text in its historical setting. The surviving copy of the York *Creation and Fall of*

---

[1] Quotations from the York cycle are taken from Richard Beadle, ed., *The York Plays* (London, 1982), except that the obsolete letters thorn and yogh are here replaced by modern equivalents.

Lucifer dates from between 1463 and 1477, when the register of the cycle as a whole was compiled,[2] but its date of composition was undoubtedly much earlier. There is mention of a Barkers' pageant on the same subject in an important civil document known as the *Ordo Paginarum* of 1415,[3] and the language of the registered copy of the play has an archaic flavour, suggesting that it is certainly older than (for example) the Passion sequence attributed to the 'York Realist', who was at work in the 1420s and 1430s.[4] If the documents are to be trusted, the *Creation and Fall* may date from as early as the turn of the fourteenth century, making it one of the oldest parts of the York cycle, which is itself for the most part substantially earlier than its congeners from Chester, Wakefield and 'N-Town'. Records of the annual performance of the cycle are available for most years from the 1390s (perhaps the 1370s) to the late 1560s, and the *Creation and Fall of Lucifer* evidently remained the responsibility of the Barkers throughout its long career. Civic and gild documents occasionally give glimpses of the financial and practical arrangements for the Barkers' pageant, but alas reveal nothing bearing directly upon the staging, or the interpretation of the text.[5] It is however possible to derive some slight assistance from the extensive documentation of the York Mercers' pageant of *Doomsday*, as the Fall of the Angels and the Last Judgement are the only two plays in the cycle which attempt to show heaven, earth and hell simultaneously, and it is natural to think that there would be some correspondence in their manner of presentation.[6]

Much has been written elsewhere on the close assimilation of the Corpus Christi drama to both the practical and spiritual lives of the community. An entry of 1417 in York's municipal *Memorandum Book* puts the matter succinctly, describing the performance of the cycle as being 'ad honorem precipue et reverenciam Domini nostri Jesu Christi, et commodum civium predictorum' (especially to the honour and glory of Our Lord Jesus Christ, and the profit of the aforesaid citizens).[7] The Barkers (or Tanners) were,

[2] See Richard Beadle and Peter Meredith, eds., *The York Play. A facsimile of British Library MS Additional 35290, together with a facsimile of the Ordo Paginarum section of the A/Y Memorandum Book* (Leeds, 1983). For the dating, see p. ix, n. 2, and references there.

[3] A. F. Johnston and M. Rogerson, *Records of Early English Drama: York* (2 vols, Toronto, 1979), pp. 16 – 24, give the best transcription of the *Ordo Paginarum* that has yet appeared, but they do not observe that the Barkers' entry is written over an erasure. This is visible in the facsimile mentioned in the previous note, f.252v.

[4] See J. W. Robinson, 'The Art of the York Realist', *Modern Philology* 60 (1962 – 3) 241 – 51, and references there.

[5] Johnston and Rogerson, *REED: York*, pp. 110 – 11, 374 – 5, 417, 421, 526 – 7, 622.

[6] For conjectural reconstructions see A. F. Johnston and M. Dorrell, 'The York Mercers and their Pageant of Doomsday 1433 – 1526', *Leeds Studies in English* NS 6 (1972) 10 – 35, and P. Meredith, 'The Development of the York Mercers' Pageant Waggon', *Medieval English Theatre* 1 (1979) 5 – 18.

[7] Johnston and Rogerson, *REED: York*, p. 28.

judging by the Freemen's Roll of the city, a large and influential gild, and something of their prestige is reflected in the tenure of the important first pageant in the cycle.[8] Existing York street names such as Tanner Row, Tanner's Moat and Barker Hill preserve traces of their once-substantial presence in the city.[9] It is not known how or why the gild came to be associated with the play, though it is of interest to note that the Barkers of Wakefield and Chester also brought forth pageants on the same subject. Their trade, preparing hides for leather manufacture, may have enabled them to illustrate a facet of their workmanship in the black leather costumes and masks traditionally worn by actors playing devils.[10]

Turning to the substance and action of the play, it is worth reiterating that the mystery cycles were probably without precedent in the portentous matter of presenting God in heaven on stage, and depicting the first sinful act and the origin of evil in Lucifer's rebellion.[11] Neither matter was to be taken lightly, in terms either of practical dramaturgy or of religious faith.

In strict theological terms, God was held not to have corporeal form in heaven but was the uncircumscribed Trinity. The visual arts of the period sometimes found means, often bizarre, of representing a concept that was clearly much better left to theology, but the playwrights had no alternative other than to have a suitably costumed actor speaking verse aimed at evoking the most rarefied and abstract of divine mysteries. Some illuminated manuscripts, and stained-glass windows such as that executed by John Thornton at the east end of the choir of York Minster in 1405, belong to the tradition perforce adopted by the plays, where God is represented as a venerable male figure, the ancient of days.[12] The impersonation of God the Creator was also a problematic issue because it was open to accusations of sacrilege and blasphemy, such as were indeed brought by Lollard opponents of the drama. (It is worth passing remark that at the first modern revival of the York cycle in 1951, God the Father was not represented on stage out of deference to religious sensibilities. His part was read in voice-over). The impersonation of God in the Barkers' pageant may also have given pause in the context of Lucifer's offence in the play, which

---

[8] See the tabulation of admissions to the freedom of the city accompanying E. Miller, 'Medieval York' in P. Tillott, ed., *The Victoria History of the County of York: The City of York* (Oxford, 1961), pp. 25 – 116.

[9] D. M. Palliser, 'The Medieval Street-names of York', *York Historian* 2 (1978) 2 – 16, provides a documented gazeteer.

[10] J. W. Robinson, 'On the Evidence for Puppets in Late Medieval England', *Theatre Notebook* 14 (1973) 112 – 7, at p. 114.

[11] For a survey of the background to the episode see R. Woolf, *The English Mystery Plays* (London, 1972), pp. 105 – 13.

[12] For references to the iconography see C. Davidson, *From Creation to Doom* (New York, 1984), pp. 27 – 9. Davidson's acceptance of the attribution of the Barkers' pageant to the dramatist of the Passion sequence, the 'York Realist' (see n.4 above), is unorthodox.

itself was open to the interpretation of being an attempt to impersonate the Creator. Dramatic mimesis of the divine and its attendant problems, therefore, constitutes the occasion of the play, and contributes centrally to its substance.[13] As we shall see, the nature of Lucifer's sinful mimesis is an interpretative and dramaturgic crux which forms a qualitative distinction between the version seen at York, and those of the Wakefield, Chester and N-Town cycles.

The *dramatis personae* of the Barkers' pageant must be inferred from the script. Five speakers are named in the manuscript (Deus, Angelus Seraphyn, Angelus Cherabyn, I Angelus deficiens Lucifer, and II Angelus deficiens), but there were evidently others on stage who do not take part in the dialogue. It is likely that representatives of some or all of the nine orders of angels created by God (line 23) were present, probably as singers and musicians, and when Lucifer speaks in hell he uses 2nd person plural pronouns, suggesting the presence of more than one other fallen angel. The augmented cast which appeared on stage was one of the means whereby spectacle appropriate to the epic character of the action could be created. The conventions governing the presentation of the scene in the visual arts yielded alternatives as to props and costumes. The angels might be dressed in leather costumes painted white and gold, with wings, preferably of peacock feathers, or they might be shown according to the iconography which had developed in relation to the nine orders of angels anciently described in the *De coelesti hierarchia* of the Pseudo-Dionysus.[14] The rebellious angels evidently had means to effect a quick-change from this kind of aspect to black-masked diabolical costumes. Indeed, it is worth emphasising that, as all the characters were supernatural, no human faces would have been visible; according to medieval dramatic convention all the actors would have worn masks or visors.[15] As has been observed, God probably took the theologically inexact form of the Father. Apart from suitably regal-ecclesiastical garments, the actor probably wore a golden mask, with golden facial hair and wig, and a cruciform nimbus foreshadowing the Incarnation and Passion. He may have held a book, or the compasses with which creation was circumscribed.[16]

---

[13] R. W. Hanning, ' "You Have Begun a Parlous Pleye' ': The Nature and Limits of Dramatic Mimesis as a Theme in Four Middle English "Fall of Lucifer" Plays', *Comparative Drama* 7 (1973) 22 – 50.

[14] Davidson, *From Creation to Doom*, pp. 29 – 32; C. A. Patrides, *"Quaterniond into their celestiall Princedomes"*: The Orders of the Angels' in *Premises and Motifs in Renaissance Thought and Literature* (Princeton, 1982), pp. 3 – 30.

[15] M. Twycross and S. Carpenter, 'Masks in Medieval English Theatre: The Mystery Plays', *Medieval English Theatre* 3 (1981) 7 – 44, and 69 – 113, esp. 69 – 90 and 96 – 115.

[16] Davidson, *From Creation to Doom*, pp. 23, 27 – 8.

Informed conjecture must serve to set the scene. The script contains no explicit stage-directions except the music cues, and directions implicit in the dialogue reveal no more than that action took place on at least two levels, the rebellious angels falling from one to the other. Entrances and exits (in the modern sense) are not marked, and one cannot therefore be certain, for example, on the crucial point of whether God exits after the creation and returns after the fall of Lucifer, or is present but silent throughout the central action. If the Barkers' pageant wagon did indeed resemble the vehicle used by the Mercers for *Doomsday*, then it was a sophisticated and complex piece of machinery by the standards of contemporary technology. God would have had the means to descend and ascend, and other machinery (perhaps including pyrotechnics) would have been used to manage the acts of creation — heavens, light, sun and moon — providing a spectacle to reinforce themes and images embodied in the structure of the action and the language of the dialogue. The bulk of the action would doubtless have been transacted, as normal, on the deck of the pageant wagon, but Lucifer's fall must have taken him to street-level amongst the audience, where (again like the Mercers) the Barkers would have required a contraption for hell-mouth, belching smoke and flames.

The action of the play occupies 160 lines of verse cast in 8-line alliterative stanzas. It begins with God identifying himself in resonant language which is effective in establishing the mysterious aura of the hypostasis:

> *Ego sum Alpha et O: vita, via, veritas, primus et nouissimus.*
> I am gracyus and grete, God withoutyn begynnyng,
> I am maker vnmade, all mighte es in me;
> I am lyfe, and way vnto welth-wynnyng,
> I am formaste and fyrste, als I byd sall it be.
> My blyssyng o ble sall be blendyng,
> And heldand, fro harme to be hydande,
> My body in blys ay abydande,
> Vnendande, withoutyn any endyng.   (1 – 8)

In his third stanza God creates the heavens, and then the angels. Lines 22 – 3 — 'In the whilke blys I byde at be here / Nyen ordres of aungels . . .' — possibly contain a cue for the entry of the angels, for they are followed by a stage-direction calling for music, specifying the opening of the *Te deum*. Music is commonly used to 'cover' stage business in the early drama. God goes on to deliver two more stanzas, in the first of which he creates the earth and hell, and in the second nominates Lucifer as his deputy — 'moste nexte after me . . . and merour of my mighte' (33 – 4). These stanzas are marked by repeated injunctions to obedience, and they are followed by a second musical interlude, the singing of the *Sanctus* from the *Te deum*. From this point in the play God is either present but silent, or exits only to return when Lucifer's rebellion and fall are over. The *Sanctus* is followed by a series of alternate speeches, consisting of a stanza apiece given to the good and rebellious angels, the former praising God, the latter themselves. It is in this area of the play that the careful disposition of its stanzaic form first becomes noticeable. Lucifer's praise of himself comes to rhapsodic climax, which is abruptly cut short by his sudden and apparently spontaneous fall from heaven to hell. In hell, the fallen angels exchange laments which develop into mutual accusations and then a fight. In heaven, the remaining angels resume their praise of God, who now speaks again, promising to create mankind to fill the place in heaven left by the fallen angels. He then makes reference to the creation of the sun and moon, and closes the pageant with his blessing upon them.

It is immediately striking that the structural organisation of the action and the dialogue is determined by a number of basic physical and conceptual oppositions, for example, God and devil, heaven and hell, virtue and evil, order and disorder, obedience and rebellion, light and darkness, height and depth, to name the most obvious. Here it is also important to bear in mind God's closing promise to create man, which provides the first component in the overarching structure of the cycle as a whole, reaching forward through the Fall, Incarnation, Passion and Resurrection to the Last Judgement. It is vital that the inception of this narrative theme should be perceived as closely integrated with the establishment of the moral correlatives of the universe as they are implied in the binary oppositions mentioned above. As consideration of the sources will in a moment show, this conception owes much to the account of spiritual history set forth by St Augustine. But it should also be noted that the Barkers' pageant displays an ordered structure of a quite different type, in that its patterns are those of the type which have been identified in ritual drama. It displays features to which terms borrowed from the criticism of Greek tragedy can readily be applied: *agon, peripeteia, threnos, anagnorisis.* (It is perhaps worth recalling here that all the actors would have been masked). The existence of such a pattern was scarcely a matter for conscious contrivance on the part of the dramatist, and in any case it was inherent in the source material from which he was working. Nevertheless the economy and sense of focus with which that material was handled suggests the work of a writer with an instinctive grasp of what we might now describe as the mythic or archetypal quality of the action.

The ultimate sources of the *Creation and Fall of Lucifer* are to be found in patristic expositions of several scattered biblical texts, which had by the later medieval period been woven into a standard narrative. New Testament passages such as Christ's words in St Luke's gospel — 'I beheld Satan fallen as lightning from heaven' (10:18) — and those of the writer of the Apocalypse — 'I saw a star from heaven fallen unto the earth: and there was given to him the key of the pit of the abyss' (9:1) — were applied to older passages in the prophets dealing with the overthrow by God of earthly potentates, such as the King of Tyre in Ezekiel 28. The principal text, however, was Isaiah's apostrophe in his parable against the King of Babylon:

> How art thou fallen from heaven, O day star [Vulg. 'Lucifer'], son of the morning! . . . And thou saidst in thine heart, I will ascend into heaven, I will exalt my throne above the stars of God; and I will sit upon the mount of congregation, in the uttermost parts of the north: I will ascend above the heights of the clouds; I will be like the Most High. Yet thou shalt be brought down to hell, to the uttermost parts of the pit. (14:12 – 15)

The York dramatist quotes this passage verbatim at the climax of Lucifer's boast in the play, 'I shall be lyke vnto hym that es hyeste on heghte' (91), the moment before his fall.

The first fully detailed exposition of the narrative of Lucifer's fall hinted at in scripture is to be found in Book XI of St Augustine's *City of God*, which is worth reading in full for the sake of Augustine's sense of the poetic and imaginative resonances of the theme. Quotations must suffice here, for example his observation on the difficult problem of how Lucifer, though created good, could fall through the depravity of his will:

> . . . even while God in his goodness created him good, He yet had already foreseen and arranged how he would make use of him when he became wicked.
> . . .
> For God would never have created any, I do not say angel, but even man, whose future wickedness He foreknew, unless He had equally known to what uses in behalf of the good He could turn him, thus embellishing the course of the ages, as it were an exquisite poem set off with antitheses. . . . As, then, these oppositions of contraries lend beauty to the language, so the beauty of the course of this world is achieved by the opposition of contraries, arranged, as it were, by an eloquence not of words, but of things.[17]

The imaginative tenor of these remarks returns us immediately to what was said above concerning the structural organisation of the Barkers' pageant around a set of oppositions which resonate through the remainder of the cycle. Augustine continues in a vein which also bears very closely on the dramatist's realisation of the oppositional theme in the language and dramaturgy:

> The angels were created when that first light was made, and a separation was made between the holy and the unclean angels, when, as is said, 'God divided the light from the darkness; and God called the light Day, and the darkness he called Night'.

---

[17] *The Works of Aurelius Augustine*, ed. M. Dods (Edinburgh, 1871), Vol. I, *The City of God*, 1, p. 457.

. . .
. . . that light, which is the holy company of the angels spiritually radiant with
the illumination of the truth, and that opposing darkness, which is the noisome
foulness of the spiritual condition of those angels who are turned away from
the light of righteousness.
. . .

These two angelic communities, then, dissimilar and contrary to one another,
the one both by nature good and by will upright, the other also good by nature
but by will depraved . . . so I think they are spoken of in this book of Genesis
under the names of light and darkness.[18]

Whether or not the York dramatist relied directly for his inspiration on such
passages in the *City of God*, an imaginative spirit strikingly similar to
Augustine's breathes in his writing.

Augustine held that Lucifer sinned through the misuse of his will at the
very instant of his creation, and he quotes with approval from the First
Epistle of John: 'The devil sinneth from the beginning' (3:8). This view was
carefully refined by the scholastic theologians, who were possibly nervous
of the Manichean construction which might be placed on Augustine's
account. They preferred to see a short lapse of time between the creation of
Lucifer and his motion to sin. Such an interpretation is found in Aquinas
(*Summa Theologica*, 1.lxiii.6), who asserted that the devil sinned
'immediately after the first moment of his creation'.[19] Though apparently a
theological nicety, the issue was turned to dramatic advantage by the York
playwright, in that he was not obliged to show Lucifer as sinful until he
came to speak. In performance, therefore, Lucifer would have appeared as
identical to the other angels, increasing the adverse impact of his first
speech. There is perhaps an allusion to this point later in the play, when the
fallen Lucifer responds to the chiding of his companions with:

> Vnthryuandely threpe yhe — I sayde but a thoghte   (114)

which aptly brings out the motion of the will, followed by the deed.

The exact nature of Lucifer's offence brings us to the interpretative and
dramaturgic crux, alluded to above, of whether his proud ambition to be like
the most high actually took the form of usurping God's throne, and seeking
to rule over the other angels as if he were a god himself. The view that he
did was widely disseminated in the later Middle Ages, and is to be found in
many standard theological works. It is this view of the action that is clearly
followed in the other three cycle plays on the same subject, where God
creates the heavens and the angelic host, then withdraws.[20] Lucifer then

---

[18] Augustine, *The City of God*, ed. cit., pp. 458, 478.
[19] Cf. Woolf, *The English Mystery Plays*, p. 107.
[20] *Ibidem*, pp. 107 – 8.

steps forward as a usurper or impostor, and takes the heavenly throne — the tableau, with its obvious secular and political overtones, can be readily pictured. Though it would probably have been possible to use the York Barkers' script for the presentation in this mode, it is evident that the dramatist wished to portray a more subtle view of the event. Instead of presenting Lucifer as a usurper cast out by God, the York version presents his offence as a kind of intellectual pride which causes a spontaneous fall, with God apparently taking no part in his expulsion from heaven:

> Ther sall I set myselfe full semely to seyghte,
> To ressayue my reuerence thorowe righte o renowne;
> I sall be lyke vnto hym that es hyeste on heghte.
> Owe, what I am derworth and defte — Owe, Dewes! All goes downe!
> (89 – 92)

In the *Summa Theologica* (l.lxiii.3) Aquinas argued that what Lucifer meant when he said he wanted to be like the most high was that he wished to be like God, but without changing his own nature or identity — that he wanted to derive his beatitude not from God but from himself. Details in the language of Lucifer's boasts leading to the above assertion suggest that it was this more subtle scholastic interpretation of Lucifer's sin which governed the dramaturgy. In line 34 God designates Lucifer as 'merour of my mighte', the suggestion being that such beatitude as Lucifer enjoys is through the privilege of reflecting God's. The mirror image is taken up immediately by Lucifer in his first boasting stanza, but he sees in the mirror only his own reflection: '. . . I so semely in syghte myselfe now I se' (51). Throughout the speeches of Lucifer and the other 'Angelus Deficiens' there is a deliberate appropriation of the style of address established by God in the opening stanza of the play, primarily by means of heavy use of first person pronouns, and misapplied repetitions of God's phrases, e.g. God's 'My body in blys ay abydande' (7), and '. . . haue all welth in youre weledyng' (39), reappear as 'Ay sall I byde in this blys . . .' (84), and 'All welth in my weelde es . . .' (67). Lucifer's relentlessly self-referential imitation of God's style expresses the scholastic notion of his sin of striving to become the source of his own beatitude, and incidentally forms the model for the narcissistic adversaries of God who appear later in the cycle, such as Pharaoh, the two Herods and Pontius Pilate. But this interpretation does not entirely resolve the practical issue of whether God withdraws, or remains enthroned but silent towards the disastrous climax of Lucifer's boast, making the following assertion figurative rather than literal in intent:

> Abowne yhit sall I be beeldand,
> On heghte in the hyeste of hewuen.
>
> Ther sall I set myselfe full semely to seyghte,
> To ressayue my reuerence thorowe righte o renowne;   (87 – 90)

There are arguments on both sides. The singing of the *Sanctus* at the end of God's opening speech may have served the practical function of covering his exit after line 40, in which case Lucifer's subsequent line 'For lyke a lorde am I lefte to lende in this lighte' (52) would be literally true. On the other hand, the (for the period) unusual oath in line 92 which marks exact moment of Lucifer's downfall — 'Owe, what I am derworth and defte — Owe! Dewes! All goes down!' [Dewes = God, not Deuce] — would have been all the more effective with a silent and impassive God gazing down from his throne throughout at the disastrous effects of the perverted will.

One further possibility is worth mentioning. It has recently become clear that medieval plays (for example, parts of the Chester cycle) were scripted in such a way that they could be played to yield differing interpretations of one and the same episode,[21] and it is possible that such was the case with the York Barkers' pageant. The signs are that the dramatist espoused the refined scholastic view of Lucifer's sin, but his script would allow a director to present the devil more straightforwardly as the familiar figure of a usurper, in common with the other cycles.

Before turning to the ways in which the thematic concerns of the play are embodied in its style and structure, it is necessary to add a word about the rôle of music. God's first speech is twice punctuated by stage-directions calling for the singing of portions of the *Te deum*, the opening, and the *Sanctus*. It is not clear exactly how much singing there was, how many singers were involved, what kind of setting was used, and whether there was instrumental accompaniment — in contemporary art some of the heavenly host were conventionally shown praising God on musical instruments. However it is helpful to consider the nature and formal qualities of the specified pieces, because there is a sense in which they were intended to function as statements of a stylistic and structural nature in a medium other than the dramatic. The *Te deum* was of course the Church's most ancient hymn of praise, sung daily as part of the liturgy of Matins, which makes it the appropriate piece for the dawn of creation and the dawn of Corpus Christi day, when the pageant was in fact played. It is equally appropriate through its conventional use on major ceremonial occasions such as coronations and the enthronements of bishops.[22] However its conspicuous importance in the dramatic context here is to establish *praise* as the dominant mode of discourse in the play, for the *agon* which follows is conducted in antiphonal paeans of properly directed and misdirected praise. The subsequent selection of the *Sanctus* passage helps the transformation of

[21] Examples from the Chester cycle are discussed by R. M. Lumiansky and D. Mills, *The Chester Mystery Cycle: Essays and Documents* (Chapel Hill and London, 1983), pp. 15–23.

[22] J. Wordsworth, *The 'Te Deum'* (London, 1902).

this idea into dramatic form by recalling the origins of its text in Isaiah's vision of heaven, with the alternating cries of the Cherubim and Seraphim, 'And one cried unto another, and said, Holy, holy, holy, is the Lord of Hosts, the whole earth is full of his glory' (6:3). The York dramatist's antiphonal arrangement by stanza of the speeches of praise which follow is most appropriate.

The dramatist's careful organisation of stanza form in relation to character, theme and action is one of the play's most striking features. The text is composed of twenty eight-line alliterative stanzas, of which God speaks nine, and the good angels four, with the rebellious angels sharing seven. The fact that God and the good angels always speak in complete stanzas whilst the rebellious angels divide stanzas between them has a significant expressive effect. God's opening monologue consisting of five stanzas is rounded off with the singing of the *Sanctus*, which leads naturally into the antiphonal stanzas consisting of opposed forms of praise, recalling St Augustine's remarks quoted above concerning the aesthetic pleasure of contraries. The workings of the passage are worth observing in detail. It is initiated by an unexceptionable speech from the Seraphim:

> A, mercyfull maker, full mekill es thi mighte,
> That all this warke at a worde worthely has wroghte.
> Ay loued be that lufly lorde of his lighte,
> That vs thus mighty has made that nowe was righte noghte,
> In blys for to byde in his blyssyng.
> Ay-lastande in luf lat vs lowte hym,
> At beelde vs thus baynely abowete hym,
> Of myrthe neuermore to haue myssyng.　　　　　　　　(41 – 48)

The audience is likely to be expecting more in the same vein, but it is Lucifer who joins the second half of the antiphon, using exactly the same tone, but praising himself:

> All the myrth that es made es markide in me!
> The bemes of my brighthode ar byrnand so bryghte,
> And I so semely in syghte myselfe now I se,
> For lyke a lorde am I lefte to lende in this lighte.
> More fayrear be far than my feres,
> In me is no poynte that may payre;
> I fele me fetys and fayre,
> My powar es passande my peres.　　　　　　　　(49 – 56)

The effect is mildly comical, given the audience's likely expectations. Lucifer's first line, 'All the *myrth* that es made . . .' (49), (picking up the Seraphim's 'Of *myrthe* neuermore to haue myssyng' — 48) is a mischievous example of the *concatenatio* often found in Middle English alliterative verse in stanzaic form. These antiphons of properly-directed and misdirected

praise continue over four more stanzas until Lucifer breaks the pattern by
venturing beyond a single stanza into a second, at the same time bringing his
praise of himself to a crescendo. At the point where Lucifer begins his
consecutive stanza, with the audience's attention suddenly aroused, the
dramatist inserts the direct quotation from Isaiah 14 upon which the weight
of patristic interpretation of the episode was concentrated: 'I sall be lyke
vnto hym that es hyeste on heghte' (91). Lucifer is permitted a few more
boastful words which take him to mid-line and mid-stanza, where he falls:

> Owe, what I am derworth and defte — Owe! Dewes! All goes downe!
>
> (92)

In the process of his falling there is the first division of a stanza between two
speakers, as II Angelus deficiens joins him, and in hell there is a brief and
perhaps ironical return to the antiphonal mode where the two fallen angels
each have a mutually recriminative stanza. The stichomythia employed in
the following stanza, where the fight breaks out, is a most unusual technique
in the early drama, and forms a striking contrast to the neatness with which
the stanzaic form is observed in the remainder of the play:

> LUCIFER:Walaway! Wa es me now, nowe es it war thane it was.
> Vnthryuandely threpe yhe — I sayde but a thoghte.
> 2 DIABOLUS: We! lurdane, thou lost vs.
> LUCIFER: Yhe ly! Owte, allas!
> I wyste noghte this wo sculde be wroghte.
> Owte on yhow, lurdans, yhe smore me in smoke.
> 2 DIABOLUS: This wo has thou wroghte vs.
> LUCIFER: Yhe ly! Yhe ly!
> 2 DIABOLUS: Thou lyes, and that sall thou by.
> LUCIFER: We, lurdane, haue at yowe, lat loke!   (113 – 120)

This metrical explosion is the most prominent instance of the dramatist's
skill at integrating theme, action and poetic form.

A number of passing observations have been made above which rely on
matters of relatively small verbal detail to support larger arguments as to
theme and style. Comment of this kind on the exact verbal texture of a
medieval play runs against the grain of modern critical practice, which
generally denies, at this level of analysis, much subtlety of intention on the
part of the author, or of perception on the part of the audience. It seems,
however, inappropriate to sustain such a view of the York Barkers' pageant.
The sophisticated way in which the minutiae of contemporary theology are
embodied in the dramaturgy, and the care with which the versification is
assimilated to character and action, suggest that it was written for an
audience accustomed to listening with a much finer sense of poetic
resonance, allusion, and wordplay than is commonly assumed. For
example, a recent history of Middle English poetry happened to quote the

first stanza of the play, to dismiss it as an example of 'sonorous empty
rhetoric':[23]

> *Ego sum Alpha et O: vita, via, veritas, primus et nouissimus.*
> I am gracyus and grete, God withoutyn begynnyng,
> I am maker vnmade, all mighte es in me;
> I am lyfe, and way vnto welth-wynnyng,
> I am formaste and fyrste, als I byd sall it be.
> My blyssyng o ble sall be blendyng,
> And heldand, fro harme to be hydande,
> My body in blys ay abydande,
> Vnendande, withoutyn any endyng.   (1 – 8)

The extreme difficulty of finding a register appropriate to the dramatic
situation here has been mentioned above, but the speech succeeds partly
because of its truth as a soliloquy, for the actor (whom, we recall once
again, is masked) addresses the words neither to the audience nor to other
actors, but only to himself. The key to its rarefied, extratemporal tone is
provided by the extrametrical Latin line, which serves as an epigraph both
to the play and to the cycle as a whole. The familiarity of the biblical texts
upon which it is based would ease the audience's recognition that it is a
conflation of 'I am the way, and the truth, and the life: no one cometh unto
the Father, but by me', Christ's words after the Last Supper in St John's
gospel (14:6), and 'I am the Alpha and the Omega, the first and the last, the
beginning and the end', from the closing words of the Apocalypse (22:13).
The placing of these numinous texts in the mouth of the Creator, evokes the
two climactic moments of the cycle about to be played, Christ going to his
Passion, and the end of time at the Last Judgement. The vernacular lines
which follow this pregnant epigraph are however more than a simple
paraphrase. The anaphora employed in the first four lines of the stanza — 'I
am . . . I am . . .' and so on — is equally allusive, and is intended to call to
mind God's revelation of his name to Moses: 'And Moses said unto God,
Behold, when I come unto the children of Israel, and shall say unto them,
The God of your fathers hath sent me unto you; and they shall say to me,
What is his name? What shall I say unto them? And God said unto Moses, I
AM THAT I AM: and he said, Thus shalt thou say unto the children of Israel, I
AM hath sent me unto you' (Exodus 3:13 – 14). The underlying cumulative
effect of the allusions in the Latin text and the repetition of 'I am' is to lend
God's speech a sense of the eternal present, a vantage point which the
audience is temporarily able to share as they view the events of the cycle as a
whole unfolding. The effect is supported by syntactical means, with the
repetition of present participles and verbal nouns ending in ' – ing', of
which there are nine in the eight lines of the stanza. And is it merely

---

[23] D. Pearsall, *Old and Middle English Poetry* (London, 1977), p. 254.

coincidence that the final word of the first line is 'begynnyng', and the last word of the last line 'endyng'? The language is indeed sonorous and rhetorical, and that is appropriate, but it is far from empty.

The presence in the text of wordplay intended to point some of the thematic concerns outlined above also deserves to be recognised. Throughout the play there are examples of words used to thicken the texture of the language by reference to more than one level of meaning. For instance when God speaks of his intention to 'enspyre' the creation with his spirit (line 18) the sense of the divine afflatus is present alongside the more generalised modern signification. But wordplay is used most extensively in the presentation of the rebellious angels, to reveal their equivocal nature. For example, Lucifer's accomplice uses lines like 'The forme of all fayrhede apon me es feste' (66), and 'My schewyng es schemerande and schynande' (69), where (as the records of usage in the historical dictionaries attest) the words 'forme' and 'schewyng' could readily be employed in suspect senses in the literary language of the period. By 'forme' the speaker clearly intends 'essence' or 'pattern', the abstruser sense in Middle English; it meant primarily an assumed or false appearance. 'Schewyng' displays a comparable ambiguity in some contexts. Similarly, in Lucifer's line, 'For in a glorius gle my gleteryng it glemes' (83), 'gleteryng', though intended neutrally by its user, often carried meretricious connotations when referred to personal appearance.[24]

Wordplay is also assimilated to the imagery and conceptual structure of the text, particularly the literal and figurative significance of 'light' and 'darkness', which the dramatist may owe to St Augustine's discussion of the episode. Lucifer bemoans his fate in hell with 'Nowe am I laytheste, allas, that are was lighte' (100), where the last word refers back to his original form and function ('I name the for Lucifer, als berar of lyghte' — 36), but in its opposition to 'laytheste' also implies the figurative sense of 'light' as 'pure' or 'guiltless'. This interplay of senses is taken up in the recriminations of the other devil in 'oure lyghte has thou lorne' (108), and extended in his pun in line 111, 'For thow was oure lyghte and our ledar', with 'lyghte' in the sense of 'guide' or 'inspiration' brought in. Wordplay associated with the various senses of 'light' also appears earlier in the text. In line 60 the Cherubim speaks of the nature of heavenly beatitude, in which, as long as the angels remain obedient, 'neuer felyng of fylth may full vs nor fade vs', where 'fade' signifies both 'to corrupt' and 'to dim the light of'. The use of 'fylth' with moral connotation in this context is strongly reminiscent of the *Gawain* poet's manner in *Cleanness*,[25] where the Fall of

---

[24] H. Kurath, S. M. Kuhn, *et al.*, *Middle English Dictionary*, (Ann Arbor, in progress), s.vv. 'forme', n. 1b. (a); 'gliteren', v., 1.(b); 'sheuing(e, ger., 1. (c), (d).

[25] *Cleanness*, ed. J. J. Anderson (Manchester, 1977), lines 205–232.

Lucifer is the first of the Old Testament exempla. Later in the Barkers' pageant Lucifer in hell says 'All oure fode es but filth we fynde vs beforn' (106), and God also opposes the literal and figurative senses of 'fylthe' and 'fade' when he says of the fallen angels, 'sum ar fallen into fylthe that euermore sall fade tham' (132). The general tenor of the language recalls part of the passage from St Augustine quoted above, concerning 'the noisome foulness of the spiritual condition of those angels who are turned away from the light of righteousness'. Though further examples of wordplay might be adduced — particularly instances which relate to episodes later in the cycle — the above must suffice to illustrate the dramatist's attention to neglected matters of exact detail in the verbal complexion of his text.

I have argued at length for a high degree of integration in the language, dramatic structure, and theological substance of the York *Creation and Fall of Lucifer*. It remains to return the play to its context in the annual processional production of the Corpus Christi cycle in the streets of fifteenth-century York. The opening of the performance was a portentous yet difficult moment, in both practical and conceptual terms, but the script provided for the Barkers' gild gave them ample means to rise to the occasion. It was proclaimed officially that performance of the first pageant at the first station should begin at daybreak,[26] a fact which the dramatist did not overlook. The combining of the themes of creation and light with the physical setting of the dawn of Corpus Christi day was a *coup de théâtre* in the grand manner, for the resonances of the cosmic event to be enacted echo down through the cycle to the performance of the final pageant, the Last Judgement, at midnight.

---

[26] Johnston and Rogerson, *REED: York*, p. 25, the 'Proclamacio ludi corporis christi facienda in vigilia corporis cristi' of 1415.

Index

Aaron 10 n
Abelard 133
Abraham 152, 176, 177, 193, 207
Achilles 141
Acts of the Apostles 180
Adam 29, 30, 34, 52, 62, 159, 206, 209
Aeneas 69, 70, 71, 72
Aeolus 69, 70, 71, 72
Aers, D. 115 and n, 165 n
Ailred of Rievaulx 36
— *De Institutione Inclusarum* 7 and n
— *Speculum Caritatis* 66 n
Alexander, J. 25 n
Alexander of Hales *Summa universae theologiae* 201 n
Aleyn 98
Alfaro, J. 32 n, 52 n
Alford, J.A. 39 n, 49, 50 n
Alfred, King *Proverbs* 195 n
Alhazen 94 n
Alla 105, 106, 116
Allen, H.E. 9 n, 10 n, 14 n, 15 n, 22 n, 23 n, 29 n, 39 n, 42 n, 44 n, 45 n
Almachius 105, 108, 115, 116
Ames, R.M. 97
Ancilli, E. 37 n
Anderson, J.J. 226 n
Andreas Capellanus 98
Andromache 143
Angela of Foligno 20 n, 37
Anne, St 24, 112
Anselm, St 36, 52 n
— *Cur Deus Homo* 209, 210 and n, 211
— *Meditatio Redemptionis Humanae* 34 and n, 42 n, 51 n
Apius and Virginia 120
Apocalypse 218, 225

Aquinas, St Thomas 34, 36, 86, 100, 153
— *Summa theologiae* 94 and n, 220, 221
Arcite 79, 99
Aristotle 100
Arnesby, J. 13 n
Arnold, T. 50
Arnould, E.J.F. 44 n
Arthur, King 79 and n, 80 and n, 81
Aston, T.H. 165 n
Atkinson, C.W. 1 n
Aubrey, J. 6
Auerbach, E. 25 and n, 75 n, 110 and n
Augustine, St 40 n, 47 n, 110, 153, 155, 180, 181 and n, 182 n, 218, 223, 226, 227
— *City of God* 219 and n, 220 and n
— *De Libero Arbitrio* 159
Ayre, J. 5 n

Balade de Bon Conseil 90
Bale, J. 15 and n, 22 n
Balthasar, H.U. von 43 n, 64 and n
Baum, P.F. 179 n, 182 and n, 188 and n
Beadle, R. 181 n, 201 n, 213 n, 214 n
Beatrice 110
Becket, St Thomas 6 n
Becon, T. 5 and n, 9
Beichner, P.E. 90 n
Bennett, J.A.W. 39 n, 44 n, 47 n, 48 n, 55 n
Benson, L.D. 83 n, 103 n, 119 n, 133 n, 142
Bent, M. 179 n
Benvenuto da Imola 110
Bernard of Clairvaux, St 35 and n, 36, 40 n, 84